EXPANSION AND REACTION

COMPARATIVE STUDIES IN OVERSEAS HISTORY

general editor

H.L. WESSELING

PUBLICATIONS OF THE LEIDEN CENTRE
FOR THE HISTORY OF EUROPEAN EXPANSION

Vol. I – H.L. WESSELING (ed.), *Expansion and Reaction.*

Essays on European Expansion and Reactions in Asia and Africa, by F. Braudel, H. Brunschwig, S.N. Eisenstadt, J.C. Heesterman, J.L. Miège, R. Robinson, I. Schöffer, H.L. Wesseling, and E. Zürcher.

Vol. II – P.C. EMMER and H.L. WESSELING (eds.), *Reappraisals in Overseas History.*

Essays on Post-war Historiography about European Expansion, by C. Bayly, H. Bley, L. Blussé, H. Brunschwig, A. Hopkins, J.L. Miège, N. Steensgaard, J. Stengers, H.L. Wesseling, and G. Winius.

(forthcoming)

Subsequent volumes will deal with Companies and Trade, the Colonial City, Theory and Practice of Imperialism, and Racism and Colonialism.

EXPANSION
AND REACTION

edited by

H.L. WESSELING

Essays on European Expansion and Reaction in Asia and Africa *by* F. BRAUDEL,
H. BRUNSCHWIG, S.N. EISENSTADT, J.C. HEESTERMAN, J.L. MIÈGE, R. ROBINSON,
I. SCHÖFFER, H.L. WESSELING, and E. ZÜRCHER.

LEIDEN UNIVERSITY PRESS
1978

ISBN 90.6021.426.9

© 1978 LEIDEN UNIVERSITY PRESS

CONTENTS

EDITORIAL NOTE

All the contributions with the exception of those by Professors Eisenstadt, Heesterman and Robinson have been translated.

PART I

INTRODUCTION

I. EXPANSION AND REACTION:
SOME REFLECTIONS ON A SYMPOSIUM
AND A THEME

by

H.L. WESSELING

I

The history of European expansion has become a problem, not only in the moral but also in the conceptual sense. A generation ago the word was just as simple as the thing itself. The history of expansion was called "colonial history" and was considered to be a chapter in the history of the mother country. In addition to sections on political, economic and cultural history, there were also chapters on the exploration and exploitation of new worlds, the establishment of European authority, the subjugation of native rulers.

This was said to have been carried out "for the honour of God, the glory of our country and our commercial interests in those regions," as so aptly expressed by an inscription on a tombstone in Westminster Abbey. In French colonial hagiography, for that matter, commerce was usually omitted resulting in a direct reliance on History and Providence. As Gabriel Hanotaux wrote in 1931, "en occupant Alger, la France remplissait la mission que la Providence et l'Histoire lui avaient confiée...."[1] But whatever the precise proportions of "God, gold and glory," European expansion was believed to be a process the historic necessity of which was no more to be questioned than the beneficial results for the parties involved.

That the colored peoples also had a precolonial history, let alone that they could have a postcolonial one, was seldom contemplated. They were after all, it was said, peoples without a history although they were not therefore happy peoples, as the well-known saying goes. On the contrary, they were unhappy precisely because they knew no progress and thus no history.

A close relationship does indeed seem to exist between history and happiness and the fact that historical writing today is still predominantly a Western affair is therefore not without drawbacks. History is a gift of the

---

[1] G. Hanotaux, *Pour l'empire colonial français*, Paris 1933, p. 41.

Greeks, but it is apparently only the West that has learnt to stop fearing the gifts of the Greeks. In the meantime, however, there have been some changes in the optics of Western historians. Journals, institutes and university chairs of colonial history have helped to replace that embarrassing word with terms such as overseas history, African history, Asian history, etc. And this is more than just a question of a name. The colonial period, formerly treated as an important chapter in European history, is reduced to a footnote in the history of Asia and Africa. Thus it would seem as if the history of European expansion, whether centres are established to study it or not, actually does not exist at all. Because if European expansion is no more than a day or an hour in the centuries-long history of highly diversified regions, it would then be ridiculous to designate this expansion as a separate field and thus group the diverse territories under one denominator. Well then, this is the question we would like to study in this volume before answering it.

It is clear that in the first place we are confronted with a problem of terminology. The term "History of European Expansion" is a result of the search for a word to replace the traditional term colonial history, which was felt to be too obnoxious. But it is still questionable whether the word is suitable as such. For many the implications of the term expansion, although not as heavily associated with a sense of grief and guilt, still tend too much towards a Euro-centric interpretation of history. For this reason the words "and reaction" were added. In fact however, the conceptual problem has not hereby been solved but instead has increased. The combination expansion-reaction appears to imply a simplicity and an inevitability in the process of the encounters between the diverse civilizations which does not do justice to its complexity. The dissatisfaction which is thus aroused was most clearly expressed by Heesterman in his contribution: "the coupling of the two concepts in a complementary pair seems obvious. In fact it is too obvious to be true."[2] And actually it is clear that such a simple dichotomy as the concept pair expansion-reaction suggests in the first instance is untenable. The words seem to imply a certain preconception about the initiators, the hierarchy of the participants and the direction of the process. But it quickly becomes evident that these preconceptions are not tenable as generalities: expansion and reaction sometimes occurred at different levels, the reactions were complicated, sometimes it was a question of reactions to reactions rather than reactions to expansion. On the other hand, the reactions at the various levels of politics, economics, etc. were not always synchronous and were different in character. Moreover, the expansion was not always a European initiative but

---

[2] See below, p. 31.

was instead in some cases itself a reaction, forced or voluntary, to local crises and requests for intervention. In any case these processes were certainly not always directed or dominated by the Europeans. In short, sometimes there is expansion without reaction and sometimes even reaction without expansion.

Not only the course but also the direction of the process appears to be more complicated than was formerly assumed when it was described in single terms such as "modernization" or "westernization." Indeed we can see that existing indigenous developments or tendencies in the non-western world have been accelerated, as well as retarded, as a result of European activity. In some cases European penetration revived indigenous modernization processes which had become bogged down, whereas in other cases the presence of Europeans suffocated the native society and led to a process of "involution," to use a phrase coined by Clifford Geertz.[3] In short the European expansionists fared no better than the sorcerer's apprentice in Dr. Faust: the spirits which they conjured up could no longer be laid to rest. And although it is frequently said that they sold their souls to the devil, they still were not able to put the spirit back in the bottle or to close the lid of Pandora's box.

The first conclusion is therefore, in short, that the concepts expansion and reaction create more questions than they answer and also produce major conceptual problems. But does this also mean that it would therefore be better to forcibly remove this concept pair from the court of history and in the future only to incorporate European expansion in a series of autonomous Asia-centric, Africa-centric, etc. histories? That cure would be worse than the ailment itself. Some of the illnesses mentioned are, after all, not incurable. To begin with, the words expansion and reaction do not have to exclude connotations such as variability and interaction. Nor need these terms imply a judgement of the direction or course. However the main problem is that, although the history of expansion is, both for Europeans and for others, no more than a part of their history, the total is certainly different from the sum of these parts. Whether, as formerly, one places an emphasis on the European part or, as now, on the non-Western part, it remains a fact that the parts together rise above the entities to which they belong. That is why we can continue to maintain that the history of European expansion does exist, because it has its own identity based on the point of view from which it selects and studies historical phenomena. The most important characteristic of modern history is the development all over the world of more or less similar systems of production, society and values, and it is this development of a universal system of civilization from which the history of expansion derives

---

[3] C. Geertz, *Agricultural Involution. The Process of Ecological Change in Indonesia*, Berkeley 1963.

its significance and coherent perspective. For this reason the history of expansion could be described as the history of the encounters between diverse systems of civilization, their influence on one another and the gradual growth toward a global, universal system of civilization. Seen from this point of view, the history of expansion is a form of world history, or perhaps more accurately an attempt to arrive at a world history which is more than the sum of the histories of the different parts of the world.

It is advisable, even if only to avoid the risk of a new Euro-centricity, to point out immediately that universality does not imply uniformity, contact does not imply confrontation, influence does not imply imitation. In addition it is obvious that this process will differ markedly from time to time and from place to place. One of the main problems is in fact when to emphasize change and when continuity, where to stress agreement and where difference, where to stress unity and where diversity. It is therefore necessary, apart from the unity of perspective, to introduce at least some major differentiations in time and space. Chronologically it appears feasible to demonstrate a qualitative difference between the 19th and 20th centuries on the one hand and the earlier centuries on the other. It is worthwhile to remember what van Leur mentioned long ago about the 16th, 17th and 18th centuries. This period, he wrote, "did not know any superior Occident, nor any self-isolating Orient no longer progressing with it. It knew a mighty East, a rich fabric of a strong, broad weave with a more fragile Western warp thread inserted in it at broad intervals."[4] For many centuries Europeans and Asians were the warp and the woof of the same commercial fabric which did not tear until the 19th century, and then through the violence of the new capitalism.

Of course this separation into periods is subject to many questions, as is the actual impact of capitalism, but still it is obvious that it was not until the 19th century that the European sun reached its zenith and the long winter of discontent made way for the glorious summer of a short-lived supremacy.

This 19th century expansion of Europe was directed in particular towards Africa and, once again but in a different manner, Asia. That is to say the "formal" expansion. It is now common knowledge that, in terms of investments and trade, both Americas were much more important – certainly for England – than Asia and Africa.[5] But if the word is used in its strictest sense, then European expansion did not exist in America. This was the result of a much earlier decision. As Braudel writes, in 1500 Europe was confronted

---

[4] J.C. van Leur, *Indonesian Trade and Society. Essays in Asian Social and Economic History.* The Hague 1955, p. 289.

[5] About this, see especially D.K. Fieldhouse, *Economics and Empire, 1830–1914,* London 1973.

with a vital choice, "either to make use of Christopher Columbus' discovery and opt for America, or to exploit the discovery of the continuous sea links round the Cape of Good Hope to its limits and batten on to Asia."[6] It is obvious that it chose to play the American card and that this choice led to a long-term development which was highly unstable but had enormous consequences for the players and their opponents. In fact, as a result, everything was over in America by the 19th century: conquest, colonization, liberation and, as far as the United States were concerned, the start of an empire of its own. Except in the economical sense, for instance in Argentina, European imperialism in the 19th century scarcely existed in the Americas.

It was quite another story in Asia and Africa where in the 19th century the cards were dealt out once again although the hands were quite different at the two tables. In Asia the issue was roughly speaking to implement existing spheres of influence, in Africa to create new ones. Of course this manner of formulation is probably too simple because the spheres of influence were only vaguely demarcated and the malleable periphery did not congeal into hard boundaries until later. In the case of the Dutch East Indies, for example, it is essential to realize that in fact this word itself is already an anachronism. In the 19th century, the "Dutch East Indies" meant actually Java, a fact which everyone at that time was very much aware of. This is apparent from well-known books such as those of Money, Chailley-Bert, Day, etc. in whose titles always appears the word "Java" and never "the Indies."[7]

This is also apparent in the international interest in the large but fragile Dutch Empire, considered by many as the most delicious of the colonial dishes but also as being too big for the Dutch appetite. However, in the end its borders were respected and the very real expansion of the Netherlands during this period was therefore completed within a given framework, at least to a certain extent. The same is applicable to British India and, although to a lesser extent, French penetration into Indochina. Whatever fell outside these spheres of influence, remained for the most part outside with the exception of the Philippines where the Americans acted as the all too greedy testementary executors of the defunct Spanish Empire. But, and that is striking, China was not divided up, in spite of the considerable interest precisely in this enormous market, and the European presence there remained marginal, both literally and figuratively. Japan on the other hand, although to some extent influenced by the West, evaded this influence fairly quickly and by a dialectic process, not of expansion and reaction but of reaction and expansion, was already an

---

[6] See below, p. 18.

[7] J.W.B. Money, *Java: Or, How to manage a Colony*, London 1861; J. Chailley-Bert, *Java et ses habitants*, Paris 1900; C. Day, *The Dutch on Java*, London 1904.

imperial power in the 1890's. Therefore European imperialism in Asia can be seen as essentially a process of consolidation and formalization, in other words of internal expansion. The key to the understanding of this process lies in the relationships between colony and colonizer and not in the rivalry between the colonial powers themselves.

The situation in Africa was quite different. In the 19th century Africa was still, as Hilaire Belloc so aptly expressed it, a "mysterious land surrounded by a lot of sand."[8] Only the major arteries such as the Nile, the Niger and the Congo were known but, as in medicine, in the 19th century blood vessels were only used for tapping blood and not for catheterization, to investigate the condition of the heart itself. Exploration of the heart of Africa did not occur until the end of the 19th century. Because the spheres of influence here were vague or non-existent, the international rivalries could erupt in complete freedom – with the well-known results. The rapid, brutal and radical division of the black continent, has, due in part to its exotic and dramatic aspects, appealed greatly to the imagination and thus became a symbol, as it were, of modern imperialism. But is this correct? Many have in fact argued that Africa was only a side stage in the imperialistic drama, and its division just a sequel. Is the answer then: expansion in Africa, imperialism in Asia?

But it is clear that the generalizations inherent in the terms Europe, Africa and Asia are also much too broad. Politically and culturally there are considerable differences between Islamized and mediterranean North Africa and continental and tribal Black Africa. Expansion in India, where the state was taken over, was quite different from that in China, where the state was maintained but society was influenced. On the other hand there was an essential difference between the colonial ambitions and positions of major powers such as England and France, and those of the Netherlands, a colonial giant but a political dwarf. These differences are clearly expressed in the analyses of the authors of this volume and in the points they choose to stress.

II

Zürcher, to begin with, sketches a picture of the precarious balance which existed in premodern China between universalism and particularism. On the one hand there was a cellular society consisting of small units and mainly dominated by the gentry as well as the dependent merchant class. On the other hand was the universalistic and bureaucratic state machinery of the

---

[8] H. Belloc, *The Modern Traveller*, London 1898.

Mandarins, who exercised the imperial power, theoretically absolute, but in practice extremely limited. Between these two spheres was a most precarious equilibrium. The essential significance of Western expansion was that it increased the existing tensions such that this unstable balance was upset and China ended up in a permanent crisis. As far as the Chinese reaction is concerned, it is important to note that it was not directly correlated with the phases of Western penetration. This correlation can only be found at the political level; socially, economically and intellectually the Chinese reactions were asynchronous and highly pluriform. It is therefore not possible to discuss *the* Chinese reaction. Rather, one should speak of a series of reactions, the most important of which were reactions to reactions and not reactions to expansion. Thus, Western expansion acted as a catalyst in a largely endogenous process of change and modernization. China did not die of the virus of expansion but of the antidotes which it developed in its fight against this virus.

Events in India, while similar in some respects, show great differences in others. These differences are due in part to the structure of Indian society and in part to the nature of British expansion in India. There was no empire in India as there was in China. The political organization was much more casual and the position of the ruler was based on pragmatic rather than on theoretical considerations. The structure was horizontal instead of vertical, based on personal relationships and loyalties and not on a pyramidal hierarchy. Paradoxically the strength of the Mughal empire lay precisely in this weakness, in the lack of an imperial center. This would have led to a stronger and more stable power but would also have been more vulnerable to attack and overthrow. Not only was there no center, there were also no borders; more accurately the boundary which existed in India was not an external but an internal one, namely that between state-controlled areas and those not controlled by the state. It is striking that both in China and in India, in spite of all differences in power and organization, the state was in fact a structure imposed by outsiders and experienced by the people as foreign. The Chinese provincial administrators even resembled colonial governors in that they too were strangers, did not speak the regional dialect and were transferred every few years. The colonial state therefore seems to differ little from the just as foreign governments of the Manchus and the Mughals.

There was of course a pronounced difference in the manner in which expansion occurred. In India where the state was only a theoretical construction, the English set up a government; in China where a strong state already existed there was no opportunity for such an operation. But because of the limited significance of the state in India, the English activities there also had little effect. Thus one could hardly speak of a relationship between expansion and reaction, because they occurred at different levels: expansion of the state, reactions in society. Instead of reaction it is better to consider it as a symbiosis, namely, one of particularistic practice and universalistic ideals. This symbiosis was possible because of Western expansion. The effect of the expansion appears to be similar to that in China: that of a catalyst. The Mughal empire was, as many have argued, already in decline before British expansion but this decline, like that of the Ottoman empire, was a structure rather than a process. Through Western expansion this structure was disturbed and the decline was accelerated.

The special position of India in the British colonial empire is clearly illustrated in Robinson's contribution about British West Africa. In India an empire was possible without expansion. This was due to the unique political structure in India: the state was powerful enough to provide money and troops but too weak to resist social developments. What the English hoped to do in Africa was the building of a "new India," – that is, of what they, to a large extent mistakenly, imagined this to be in terms of political organization. In the period 1895–1900 in particular attempts were made in this direction. They failed, however, due to the political and social structures in West Africa. The discovery of the power of the chiefs resulted in resignation on the part of the English which was elevated to a principle in the theory of Indirect Rule. In fact this was a rationalization of impotency. The limits of English power were determined by the willingness of the Africans to collaborate. What took place during the colonial period was therefore in fact only the spread of precolonial collaboration systems from the coast to the interior.

The essential significance of the willingness to collaborate is also apparent in Brunschwig's contribution on French Black Africa. The similarities with England are striking: a lack of economic interest, reluctance to invest, concern about whether the profits would ever cover the costs. This "bienveillante indifférence," as Doumergue called it, which was so typical of France is incidentally just as evident in Churchill's statement concerning Africa made in 1906, "I see no reason why. . . . these savage tribes should not be allowed to eat each other without restraint."[9] As a result of this lack of interest the autonomy of the local governors was considerable and their quarrels among themselves numerous. Thus reality was closer to anarchy than a colonial system. The presence of the white man was predominantly official (behind

---

[9] For Doumergue see: *Journal Officiel, Chambre, Débats*, 22 november 1894, p. 1955, quoted by H. Brunschwig, "Vigné d'Octon et l'anticolonialisme sous la Troisième République (1871–1914)," *Cahiers d'Etudes Africaines*, 54, XIV – 2 (1974), p. 295; for Churchill: see below, p. 160, note 45.

every colonist was one official) and quantitatively very small: even in 1914 there were only about 3000 people for an area seven times the size of France. The general conclusion would seem to be that there is little evidence of Western expansion in Black Africa before 1914 and that the most important decision was taken by the Africans, namely the choice between collaboration and resistance.

The situation was totally different in the Maghrib, a region that had been part of the Mediterranean system for centuries. Actually the word Maghrib is too broad because it does not do justice to the differences in phase and character of the French penetration in Algeria, Tunisia and Morocco, respectively. The resemblance however lies in the fact that here one can speak of a true presence. There was a large white population, with all of the related problems of land ownership and so on, and a substantial military force (150,000 men, ten times as large as in Black Africa). Interest in the Maghrib was the result in particular of a widely accepted geo-political concept of France's role as a Mediterranean power. Because the French administrative apparatus was relatively understaffed, there was still sufficient room for the indigenous exercise of power. We see increasing tensions between the traditional chiefs and literati and the rising intellectual and commercial bourgeoisie which was mainly pro-French. The French attitude toward these phenomena was ambiguous: the official ideal of assimilation was contradicted by actual practice, which in reality left no room for it (thus, schooling was very limited, and naturalization policy very reserved).

This ambiguity, characteristic of the colonial situation *tout court*, forms the background for the colonial dilemmas which are the central theme of Schöffer's contribution. Dilemmas existed for the colonial ruler, such as the relationship between the traditional and the new elites, the strain between the educator-and-guardian dream on the one hand and the actual position of being the colonial masters on the other, as well as for the Indonesians, for example, their desire to achieve modernity but their reluctance to accept westernization, etc. In the period 1870–1920 these problems became more pronounced as a result of the increased expansion and the late but still very real reactions to it. Dutch expansion in the late 19th century, a result of external rather than internal problems and in fact part of a much longer process, definitely has a distinctive character. It was however not an economic necessity for the Netherlands, nor the result of an intentional forward policy, but rather of internal migration and the activities of local entrepreneurs.

The Dutch regime was characterized by a marked duality. Not only was there Dual Rule – there was also a Dual Economy: a colonial economy directed towards the world market controlled by the Dutch next to an autarchy and local indigenous economy. Yet the colonial economy affected native society in many ways (population growth, monetary economy, internal migration and communication) so that changes occurred in society which also gave rise to various Indonesian reactions. However vague expectations for the future on both sides may have been, they were quite different from what would become reality.

III

The conclusion of this volume appears surprising: no European expansion in British or French Black Africa, little in China and India, some expansion in North Africa and Indonesia; as for reactions, they were rather effects, side-effects mostly of widely different types. If some expansion did occur, then it was for the most part unintentional, undesired and uncontrolled. The process was not directed by a Western hand, the results were not foreseen by a Western eye. The question arises once again: has European expansion ever really existed?

The first comment which must be made before trying to formulate an answer to this question is that we have here once again the contributions of European historians. Does their strikingly negative and sceptical evaluation of the significance of European expansion imply a certain pessimism, a doubt about the actual and future position and significance of Europe? Do we see here the same phenomenon, but with the opposite sign, as found in the older colonial historiography, namely historians who allow their judgement of the present to influence their interpretation of the past? For Europeans before 1914 the world resembled Shakespeare's dawn, "Night's candles are burnt out and jocund day stands tiptoe on a misty mountain top." This lucid light so strongly reflected on the Europeans' image of history that the autonomous role of the East, which in an earlier period had been clearly recognized, paled. Modern historians know all too well that this "jocund day" would in fact turn out to be a "false dawn."[10] Has this led to an interpretation of history in which there is also little or even no place for a European role in the past? It is in any case striking that the historians of the Third World often assume that the influence from the West was stronger than do the Westerners themselves – although of course this need not imply a positive evaluation of it.[11]

[10] Compare R.F. Betts, *The False Dawn. European Imperialism in the 19th Century.* Oxford/Minneapolis 1976 ("Europe and the World in the Age of Expansion," Vol. VI).

[11] See for example, M.S. Rajan, "The Impact of British Rule in India," *Journal of Contemporary History*, Vol. IV, no. 1 (1969), pp. 89–102.

However a more fundamental consideration can also be introduced. When we discuss European expansion then it must be remembered that this refers not only to a number of more or less expanding states or even an expanding European economy but also to something more comprehensive, namely an expanding society or if one prefers an expanding civilization. European expansion led, especially in its later phase, to an encounter between a European industrial-technical mass society with its more or less egalitarian and democratic values on the one hand, and the predominantly agrarian, feudal and autocratic societies on the other. This type of contact continued even after the colonial period and seems to be the most important consequence of expansion.

Eisenstadt considers this problem in his contribution. He is opposed to the old modernization theories in which it is postulated rather naively that the traditional societies, once infected with the virus of modernity, would evolve on their own, automatically, and in a uniform fashion to a genus oriented towards the West. In fact it was not that simple. The constituents tradition and modernization appear on the contrary to combine in highly diversified ways. The history of Western expansion is therefore complicated because the result is quite different from anything ever foreseen or planned and Western civilization itself has changed as a result of and during expansion. But the existence of an influence of this "civilization of modernity," which in time also became a "great tradition" like Christianity or Islam, need not be questioned. Western expansion led to the creation of various world systems – economical, political, ideological. As of the 16th/17th century new areas were continually being incorporated in an economical world system, which was a system of unification and hierarchization. But political and ideological systems also affected the traditional societies: corrosion of traditional political legitimacy, changes in the relationship center-periphery, institutionalizing of protest movements and ideologies. The results of this however depended greatly on the nature of the endogenous tradition, as is demonstrated by the spread of socialism which took root in many different ways according to whether it corresponded with universalistic elements in the existing tradition or could fill an ideological vacuum.

One of the world systems described by Eisenstadt, namely the economical one; is also the central theme in Braudel's contribution. Braudel of course writes from the chronological perspective of the "longue durée." He wants to view the history of expansion in its totality, thus since the 16th century, and describes it as the history of our modern economic world-system. The division of the world and the accompanying economic hierarchization are the essential features of Western expansion and this permanent preoccupation with the division of the world gives European history its unique character, from the standpoint of world history. This brings us back to the previously mentioned problem, namely that of continuity. Is the "longue durée" indeed the most fruitful perspective for viewing European expansion? Will not possible essential changes in its character thus be neglected?

This difficulty is not new. It is known from the discussions surrounding the attempts to distinguish periods in imperialism. Here the theory of the continuity of expansion, in any event that of England, has won ground in recent years – especially under the influence of English authors.[12]The time perspective has more and more been extended from the late to the entire 19th century. The problem has also been considered in an even broader perspective by the Indian historian Panikkar who wants to refer to a "Vasco da Gama epoch" extending from 1498 until 1945 (or 1947); in contrast Lüthy stresses phase differences and does not distinguish a true impact of the West until the third and last period, that following the Industrial Revolution.[13]

The problem as a whole cannot be solved because it is a question of assessment and interpretation. On the one hand it is clear that this late-19th-century imperialism was built on foundations laid much earlier and continued working after old patterns; on the other hand it is impossible to negate the dramatic revisions which took place in the period called "Achsenzeit" by Jaspers, "Breukvlak" by Romein and "watershed" by Barraclough. The release of Prometheus in post-1870 Europe had tremendous effects, both in Europe itself and beyond. Some figures will suffice to illustrate this "acceleration of history," to use the phrase by Halévy. Between 1883 and 1913 the export from the tropical regions, which initially had remained constant, grew on the average as quickly as that of the industrialized West, i.e. by 3.5% per annum. In India and Indonesia the rate of growth in the 15 years before 1914 even reached a total of 150%. The population of Java increased between 1880 and 1905, thus within one generation, by 50% from 20 to 30 million.[14]Although the rapids and cataracts of demographic and economic developments in Africa are less spectacular, it is impossible not to see looking back now how much the capricious and arbitrary lines which were drawn in the few years between 1885 and 1905 in dusty chancelleries on inadequate maps influenced vital present-day facts such as borders, language, politics,

---

[12] See for example, R. Hyam, *Britain's Imperial Century* 1815–1914, London 1976 and Fieldhouse (see note 5).

[13] K.M. Panikkar, *Asia and Western Dominance. A Survey of the Vasco da Gama Epoch of Asian History, 1498–1945*, London 1953, p. 11–12; H. Lüthy, "Colonization and the Making of Mankind," *Journal of Economic History*, Vol. XXI, no. 4 (1961), pp. 483–495.

[14] See W.A. Lewis (ed.), *Tropical Development 1880–1913*, Evanston 1970, pp. 46–49.

social systems and ideologies. The question arises as to whether a certain Euro-centricity does not in fact lurk behind such a global and long-range view, which brushes aside the distinction between formal and informal rule and relegates political seizures and rivalries to the playrooms of childish historians. An historian of Africa such as Thomas Hodgkin, for example, emphasizes that from the African perspective the changes in the political and ideological superstructure in this period were more important than the continuity in the economic substructure. He mentions the concern of African theorists with what they consider to be the central fact of the age of imperialism: their nation's defeat and loss of sovereignty at the hands of Europe. He notes too that "they had in general no doubt that they had moved into a new phase of history...."[15] Of course "nation," "sovereignty" and even "history" are, in turn, typically European concepts, and this modern perception of reality may – influenced by the very contact with Europeans – be different from the contemporary one. But it is still obvious that the 19th century change from informal to formal rule left its marks on the world today. Thus the concept of modern imperialism, after having been pushed out the door with such force, has come back in again through the window. Possibly the essential difference between the 19th century and earlier periods lies in the qualitative changes in the instruments of power. The desire for power, the disparity in power and thus expansion are phenomena found in all periods. The new aspect was that as a result of the Industrial Revolution the instruments available for the exercise of power were enlarged in an unprecedented manner. The characteristic of European development since the "long 16th century" is the separation of the state, of a "public domain," from the original diffusion of politics, economy, culture, etc. "Der Staat als Kunstwerk," to quote Burckhardt. Since then the historical drama in Europe was acted out on two separate stages: politics and economy, state and society. Whereas the social process was dominated by the struggle for the control of nature, the concern in politics was the exercise of the existing but limited power. During the Industrial Revolution however these two stages gradually merged again, albeit in a different manner. The control of nature had been achieved but, and this is the new aspect, it was subsequently turned over to the state. The state won over society. Thus the Industrial Revolution led to a political revolution, that is, a revolution in the true function of politics. The

---

[15] See R. Owen, "Introduction," p. 7 in R. Owen and B. Sutcliffe (eds.): *Studies in the Theory of Imperialism*, London 1971. See also (*ibid.*, 11): "Even though the third world theorists (...) believe that imperialism is, at root, a system of economic exploitation, *a more important fact for them* was that their people had actually been politically subordinate to a foreign power" (my italics, W.).

distinction between political and economical factors loses its significance, because politics henceforth implies economics. Political history is after all the history of power and as that power becomes total, political history becomes total history instead of a segment of it. This explains the primate of power in contemporary history and the preoccupation of contemporary historians with external and internal shifts in power, with war and revolution.

Modern imperialism was nothing more than the first effect this new situation had upon international relations. The result was a change from informal to formal empires. But to a certain extent it can be said that European societies never followed this process through to the end, that they never became truly "modern." They remained imprisoned between old and new, between state and society, between a political desire for power and economic freedom. This tension between totality and pluriformity was also evident in the continuing doubts about the desire for and the exercise of power outside Europe.

On the other hand it should also be pointed out that European expansion ultimately evolved through and was based on naval power. This alone made it possible to initiate an enterprise which far exceeded the demographic capabilities of this "Cap d'Asie." But this strength was also a weakness. As Braudel states, maritime hearts are good hearts in contrast to landlocked hearts,[16] but kindheartedness is not always a source of strength. Maritime orientation provided a greater freedom within the country and a certain looseness without. Even the formal empires retained a loose structure in spite of economic ties and social-cultural influences. The political power remained foreign and not legitimated, and therefore vulnerable and fragile. Deterioration of the empires could therefore proceed even more quickly than their construction. The only empire which survived decolonialization was the Russian empire – an empire with a bad, landlocked heart – but based on continental expansion and forged with the instruments of modern times: state power and ideology.

The boundary between history and the future is determined by that short and elusive moment, the present, and it is perhaps better for a historian not to cross this threshold. Be that as it may, it is clear that for the historian of the "longue durée" as well as for the sociologist concerned with understanding the present, European expansion not only existed but was, and to a certain extent still is, a process with a unique significance for world history. For the time being therefore historians would be wise to continue their careful studies of it.

[16] See below, p. 22.

PART II

PROLOGUE

2. THE EXPANSION OF EUROPE
AND THE "LONGUE DURÉE"

by

FERNAND BRAUDEL

If I had had to chose the title of this lecture, I would have spoken of *Le partage du monde*. That is the title of the third and last volume of my work *Civilisation matérielle et capitalisme*, which will soon be published.[1]

The division of the world has been Europe's deepest vocation. It was its structural vocation: it has been so busy dividing up the world that, in the last resort, there has been nothing left for the others. This division has not been a peculiar honour to Europe, but Europe has been caught in a process, which has outstripped it, of economic hierarchisation and of dividing the world, so that I would be quite prepared to plead extenuating circumstances in its favour.

Yet, not without a certain amount of humour, the chairman of our symposium has slipped into the title of my lecture the words "la longue durée." I am sure that any time someone wants to put me, not in a difficult, but in an amusing position, he speaks of the "longue durée." But "la longue durée" allows me to wear seven-leagued boots. Thus, I have the right to traverse a century in a few seconds and to extend my field of operations considerably, as the centuries themselves do not frighten me.

Moreover, as will appear, I will quickly leave Europe aside, to talk of the world and, above all, of *expansion*; this word which, despite appearances, is so confusing that, in the papers presented here, you have been forced to make two or three attempts to define it – and you are still not satisfied with the definitions since, apart from expansion, you have had to draw attention to its antithesis, the *reactions*. You speak of expansion and reaction and you have even used the word *penetration* in place of expansion. It thus seems to be a word full of meaning and of difficulties, on which I would like to expound at some length.

[1] One volume has been published so far: F. Braudel, *Civilisation matérielle et capitalisme (XVe–XVIIIe siècle)*, Paris 1967. English translation: *Capitalism and Material Life 1400–1800*, Glasgow 1973.

The expansion of Europe, in the general sense of the term, is not a difficult subject. In so far as one wishes simply to note the major turning points, one can accept without too much difficulty that European expansion, at least of any consequence, began in 1492 with the discovery of America or in 1497, when Vasco da Gama rounded the Cape of Good Hope. This is a simplification, to be sure; before 1492, Europe was already a unity, and this aggregated space had succeeded in pushing back its eastern frontiers a good way, at the expense of the Slavs. This European world had also succeeded in mastering the arts of seafaring in the Baltic, the North Sea and the Channel and in sailing on through the Atlantic and the roughest sea in the world to Gibraltar and the Mediterranean. Admittedly, Europe had not taken control of the whole of the Mediterranean world before 1492. The Crusades did not succeed in it, and indeed they failed as regards territorial conquests; in 1291, when the Muslims re-captured Acre, the Holy Land ceased to be one of Europe's possessions, but the watery space of the Mediterranean as a whole, and the traffic on its surface, remained under the domination of the Mediterranean world.

In short, and with these reservations, it can be said that European expansion began in 1492 or 1497. This forced on Europe an extremely grave choice: either to make use of Christopher Columbus' discovery and opt for America, or to exploit the discovery of the continuous sea links round the Cape of Good Hope to its limits and batten on to Asia. At some times Europe has been obliged to go one way, at other times the other. In the short term, in 1497, or rather in 1498, it was more profitable to exploit Asia, because there, everything was already in place. Exploitation, parasitisation, even sometimes the seizing of ships belonging to Muslims or Gujeratis, that was all that was necessary. There was a period of predation across the Indian Ocean. On the other hand, in America, it was necessary to build or rebuild. The arrival of gold or silver out of the American continent should not be put too early. The New World did not deliver any considerable quantity of precious metal before 1550. Therefore, it was necessary to build America, which was Europe's task, in the *long term*. I do believe that the long term was ultimately more profitable than the short. But everything had to be built, plantations, mines, gold washings, the peopling of this great area. However, Europe had the great advantage of being able to take its time here. Elsewhere, it was always confronted by indigenous societies, while in America, their reaction was extremely feeble.

American Europe began with towns, genuine ancient towns like Sparta or Thebes, very small towns with ancient, patriarchal families. In time, there developed phenomena well known to specialists of the Middle Ages, such as pioneer zones. Even in modern America – I am not referring to the United States but to certain regions of Latin America – the atmosphere of Europe before the Reformation can still be recognised. If you want to understand that time by seeing it, look at how religious questions present themselves in the interior of Brazil today. I am well aware that talking of the recommencement of Europe allows for certain nice pleasantries. In my youth, I had an American professor, Van Norden Shaw, a journalist and historian, as a colleague. He used to make fun of me saying: "Your American Middle Ages contain Ford motor cars." But, after all, are Middle Ages with Ford cars impossible?

Without wanting to go into retrospective argument at too great detail, it is clear that Europe only grew in power and vigour to the extent that America, as it grew, gave it its full support. America gave Europe the means to seize the world, in a much more brutal and complete manner than would have been possible if it had been limited to its own resource. As for precious metals, these began with a little gold at the start of the sixteenth century, to continue with silver, great quantities of the white metal in the sixteenth and seventeenth centuries and then, at the end of the seventeenth, from 1680 on, with the products of the gold washings in Brazil and, at the same time, of the reopened silver mines of Potosi and, even more important, of New Spain. Now, Europe did not keep these precious metals for itself, but sent them to Asia, and not just in trifling quantities. The historians of India have told us of a price rise there, with a delay of twenty years or so, that is to say in the years 1590, 1610, 1620. We also know that the arrival of silver had considerable consequences in China. At least one third of the mineral production of the New World – which is a sizeable sum – went to China. This represents considerable instances of transfer.

Economic historians claim that, for centuries, Europe was in a deficit situation as against the Far East, and this deficit created a sort of haemorrhage, a permanent and profound cause of weakness. Now, I consider that, on the contrary, Europe's strength allowed it, as it were, to bombard the rest of the world with its coins and its precious metal, and thus to force open the doors of the markets, which might otherwise have remained closed to it. That is a proof of its strength, and it would be difficult, on the level of world history, to maintain the contrary.

So one might say that every European domination gives notice of itself in advance, being outlined beforehand on the map of America. Thus, although any attempt to present a balance sheet for the Golden Century in Holland is difficult – especially if one is not a Dutch historian, and therefore has three-quarters or nine tenths of the evidence outside one's direct acquaintance –

from this point of view it would seem that the first sign of decadence and the first set-back came in 1654, when the Dutch abandoned the North East of Brazil. They could have stayed there, because there was scarcely any opposition to them, except for large landlords, Portuguese merchants, slaves and half-castes. They could have stayed right there. But they did not. Also, note the abandonment, ten years later, of New Amsterdam by the Dutch in favour of the English, an extraordinary gift, because New York's position is certainly a key one.

I would argue the same thing with regard to France. France did not loose the competition with England during the Revolutionary and Napoleonic wars, but earlier, in 1762, when with remarkable unconcern, the government abandoned Canada; we could have defended it, kept it or recovered it. But French political understanding consisted of a preference for the sugar islands – Santo Domingo, Martinique, Guadeloupe. You will admit that, in the long term, this was a miscalculation.

I could easily continue and complete this barely outlined pattern, which you are quite capable of filling in for yourselves. But would it be worth the trouble? After all, my problem is not a history, or a description of European expansion, but rather it is the outline of a general model which, transcending Europe, would possibly encompass the expansion process as a whole.

Ladies and Gentlemen, You may think that by using "la longue durée" to make giant leaps, I have finished my lecture quickly. Well, you are wrong! My lecture is now beginning. Its intention is to move outside the restless, obsessive history of Europe. Europe, or to be more exact, Ancient Greece, invented the profession of the historian. But Ancient Greece is already Europe, and this has put the invention to its own use. It is in the centre of the stage, it is always prepared to plead for itself and it encumbers the history of the world.

Any attempt to explain expansion as such is one of model-building. I am therefore going to construct a model, a sort of cage in which to lock up the word expansion. I will only half succeed, or less. But no matter! Imagine that behind me there is a board; that I draw a circle on it; and that that circle is the space at issue. It is a space with limits, with a frontier or, in mathematical terms, an *envelope*, which can be distorted. Clearly, this *envelope* is something important. Also you may presume that this space is unbroken and that, in so far as it is made up of parts, they are dependent on one another. It is not a space without a certain hierarchy, since the various spaces are interdependent, enclose each other and converge in something like a centre. The centre is also extremely important.

This space might be the Mediterranean. Many German historians, geographers and economists say that "Das Mittelmeer ist eine Welt für sich" (a world in itself). Or they would say "Das Mittelmeer ist ein Welttheater" (a theater of the world). Or, and this is the word I like best: "Das Mittelmeer ist eine Weltwirtschaft." If you translate this as "économie mondiale" or as "world economy," that does not work; a world-economy is an economy encompassing the whole globe. The only translation I would propose is "economic world" (*économie-monde*). The Mediterranean is a *Weltwirtschaft*, that is to say, it constitutes an economy, a world for itself alone, a part of the surface of the globe. This is the concept of "Weltwirtschaft" that I will take as my starting point.

You may have noticed, in passing, that I have not been entirely consistent, in that *Weltwirtschaft* is an economic space, but that *expansion* is not only economic, but also political and cultural. However, political expansion does not last very long, and cultural expansion often only extends over a few summers or a few decades. Eighteenth century France spread its light throughout Europe, but this brilliance did not really last a long time. For innumerable reasons, an economic radiation is, in my opinion, much more important. To support my view, I would like to cite a book which you will know or would do well to get to know soon, by Immanuel Wallerstein, an anthropologist who suddenly decided to write history and has done it brilliantly. In 1974 he published his book, *The Modern World System*.[2] This book depends to a good deal on my work, but it has also taught me a great deal. Wallerstein believes that, from the sixteenth century onward, the economy with its successive expansions grew much faster than either the political or the cultural sphere. The economy has an advantage right from the start. Thus perhaps I may single out the most rapid among these movements, to emphasise it and to speak of the *Weltwirtschaft*, leaving aside the other problems.

Moreover, I believe that the process occurs fairly frequently. The Roman Empire was a political unity. But if you think of the Roman Empire as a *Weltwirtschaft*, it still had to bring its silk from China and its spices and pepper from India. The dimensions of the economy were greater than those of the polity. As for China, from an economic and cultural point of view, classical China overflowed into Japan, the Philippines, Indonesia, the north of Vietnam, Yunan, Tibet, Szechuan, Manchuria and Mongolia. China had an enormous economic *envelope*, from which it undoubtedly profited. And what was very important to China: wood, gold dust, silver, copper, all these

[2] I.M. Wallerstein, *The Modern World System. Capitalist agriculture and the origins of the European world-economy in the sixteenth century*, New York etc. 1974.

commodities and more it found in the colonial world by which it was encompassed. It even found those things for which it had a passion, such as salted bears' feet from Tibet or swifts' nests from Indonesia. In the period before Vasco da Gama's arrival, India as well was a great power, extending outside its own boundaries. The Indian Ocean was a *Weltwirtschaft* with India at its centre. Islam could be considered one too, during the centuries of its greatness.

Our economic worlds are thus economies with boundaries, a centre and a hierarchisation of the component spaces. Would you like me to attempt to explain this language, for it is a language? To emphasize the frontiers and to give two examples – historians give examples, in place of proofs, which is a way of avoiding the problems – I believe that in 1583 a world like Muscovy, primitive Russia, ceased to be touched to any great extent by the European economy. There was still the outlet through Archangel, but that through Narva on to the Baltic had just been shut, and the Russian economy was an economic world in itself, centred on Moscow, that is to say, on a landlocked heart, which means a bad heart – the good hearts are the maritime ones. A remarkable contradiction was established between the European economy, extending as far as Poland, and the Russian economy to its East. In Poland the nobility "rose," exploiting the peasants and sending wood and grain to the Baltic. On the other hand, the Russian state made its fortune and maintained control over the Boyars as well as over the peasants. The right policy was followed in Poland, the wrong one in Moscow.

Secondly, if you think of the economic world covering Europe at the end of the sixteenth century as a vast hat, you should not spread it any further than the Cape of Good Hope. That was the boundary. Europe has been able to send its ships, merchants, masters and so on further than that, to Asia, but the Indian Ocean was not part of the European economic world. This did not extend round the southern tip of Africa, which itself was included in its area. At the same time, as I have no need to emphasise, the great mass of America was a part of the European economic world.

In coming now to the importance of the centre of an economic world I am overwhelmed with examples, all of them pointing the same way. Before the end of the eighteenth century, the centres of economic worlds were cities, urban economies, limited bodies; even Venice, during its splendour in the fourteenth and fifteenth centuries, could be held in the hollow of the hand. There was a vivid contrast between the urban economy at the centre and the breadth of the economic world. In the eighteenth century, supremacy passed from Amsterdam to London, but behind London there was a *national market*. Similarly, when the centre passed from London to New York, there was a national market behind London, but a continent behind New York. The central base of the modern economy is infinitely larger than in previous ones.

Thus the most curious, and the one that you know best, of the old cities was Amsterdam. Even if you have never thought of it in this way, Amsterdam was the last polis. Venice was not the last, although it would be romantic to say that, until the terrible Bonaparte arrived in 1797, Venice was a polis, a city-state. In fact, by then it was only a local power, with nothing left to dominate, while Amsterdam had for a long time dominated the whole world, which was a fantastic prowess. I would not say that Amsterdam could be held in the hollow of one hand, but we could, I think, hold it in two.

The first town to be at the centre of a European economic world was an artificial one. Throughout the thirteenth century the fairs of Champagne and Brie, at Troyes, Bar-sur-Aube, Provins or Lagny, were the centre of the European world. It was a powerful centre in that the city of Paris was behind the fairs of Champagne and Brie, and profited from their brilliance. To be sure, it is remarkable that – doubtless because the economy did not interest them – French historians have never included the fairs of Champagne in the greatness of France under Saint Louis. After all, if with its university, with the Aristotelian revolution, with the rise of the Monarchy, Paris was remarkable, it was because the fairs of Champagne were nearby. In the shadow of the fairs, Paris became a centre of trade, which it would no longer be in the fifteenth century. This is very curious: it was the only time in France's history that we held the centre of the world. Since then, I do not know how many times we have attempted to seize or to appropriate the centre of the world, always without success, not even under Louis XIV or Napoleon. Let me put forward a detail: many years ago one of the great historians of humanism, Giuseppe Toffanin, published a book titled *Il secolo senza Roma* (The century without Rome) that is to say, the thirteenth century.[3] And to be sure, that was the century of the fairs of Champagne, when the intellectual centre could be found, strangely, in Paris, rather than in Rome.

After this era ended, at the beginning of the fourteenth century, the fairs of Champagne no longer mattered, and the centre of the world moved south, to the Mediterranean; and for a long time there was a violent struggle to decide which of two cities would seize it. One of these was Venice, a city which you no doubt love, and the other was Genoa, which you probably, but wrongly, like

---

[3] G. Toffanin, *Storia dell' Umanesimo*, Bologna 1950, 3 vols. *Vol. I, Il secolo senza Roma (Il duecento)*. English translation: *History of Humanism*. New York 1954.

less. Genoa was infinitely more modern, more violent and more extraordinary than Venice. Now, Genoa nearly won. In 1378, the Genoese managed to establish themselves at Chioggia; they held the Lion of Saint Mark by the throat. They were going to win. But everything changed. The courage of cities is something extraordinary. They invented patriotism. The whole Venetian populace threw itself on Chioggia, because gossip said that a number of *bombardes* had been installed there; so one could say that gunpowder saved Venice in 1378. However that may be, Venice was the victor when peace came in 1381. Its rival became second in rank and, for more than a century, until about 1500, Venice was the centre of the world. At that time the great maritime discoveries were made. After a few years, Lisbon, taking off, should have become the centre of the world, but no such thing happened, because the centre moved north–east. Antwerp was to succeed to the domination of the world: what Charles V wanted to do, but did not succeed in, the town accomplished without even thinking about it. In this case it is rather amusing to compare, in passing, economic and political expansion. Antwerp became the centre of the world without having really earned it, even without seeking it. Antwerp was built from outside.

Pepper had been the motor. The great market for the consumption of pepper was in fact in northern Europe, not in the Mediterranean. In the Mediterranean we had been accustomed to using pepper for too long, and were satiated by it. Nine out of ten consumers of pepper in Europe were in the north, that is to say in the Low Countries, in Germany, in Scandinavia, in Poland and so on, where even today pepper and spices have a role. This was one of the reasons why Antwerp became the centre of the world. But its sovereignty did not last long.

There were repeated crises at Antwerp, so that, in 1557, 58 and 59, the centre of the world shifted suddenly to the south, to the advantage of Genoa. This is a fact which you may not have been aware of. Everyone has read the magnificent old book by Richard Ehrenberg, *Das Zeitalter der Fugger* (The Fugger Era).[4] But the Fugger era was the era of Antwerp. The Fuggers, the great merchants of Augsburg, were to some extent the kings of Antwerp. Now, from 1557, began what Felipe Ruiz Martin, a modern Spanish historian, has called *El Siglo de los Genoveses* (The Era of the Genoese).[5] This

---

[4] R. Ehrenberg, *Das Zeitalter der Fugger. Geldkapital und Creditverkehr im 16. Jahrhundert*, Jena 1896, 2 vols. English translation: *Capital and Finance in the Age of the Renaissance: a study of the Fuggers and their connections*, 1928.

[5] F. Ruiz Martin, *El siglo de los Genoveses en Castilla (1528–1627): capitalismo cosmopolita y capitalismos nacionales*.

Genoese era was a complicated one, based on credit, paper and the great fairs of Piacenza. It lasted to 1627. Then there were two centres in Europe, Amsterdam, whose growth and emergence began around the 1580s, and, far to the south, Genoa. It would take a long lecture to tell you under which circumstances Genoa lost its primacy, the more so after a recent discovery made by Franco Berlandi. There used to be no correspondence of Genoese bankers available. He has brought to light 240 registers and thousands of letters so that we may be forced to begin our study and our explanations of Genoa's fortunes all over again.

Amsterdam's fortune, which began with the seventeenth century, was based on trade. It started from the zero level of economic life, and it lasted. Only in the eighteenth century was Amsterdam faced with a rival city, London. I have maintained (and this might amuse you in passing) that if Louis XIV had captured Amsterdam in 1672 (and he could have captured it), France would not have gained the mastery of the world. Rather, London would have declared its power a century earlier, and the centre of the world would have crossed to the other side of the sea.

I have now come to the heart of the argument, which is the hierarchisation of economic space in any economic world. A little while ago, I drew a circle. Suppose now I draw three concentric circles, representing the heart, a middle zone and a marginal zone. It is thus a heart with two coronas, one after the other. At the core of the central zone can be found everything that is best and most alive in the economy of the time, including credit, banks, gold (the gold travels towards the centre, while silver moves to the middle zones). Towards the centre can be found all the advantages, the profitable businesses and the nascent industries. There, too, can be found capitalist success, even, when its time has come, the industrial revolution, the intellectual revolution, the scientific revolution and, as well, liberty. Liberty is not everywhere in the world. That liberty we love, Western liberty *par excellence*, is to be found in Amsterdam or London. Voltaire went into exile in London, just as, before him, Descartes had gone to Amsterdam, as these were the only places in the world where men could be free.

As against this, on moving to the middle zones, to France, to Italy, even to Spain, there could be seen an economic life that was much less vibrant, an agriculture still bound, to a certain extent, by seigneurial or feudal ties, an industrial sector scarcely moving and a capitalism which if it existed at all, was in contradiction with the rest of society. But looking at the margins, the contrast is overwhelming. To the east there was serfdom, a level of industry very much behind the times, and no liberty. And in the western margins, in America, there was slavery too. This, in short, is a complete vision of the world. Acceptance of this schema, of this matrix of the *Weltwirtschaft* leads to a new, even revolutionary vision of the world.

We are, whether we like it or not, influenced by the Marxist way of thinking. We have all undergone the shock of Marxist thought, which is linear – a few years ago it would have been called diachronic – and in which slavery, feudalism and capitalism succeed one another; thus, a linear vision. On the other hand, if you have a synchronic view of the world, you find that slavery, feudalism and capitalism coexist and that a certain hierarchisation takes place. This phenomenon, then is the matrix of both capitalism and non-capitalism at the same time.

When the world changes, the consequences are felt over fabulous distances. It should not be thought that phenomena of this sort have passed unnoticed, either today or yesterday. In 1929, when New York became the economic capital of the world, the whole globe felt the repercussions. Everything shifted at the same time. Alberto Grohmann, an Italian historian, claims that, at the time of the ending of the fairs at Champagne, a very remote event, suddenly the situation changed in the Kingdom of Naples; plenty of supplementary fairs suddenly rose there. When the primacy passed from Genoa to Amsterdam, changes occurred all over the world as well, as they did when England became the core of the world or when, around 1929, England gave place to New York. The decentralisation and recentralisation of the world have come to be major problems. Now, each time when a shifting of the centre takes place, the world finds itself at a low economic tide. One of the manias of French historians is sacrificing at the altars of "conjonctures": of prices, of wages, etc. If you accept this correlation, the end of the fairs of Champagne corresponds to the onset of the recession at the beginning of the fourteenth century. When Venice had the last word with Genoa, there was the regression which divided the fourteenth century in two. When Amsterdam took the dominant position, 1590 was already the beginning of a decline; similarly when Genoa became the temporary mistress of the fate of the Spanish Empire in 1557, the century was cut in two as if by an axe – as the happy France of Francis I gave way to the sad France of Henry II. Again it is to be noted that 1929 opened a period of acute crisis, as the transition from London to New York was accomplished. What was the reason for this? In fact, in an economically active period there is room for two, or several; both Genoa and Venice can exist at one time. There is wealth for everyone. As against this, in times of trouble, there is only room for one left.

Perhaps I am only talking common sense, but common sense has its uses. You may be saying: "Oh, he has just forced an open door," but open doors are still useful, much more so than closed ones. It does not matter if a truth is banale if the truth itself matters. We are thus faced with an open door, a truism, but this allows us a little game of prognostication, of foresight.

In 1975, we are facing a turning point of the world. From all appearances, nothing is going well. Is this 1929? The repetition is not certain. Nevertheless, we are witnessing a turn in the economy. Now, if what I have put forward is valid, there is a chance that this regression will be marked by changes in the centering of the world. Either the world will recentre itself on New York once again, which is possible, and appears to me to be the most likely outcome, or it will do so elsewhere. There are three possible candidates. The United States might maintain their leadership. It is not because they have devaluated the dollar that they are not doing good business. I do not believe that the devaluation of the dollar was done purposely, but so much the worse for those who aren't strong enough to cope. There is the U.S.S.R., but I consider that they are very behindhand in technological matters. Finally there is Europe. If Europe became the centre of the world (which would surely be amusing for the historians, as it would be a countercheck for the Europeans), then the center would be, not Amsterdam, but Rotterdam. (It would not be Leiden, but Leiden could profit enormously in its wake).

Putting the question in this way may not seem reasonable. Nevertheless Europe represents, economically speaking, the greatest power in the world. It has all it takes for future greatness. But it would need a will, which does not exist, and also it needs to accept the struggle. No-one can become the centre of the world without struggling. You are aware of the ways in which, during the Fourth Anglo-Dutch War, the English smote the Dutch with unparalleled brutality; it is necessary to smite to become the strongest. You may recoil for a moment in face of so simply outlined a task. You do not covet the domination of the world, nor covet the recommencement by Rotterdam of Amsterdam's glorious career, but this question is an important one, and on this importance and the doubts which surround it I will finish my lecture.

PART III

EXPANSION AND REACTION IN ASIA

3. WAS THERE AN INDIAN REACTION?
WESTERN EXPANSION
IN INDIAN PERSPECTIVE

by

J.C. Heesterman

I

Expansion and reaction: the coupling of the two concepts in a complementary pair seems obvious. In fact it is too obvious to be true. Expansion of Western, specifically British, control over the Indian subcontinent there certainly was – even though our understanding of this complex phenomenon is less than perfect. But what about its counterpart, the Indian reaction? One is even tempted to ask: was there a reaction at all? Such a question flies in the face of the consecrated rhetoric that glibly speaks of the defense of traditional values, national identity and the struggle for freedom. But then the same goes for the countervailing slogans of the white man's burden and the *mission civilisatrice*, – not to mention the ambitious utterances of our latter day development ideologists which make the rhetoric of their colonial predecessors look rather pale and shame-faced. The point is, of course, that all this rhetoric – whether of the old-fashioned colonial, the equally old-fashioned (though hardly out of fashion) nationalist, or the brand-new foreign aid variety – will not help us to understand what has happened and is still happening. If we want to give substance to the theme of expansion and reaction, we shall have to interpret it in a radically different way. First of all we shall have to avoid the obtrusive logic of the action-reaction type, which traps us into viewing the story of European involvement exclusively in terms of a clear-cut confrontation. Even when the swelling tide of nationalism produced the non-cooperation and civil disobedience movements and the clashes of 1941, the confrontation kept a curious air of tepidity, which led one historian to speak of "a Dasehra duel between two hollow statues, locked in motionless and simulated combat."[1] It was only with the break-away of the Muslims that "a real ferocity appeared – between Indian and Indian." Nor is

---

[1] Anil Seal, *The Emergence of Indian Nationalism*, Cambridge, 1968, p. 351.

this a peculiarity of the Indo-British entanglement. Other cases of expansion – take for instance Islam or Buddhism – similarly refuse to respond to the action-reaction logic.

Admittedly the story is a complex and often contradictory one, which moreover ranges over a huge and diverse sub-continent. It seems then a natural step to take refuge in breaking up the all too global picture into probably endless series of areas, sectors, groups and instances, where confrontation and reaction did in different ways and with different outcomes occur. No doubt such case studies do contribute most valuable material for our understanding of the structures and processes involved. Moreover it is clear that the two parties to the expansion-reaction game were far from being unified blocs.

Even the British Indian government and its prestigious "steel frame," the Indian Civil Service, hardly resembled the powerfully monolithic juggernaut of popular imagination,[2] so that here too there is unlimited scope for fragmentation. The main trouble with this break-up, however interesting its results, is that it can only lead to ever further atomization, while a comprehensive view recedes more and more behind an impenetrable screen of monographs on unique situations and events – as indeed seems to happen to modern Indian historiography.

The fragmentation inherent in the expansion-reaction paradigm seems, however, to cover another, perhaps somewhat unexpected but fundamental fact. Namely that the aims, terms of reference, modes of operation and organization of the parties involved had little if anything in common.[3] In other words: what we should like to construct as the complementary expansion-reaction pair takes place on two different and separate planes, in two distinct worlds as it were. Their contacts and confrontations could only have an incidental and episodic character for lack of common ground. Even in those instances where it was actively pursued the "dialogue" is more often than not a dialogue of deaf-mutes, or at least one of misunderstandings.

Does this mean that we have to resign ourselves to this atomization or alternatively have to fall into the trap of another fragmentation along the lines of Euro-centric, Indo-centric, Sino-centric, etc., historiographies? I do not think that we have to submit to either of these unattractive alternatives. But first we should try to characterize the society where since the second half of the 18th century the expansion of British control took place.

---

[2] Interestingly the organization of the British Indian administration seems to have been very well geared to accommodate dissension through its "dual alignment" of authorities at each rung of the hierarchy. Cf. R.E. Frykenberg, *Guntur District*, Oxford, 1965, pp. 237 f.

[3] Cf. author, "Political Modernization in India," in: J.D. Legge (ed.), *Traditional Attitudes and Modern Styles in Political Leadership*, Sidney, 1973, pp. 29–56, esp. p. 48.

2

The first thing that strikes us is – in contradistinction to e.g. China – the virtual absence of an empire commanding active and unquestioning allegiance. There was, of course, the Mughal empire. But what was the extent of its effectualness, what the reality covered by its prestigious name? It is not that its origin in conquest by Central-Asian warriors in any way impaired its acceptance and legitimacy, nor was its explicit Islamic character a serious impediment to acceptance by its largely non-Muslim subjects. In both respects the Mughal empire had old and venerable precedents in the Delhi Sultanate. The truth is that – again in contradistinction to China – no ruler, whether Hindu rājā or Muslim bādshāh, could have ultimate authority and legitimacy. For these belonged to the ideal brahmin, that is to the ultra-mundane renouncer, and on condition that he kept himself free from entanglement in society,[4] so that the ruler was barred from access to the source of ultimate authority. A comparable situation obtains in Islam where the separation of secular power and spiritual authority equally keeps the ruler under a cloud of suspicion. Paradoxically, where no grave questions of the divine right of kings, the mandate of heaven or similar transcendental concepts were directly involved, the position of the actual ruler was unproblematic. Whatever his origin or confession, he could be accepted with comparative ease and even enjoy a modicum of effective allegiance – as was also the case with British rule. So there never was a serious problem of the Mughal's legitimacy. Whatever legitimacy and authority was possible under these circumstances, he certainly possessed. If we may attach any value to the reaction of an old man in a Rajput town, who, when told of the British departure from Delhi, ponderously supposed that in that case the Mughals would be back in power,[5] the legitimacy of Mughal rule vastly outlasted even the twilight of their declining presence.

The doubts about the Mughal empire are in another area. The extant administrative documents, relatively few though they may be, conjure up a most impressive picture of a centralized bureaucratic empire, efficiently run on lines of adequate regulations.[6] No doubt, if more of the Mughal archives had been salvaged, or if more official documents would come to light, this impression would only be further substantiated. However, even the most

---

[4] On this problem, cf. author, "The Conundrum of the King's Authority," forthcoming.

[5] Cf. G.M. Carstairs, *The Twice-Born*, London, 1957, p. 143.

[6] Cf. Irfan Habib, *The Agrarian System of Mughal India*, Aligarh, 1963; J.F. Richards, *Mughal Administration in Golconda*, Oxford, 1975.

complete of archives can not tell the whole story. Perhaps we should even say that the greater their precision of focus and formulation the less they will fit untidy reality. And so we should perhaps not be surprised that at the same time the empire appeared to observers as singularly ineffectual. Or, as the comment of an English factor has it "every man honours the king, but no man obeys him."[7]

This inconsistency can, of course, be explained away by invoking an organic scheme of rise, decline and fall that explains itself and only needs to be filled in with details. In this view the Mughal empire had its day of youthful vigour in the sixteenth century under Akbar. Its middle age in the seventeenth century sees the beginning of decline – notwithstanding the fact that it reaches its greatest expansion at the end of the century –, while old age is reached in the eighteenth century when the empire founders in chaos, its remnants being salvaged by the incipient British-Indian empire which then starts on a new cycle of rise and fall. Such a view, however, does little to provide adequate reasons for the fatal decline of the once impressive imperial administration. The reason can not be found in the personalities and capacities of the successive rulers. For the prime requisite of an adequate and well-established bureaucracy is that it withstands just such vagaries. Indeed a good case can be made for the strength of Mughal administration even under the strains and stresses of Aurangzeb's Deccan campaigns (esp. since 1689) and of his declining years.[8]

So the discussion centres not on the nature of the empire, but on possible explanations for its decline and break-up. The doyen of Mughal studies, Sir Jadunath Sarkar, has given strength to the argument that the empire was fatally impaired by the break between Hindus and Muslims caused by Aurangzeb's religious policies.[9] Recently a variety of other explanations have been brought forward. Satish Chandra has pointed to the disruptive effect of intense factionalism over the allocation of increasingly scarce land assignments among the vastly increased service nobility,[10] while Irfan Habib sees the decisive factor in over-exploitation of assigned lands leading to flight and finally rebellion by the oppressed peasantry.[11] J.F. Richards stresses

---

[7] Cf. W. Foster (ed.), *The English Factories in India*, Oxford, 1906–27, vol. 5, p. 204.

[8] Cf. J.F. Richards, *op.cit.*, p. 311: "Ample evidence from the archival remains demonstrates that the organization of the empire was both impressive and effective. The total impression conveyed by these documentary sources is that of a great machine, built and organized for continuous expansion and gradually intensifying control from the centre."

[9] J.M. Sarkar, *History of Aurangzib*, 5 vols., Calcutta 1912–30, vol. 3, pp. 283–364.

[10] Satish Chandra, *Parties and Politics at the Mughal Court, 1707–1740*, Aligarh, 1959, pp. XLIII–XLVII.

[11] Irfan Habib, *op.cit.*, pp. 317–51.

Aurangzeb's decision to direct his efforts at subduing the Marathas instead of coming to a settlement with them so as to round-off the Deccan conquests and integrate them, with the result that "the imperial administration and military machinery was stretched past its capacity."[12] Finally M. Athar Ali seeks to place the crisis of the Mughal empire in a global context by contrasting the growing preponderance of Northwestern Europe with the economic stagnation of the Islamic empires, which in the last resort he ascribes to a cultural failure of the entire Islamic world.[13] The debate is certain to continue for some time to come,[14] but the divergence of even the most recent opinions seems to suggest that in the end we may have to admit defeat in the face of an inextricable complex of interacting causes – a formula often intoned in such cases.

In the mean-time we might consider, albeit tentatively, whether we are asking the right question. Our perception of the Mughal break-down is, of course, conditioned by our knowledge of what happened afterwards, namely the unforeseen take-over by the British. In other words, was the break-down as absolute and irreversible as India's subsequent history has made it? Questions about what might have been are notoriously vacuous. We should, however, not forget that there was at least one other Islamic empire, the Ottoman, whose doom was already spelled out in gloomy terms in the beginning of the sixteenth century. All four pillars of the state – religion, justice, the council and finance – are broken, and one wonders whether matters can continue in this way, a Dutch consul reported in 1626 from Aleppo.[15] Well, as we know with the inexorable certainty of hindsight, matters were to continue for another three hundred years, and it took a global conflagration to put an end to them. When such time spans are involved we may wonder whether we should not look rather for the reasons of the remarkable resilience than for those of the decline. Both sets of reasons may be largely the same. Most, if not all, is in the eye of the beholder. In other words, what we perceive as a process of decline relentlessly leading to an unavoidable and definitive fall, may well be not a process but a structure – and

[12] J.F. Richards, op.cit., pp. 306–10.

[13] M. Athar Ali, "The Passing of Empire: The Mughal Case," Modern Asian Studies, 9 (1975), pp. 385–96.

[14] See now also the Symposion on the Decline of the Mughal Empire by M.N. Pearson, J.F. Richards and P. Hardy in Journal of Asian Studies, 35 (February 1976), pp. 221–63.

[15] Cf. H. Dunlop (ed.), Bronnen tot de geschiedenis der Oostindische Compagnie in Perzië, The Hague, 1930, p. 204. This Dutch opinion was not isolated or particularly original. For contemporary Turkish opinions to the same effect, cf. B. Lewis, Some Reflections on the Decline of the Ottoman Empire, in: C.M. Cipolla (ed.), The Economic Decline of Empires, London, 1970, pp. 215–34. Cf. also F. Braudel, La Méditerranée et le monde méditerranéen à l'époque de Philippe II, 2d ed., Paris, 1966, vol 2, p. 47.

a remarkably resilient and durable one at that, allowing for dramatic ups and downs without an irreversible collapse being unavoidable.

The Mughal empire, it would seem, fits very well into such a perspective of resilience and durability. Thus J.F. Richards convincingly concludes that "the vector of change was always in the direction of centralized power exercised by an Islamic ruler." "Despite the extent and severity of revolts and disorder in the first half of the eighteenth century Muslim rulers and Muslim institutions retained a tenacious hold on power."[16] If this is the case, the question as to how the empire actually worked rather than how it declined and collapsed imposes itself.

3

In the centre of the stage were the Mughal and his retainers, the *mansabdārs*, whose primary function was the recruitment and maintenance of specified contingents of the Mughal heavy cavalry, the prescribed size of the contingent indicating the *mansabdār's* rank. These ranks, it should be noted, did not derive from a hierarchical command structure, but only represented a gradation of status. A military command structure was largely missing. This made for maximal flexibility, but it also meant that the Mughal was not comfortably situated at the apex of a vertical military hierarchy, but had to move in a horizontal field of personal relationships with at least the higher ranking *mansabdārs* or nobles – this being possibly the reason for the utterly complicated rules of court etiquette. In other words, the central or at least most conspicuous organizational principle was that of an elaborate predatory war band stressing an ethos of martial panache and personal loyalty to the Mughal proven on the battlefield and rewarded with heroic titles. So the Mughal primarily worked through a personal network of high ranking retainers that was ideologically oriented towards conquest.

However, this was only part and perhaps not even the most important part of the picture. The actual base of the empire was clearly agrarian, which means that the central concern had to be the extraction of whatever agrarian surplus could be made available. For this had to pay for the *mansabdārs* and their troopers, either indirectly through salaries derived from the crownlands or directly through assignments of taxable land (*jāgīr*). So the main problem was not conquest but the extraction and management of the agrarian surplus

---

[16] J.F. Richards, *op.cit.*, p. 316. In this respect the evidence, given by the same author, for the remarkable recovery after a period of confusion and decay of the two main centres of Golconda under a forceful governor in the 1720's seems indicative of the system's resilience (*ibid.*, p. 304 ff.).

from the tracts that could be controlled. This obviously called for intensive regulation and considerable bureaucratic effort. The *mansabdārs*, therefore, were not only warriors and courtiers; they had to be competent administrators as well, so as to be able to head the bureaucratic establishments at the centre and the provinces – not to mention the supervision of the management of their land assignments. That there was indeed an impressive bureaucracy which administered the complicated regulation system is, as already mentioned, amply attested. However, even the best of military and administrative systems can not by themselves produce the agrarian surplus, which they need for their own maintenance. This meant that the imperial undertaking – apart from its being a "gamble on the monsoon" – essentially depended on the degree of cooperation that could be obtained from the local producers or rather from their leaders, the local men of substance. Over the centuries a considerable store of mutual accommodation as well as of technical experience with assessment had been built up, but the yearly realization of the agrarian revenue always remained a precarious matter of what in each case the trade could bear.

Because of the always precarious agrarian base conquest remained a necessary complement to the management of the areas already under control and, as we saw, the central organization and ideology were in principle geared to that purpose. However, conquest – as distinct from mere raiding – not only meant a fairly heavy outlay in campaign costs, but also, and more importantly, the winning over of the local men of substance and their retainers, who were in actual control of the agrarian resources in the areas to be conquered. This in turn meant that they had to be rewarded, preferably by integrating them into the *mansabdār* corps and giving them the corresponding salaries in cash or taxable land. Thus, for instance, the conquests in the Deccan resulted in the influx of a great number of Deccani notables into the higher *mansabdār* ranks.[17] This investment in local influence was always a risky one. For whatever was to be added to the central resources in crown lands and the revenue to be derived from them were in fact already largely pre-empted by the demand for salaries and assignments to pay the rising number of *mansabdārs*. In the case of the Deccan the conquest conspicuously failed to produce the expected returns and even seems to have created a severe shortage of assignments. Even the newly won crownlands of Golconda which were left relatively undisturbed by the Maratha inroads, could not remedy the pressing demand created by the expansion of the *mansabdār* corps.[18] In this way the

---

[17] Cf. M. Athar Ali, *The Mughal Nobility under Aurangzeb*, London, 1966, pp. 92–94, 173; Irfan Habib, *op.cit.*, pp. 269–73.

[18] Cf. J.F. Richards, *op.cit.*, pp. 157–62.

effects of direct military failure in open battle were less damaging than the risks of succesful conquest – the more so, since the Mughal heavy cavalry usually remained master of the battlefield till they were outdated by the firing power and organization of the sepoy battalions. The danger was in the aftermath of conquest.

So the empire remained precariously suspended between the opposite needs for careful husbanding of its resources and risky investment in conquest. But in order to put this dilemma in its proper context two further points must be considered, namely the role of trade and the problem of the frontier.

4

While there is no doubt that the main prop of the Mughal empire was agriculture, it would seem that trade and finance as important, even pivotal, factors are left somewhat in the dark. The language of the official documents and the chronicles puts almost exclusive stress on the warrior-administrator with his troopers and clerks on the one hand and the peasant or *ra'īyat* (ryot) on the other, with nothing in between. The situation looks as if the administration was in direct contact with the peasant-producer who provided the sinews of war as well as of peace. Such a situation, where all manner of intermediaries are excluded and dealings are directly with each peasant separately seems indeed to have been the ideal, as it equally was of the British administration.[19] And it stands to reason that the bureaucratic idiom was geared to this ideal. However, the various ways in which the sources insist on direct relations with the peasant – to the point of encouraging him to pay his revenue directly into the treasury, bypassing the revenue collectors[20] – suggest that there were good reasons for this repeated insistence, and, consequently, that actual practice will have been rather different. In fact, it could hardly have been otherwise.

The point is that at least from the thirteenth century onward the revenue was assesed and paid in cash.[21] So the crux of the matter was the conversion of the extracted surplus into money. The relationship between warrior-administrator and peasant could therefore hardly be a direct one. In between the two was the cash nexus. Short of an enormous state trading organization –

[19] Cf. Irfan Habib, *op.cit.*, p. 230.

[20] *Ibid.*, p. 242; W.H. Moreland, *The Agrarian System of Moslem India*, Cambridge, 1929, pp. 107, 133 ff.

[21] Cf. W.H. Moreland, *op.cit.*, p. 204; Irfan Habib, *op.cit.*, pp. 236 ff, 249.

even with the help of modern facilities such ventures are beset with dismal failures – the administration was unable to handle the cash nexus by itself. The only possibility was to shift the burden of the problem to the peasant and let him cope as best he could with the conversion tangle. Now "peasant" is a reputedly vague category – in fact, something of an abominable snowman of Indian history, ubiquitous but elusive. But so much is clear that the actual tiller or cultivator could hardly be called upon to make revenue payments in cash. The evidence is scanty, but what we know clearly indicates an utterly depressed condition of the country people.[22] The cultivator must have been singularly denuded of money. As a Dutch observer noted about 1614, "when travelling through the country, I have often wondered whence so much money could be collected, for they live extremely poorly and meanly."[23] Even the growers of an important crop like indigo near the great centre Agra were "constrained to sell to engrossers at very low prices for want of money to supply the needful."[24] The cultivator then appears to be generally unable to deal with the revenue demand by himself, nor can he have been an interesting counterpart for the revenue authorities. So both "peasant" and administrator needed an intermediary class of financiers and merchants, such as the indigo engrossers in the last quotation, who had sufficient liquid capital at their disposal to handle the cash nexus. Although the sources have little but disparaging remarks to offer on the class of merchants and moneylenders, it seems safe to infer that they actually were the pivot of the imperial enterprise.

That the sources nevertheless tend to ignore this class need not surprise us, since they stress the warrior-administrator's outlook and values. Generally speaking, the merchant is, from the point of view of agrarian society, a marginal figure, if he is not roundly deprecated as a dangerous interloper. Thus the ancient Indian book of statecraft, the Arthaśāstra, ranges the merchant with the "thieves known under other names" and as a "thorn" in the body politic.[25] Possibly his pivotal importance made him even more

[22] Cf. W.H. Moreland, *India at the Death of Akbar*, reprint, Delhi, 1962, pp. 126–29, 248–53; *From Akbar to Aurangzeb*, London, 1923, pp. 202 f, 256 f, quoting Bernier's Letter to Colbert.

[23] Cf. W.H. Moreland, *Relations of Golconda*, The Hakluyt Society, 1930, p. 77. Though the reference is to Golconda, there is no reason to assume that the picture of the countryside in the Mughal area was essentially different.

[24] W.H. Moreland, *India at the Death of Akbar*, p. 104; also Irfan Habib, *op.cit.*, p. 78.

[25] *Kauṭilīya Arthaśāstra* 4.1.65. Perhaps a not unsimilar outlook, stressing the "warrior-administrator's" point of view, while disregarding commerce, can also be found with the British-Indian administration. For instance, it is at least remarkable that, while the governor-general Wellesley like a true "warrior-administrator," discussed the annexations of 1801 exclusively in terms of their strategic importance and their revenue resources, his brother Henry was particularly enthusiastic about their commercial potentialities (cf. P.J. Marshall, "Economic and Political Expansion: The Case of Oudh," *Modern Asian Studies*, 9 (1975), pp. 465–82, esp. p. 481; cf. also E. Stokes, "Agrarian Society and the Pax Brittanica," *ibid.*, pp. 505–28, esp. p. 507). Even though

suspect in the eyes of those who depended on him. On the other hand the commercial class was far from being easily definable. The variety of its operations made it perfectly possible to classify the merchant and financier in other ways. His access to local or regional markets meant that his function was the marketing of the agrarian surplus. This enabled him to act as a source of credit and to "engage for the revenue." And this in turn was practically tantamount to land control. He could then quite naturally be labelled as a landholder, while conversely the landholder had to have liquidity and credit at his disposal. Superior rights in land had by nature a commercial aspect and we do indeed meet such landholders of different denominations who at the same time had important commercial interests.[26] The fact, attested already by surviving sixteenth century documents, that superior rights in land were a perfectly saleable commodity, equally bears out the connexion of landholding and commerce.[27]

In the same way the merchant and financier found his way into the bureaucracy to which he was anyhow indispensable. For tax collecting and "engaging for the revenue" look very much like the two faces of the same Janus – if they were not identical –, and we can readily understand the orders, which, as already noted, attempted to bypass the *'āmil* or tax collector. As one *mansabdār* complained with characteristic literary flourish, "the boat of his jāgīr was floundering in the flood of misappropriations raised by his tempestuous *'āmils*." And this was only a jāgīr; the vast imperial and provincial bureaucracy must have offered staggering opportunities to the tempestuous. At any rate, whether "tempestuous" or not, the official tax collector needed to have the same financial expertise, knowledge of the district and understanding of the market as the grain dealer and moneylender. Even though the Mughals clearly strove to keep commercial interests and official administration apart, they badly needed the cooperation of these

"there is no evidence that commercial considerations played a part in his brother's (the governor-general's) decision to take territory," the two sets of considerations were, of course, to a great extent interdependent. The governor-general's exclusive emphasis on strategic and land revenue arguments may then have been determined by the boundaries of the warrior-administrator's legitimizing idiom, which blocks the commercial argument from being expressed. Generally speaking, the British-Indian administration's marked preference for peasants and landlords and its disregard or contempt for urban traders and financiers would seem to have the same background.

[26] For a good example see, for instance, one Koldinder Ranga Razu, mentioned by Richards (*op.cit.*, p. 270), an important landholder and deshmukh of Eluru, who equally owned ships and carried on coasting trade. In fact this is not very surprising except when we think, as we are prone to do, in terms of the neat Census of India categories.

[27] Cf. Irfan Habib, "Aspects of Agrarian Relations and Economy in a Region of Uttar Pradesh during the Sixteenth Century," *Indian Economic and Social History Review*, 4 (1967), pp. 205–232, esp. p. 216.

experts and they could hardly avoid to recruit them to the financial departments of their bureaucracy. Thus the repeated injunctions against the farming out of revenue rights rather seem to indicate that this was more of a practice than the sources want us to believe. And, anyway, it is difficult to see how, for instance, the holders of land assignments (*jāgīrdār*), often posted at a great distance from their assigned lands could manage them without leaving a great measure of freedom to their '*āmils*. The question whether the actual arrangement was technically one of farming or not, seems largely an academic one. In fact the practice of farming out the collection of estate rents to groups of local financiers who then provided for the management of the estate while being equally involved with the district administration through family connections, seems to have remained a common practice in the nineteenth and even twentieth centuries.[28] On a far larger scale we know the difficulties that the incipient English administration experienced in the second half of the eighteenth century over the problem of divorcing commerce from administration.

So it cannot come as a surprise when we learn that local governors seem in practice to have been free to enter the market on their own initiative, while on the other hand we see merchant community leaders in political roles, financing pretenders to imperial succession or negotiating political settlements. No less indicative are the fairly common instances of public authorities lending money to merchants and vice versa in the sixteenth and seventeenth centuries[29] – that is long before the time of the empire's break-up. Nor was there a serious barrier for the merchant-financier to enter the ranks of the *mansabdār* nobility.[30] Even military roles came easily within his purview since his operations would anyhow have acquainted him with this aspect, both for the control of the revenue paying estates and for providing protection to his transport.[31] The cash nexus made the combination of commercial and financial operations with land control on the one hand and

---

[28] Cf. J.P. Musgrave, "Landlords and Lords of the Land: Estate Management and Social Control in Uttar Pradesh, 1860–1920," *Modern Asian Studies*, 6 (1972), pp. 257–75, esp. p. 268 ff.

[29] Cf. M.N. Pearson, "Political Participation in Mughal India," *Indian Economic and Social History Review*, 9 (1972), pp. 113–31, esp. p. 129.

[30] A well-known example is the carreer of Mir Jumla, who started out as a self-made merchant, became a powerful minister of Golconda and went over to the Mughal side as a high-ranking *mansabdār* (cf. Manucci, *Storia do Mogor*, Transl. by W. Irvine, London, 1907–08, vol I, p. 231). His official position seems to have been closely tied in with his extensive commercial operations.

[31] See, for instance, the case of Chinana Chetti, younger brother and successor of the commercial East coast magnate Malaya, who equally appears as holding various public offices and on occasion as commanding troops in the field (cf. W.H. Moreland, *From Akbar to Aurangzeb*, p. 156).

official administrative, on occasion even military, functions on the other rather natural and unavoidable.

The point of all this is, of course, not to celebrate the period as one "of equal opportunities" and "careers open to talent." The essential point is that we should be wary of viewing the empire mainly as a rigidly centralized and hierarchical bureaucratic structure rationally extracting and managing its agrarian resources. Such the Mughals certainly wanted it to be, but their imperial pyramid had to be built on the quicksands of personal networks with variously overlapping personnel and interests, which controlled the local and regional markets and thereby the surrounding agrarian tracts. It was these groups and networks that were in actual control of the sources of revenue on which the empire depended. Instead of controlling them from a commanding height the Mughal, in order to get at the resources necessary for his survival, had to involve himself all the time in local influence and to stake his power in the ever-changing alignments of factions jostling for local and regional predominance. By the same token local influence was free to encroach on the imperial centre. The integrity of the whole was therefore in the intertwining and overlapping of interests competing for the distribution of power, rather than in the spectacular use of superior force, which moreover could all too easily lead to over-extension. The system then was one of a "balancing of relative weakness," managed by conflict[32] in which the Mughal could at best be a superior arbiter arranging and re-arranging the distribution of power by a judicious and sparing use of his resources. Viewed in this perspective the imposing pyramid of imperial power had in reality to sag into a rather shapeless horizontal plane, formed by constantly shifting power configurations and governed by pervasive conflict.

5

The resulting diffusion of power was, however, not a matter of mere confusion and chaos. The neat picture, propounded by the sources, which opposes the peasant-producer and the warrior-administrator as the two poles of the empire, is broken in the middle by the operation of the cash nexus. But the same phenomenon can also offer us a vantage point for discerning a certain leading principle in the seemingly chaotic free-for-all. This principle

[32] Cf. B.S. Cohn, "Political Systems in Eighteenth Century India: the Benares Region," *Journal of the American Oriental Society*, 62 (1962), pp. 312–20, esp. p. 313. Though Cohn refers to the 18th century, the system of relative weakness and management by conflict is equally relevant for the 16th and 17th centuries – as it is for the traditional empire in general.

would, as we saw, be hard to find in the formal administrative and military structure of the empire, but rather in the movements of trade.

Though the imperial administration held on to an exhaustive organization of the total area, claimed by the Mughal, in nested territorial units – *pargana*, district, province –, it would be misleading to view the empire as an integrated territorial whole, pushing its boundaries even further into the sub-continent. Rather we have to think of the empire in terms of strings of greater and smaller centres controlling their immediate hinterlands. These centres were the market towns, where the cash nexus found its natural solution. From these market towns the business communities could control the immediate agrarian hinterland, extract the marketable surplus, convert it into cash and pay the revenue. These greater and smaller market centres did not exist in isolation. They were linked with each other by an extensive network of trade routes. In an ancient trading area like India with its strategical position in the Indian Ocean and its overland connections with Western and Central Asia such trade routes did exist together with a well-developed system of long distance transport and finance. "All nations bring coin and carry away commodities for the same; and this coin is buried in India and goeth not out" as an early English merchant succinctly put it.[33] The actual framework of the empire was formed by the market towns strung along the trade route which carried the streams of goods and money.

Rather than the actual control of vast territories, which anyhow had to be left to all manner of intermediaries, the leading principle appears to have been the control of the trade routes and the market towns along them. The emphasis on the protection of the roads and the principle that the officer in whose jurisdiction a robbery or theft had been committed had either to recover the stolen goods or pay compensation,[34] were obviously dictated by more than a simple concern for public order as an aim in itself. The safety of the trade routes clearly was of vital importance to the empire. The remittances of revenue depended on the capacity of long distance trade and finance for this essential service. The breaking-away of provincial administrations and their becoming independent sultanates – as happened to the Delhi Sultanate – may well have been occasioned by severe imbalances in interregional commerce and re-routing of trade rather than by purely military weakness. Conversely, the Mughal empire's holding together may again have had the strength of inter-regional trade as its mainstay, since the revenue transmitted

[33] William Hawkins, in *Purchas his Pilgrimes* (Hakluyt Society, 1905) For this well-known stereotype, cf. also Bernier's classical statement in his letter to Colbert (A. Constable's édition, rev. by V.A. Smith, of *Bernier's Travels in the Mogul Empire.*, Oxford, 1914, pp. 202 f.).

[34] Cf. Irfan Habib, *Agrarian System ...*, pp. 68 f.; J.F. Richards, *op.cit.*, p. 190.

through the channels of interregional commerce was an important factor in financing this trade. That the Delhi Sultanate, as so many other Indian empires, had a history of repeated break-ups while the Mughal empire did not, would seem to be a tribute to the increased strength of interregional commerce, stimulated by the growth of overseas trade. The weakening of the Mughal empire may then have had its cause in the impossibility to control the sea lanes and to force the seaborne trade to use the ports that it favoured. The growing concentration on Calcutta in the eighteenth century, corresponding to a re-routing of trade and a falling-off of other trading areas, including the routes to Western and Central Asia, may have had more to do with the declining effectivity of the empire than its military-administrative weakness.

Admittedly this line of reasoning raises more questions than this essay can even begin to answer. But it seems safe to assume that roads and their trade provided the basic framework of the empire. It was only through the intermediary of the market towns along the trade routes that the cash nexus could be handled. This meant that the Mughal's effective power and authority – as distinct from mere ritual suzerainty to be invoked or disregarded at will – was virtually limited to the trading centres and their immediate hinterlands. As the Dutch Company merchant Pelsaert reported, the Mughal "is to be regarded as king of the plains and open roads only."[35] The expansion of the Mughal empire was therefore as much a matter of extending control along the main routes as of developing lateral feeding roads and *qasbahs* in the further hinterlands.

But by the same logic the limited areas of effective control interconnected by the main and lateral roads left large interstices where the Mughal had to content himself with, at best, a nominal overlordship, leaving the management of affairs to the local "magnati et potentes." That the latter were either recognized as tributary chiefs or known as rebels and robbers, if they could not be made to agree to a tributary arrangement, was, of course, a fine but largely theoretical distinction. In practice the personnel of both categories could and did change from one category to the other with disconcerting ease. Thus Pelsaert, after stating that the Mughal's rule only extended over the plains and open roads, continues by saying: "for in many places you can travel only with a strong body of men or on payment of heavy tolls to rebels. The whole country is enclosed and broken up by many mountains and the people who live in, or beyond the mountains know nothing of any king or of Jahangir; they recognize only their rājās who are very numerous. Jahangir, whose name implies that he grasps the whole world, must therefore be

[35] Cf. W.H. Moreland, *Jahangir's India: The Remonstrantie of Francisco Pelsaert*, Cambridge, 1925, p. 58.

regarded as ruling no more than half the dominions which he claims."[36] This would not have been so serious a limitation, if the situation could have been stabilized in a durable manner. But, of course, that would have been too much to expect and it stands to reason that the activities of the "rebels" in the interstitial areas were primarily directed at the trade routes, where sizable gains, ranging from simple plunder to regular transit dues, could be made.[37] Tolls and transit dues, though certainly an object of imperial regulation, were levied not only by "rebels," but equally by tributary rājās and even imperial officers whether authorized to do so or not. An instructive case is provided by the transit dues levied by the rājā of Dhaita – not even a "rebel" – on the road from Surat to Burhanpur. When the English complained on the ground of the exemption from transit dues granted to them by the emperor, they were made to understand that the emperor could not interfere. The interesting point is that this was not so much a matter of the rājā's autonomy as, on the contrary, because of the tributary arrangement. For, as the emperor somewhat lamely but understandably explained, it was out of the transit dues that the rājā paid his tribute.[38] Obviously, the empire was not a compact territorial unity, but this case also shows the degree to which the emperor not only acquiesced in, but depended on local situations and arrangements that went against the grain of unitary regulation. Quite apart from tributary rājās, there equally were cases of villages, even within a few miles of the imperial centre, Agra, forcibly exacting transit dues. Even worse is reported by Pelsaert mentioning an unidentified rājā whose forces came pillaging up to and even inside Surat. Nor was the immediate neighbourhood of even greater centres, such as Ahmadabad, Agra, Delhi and Lahore, spared the inroads of "thieves and robbers," coming "in force by night and day like open enemies"[39] – all this in the twenties of the sixteenth century, that is long before there was any question of an impending break-down of the empire.

The point to be stressed is not the deficiencies of public order – in fact the situation seems to have compared favourably with that in other areas as, for instance, the Deccan sultanates –, but the fact that observers seem to have taken such disturbances as in the nature of things, as a structural fact. The basic structure then, to which one had to adapt oneself, was the precarious balance of "regulation" tracts round the market towns and uncontrolled interstitial areas with their numerous rājās beyond the Mughal's effective

[36] *Ibid.*, p. 59.
[37] For the easy transition from robbery to blackmail and transit dues, cf. W.H. Moreland, *From Akbar to Aurangzeb*, p. 289.
[38] *Ibid.*, p. 288.
[39] As above, n. 35. Cf. also Irfan Habib, *op.cit.*, p. 69, n. 42, for references to the activities of Meos and Jats between Agra and Delhi, the Rajputs of Baghelkhand and the Kolis in Gujarat.

grasp. Or, in Mughal terms: revenue-paying or *ra'īyatī* areas as against the "rebellious" ones known as *mawās*.[40] Since the Mughal could not hope definitively to subdue the *mawās*, he had to settle for an uneasy and constantly changing balance of forces.

6

In this context we can perhaps better understand the problems involved in the dual aim of conquest and careful management of already controlled areas. As already pointed out, the precariousness of the agrarian resources base often made conquest a likely or even unavoidable proposition. But we equally saw that conquest could well turn into a self-defeating venture. The Mughals must have been perfectly aware of this risk. That they nevertheless gave prominence to conquest seems to have another reason. This is that there was not just an external frontier which one could either choose to round off and secure or to push further out. The real frontier was a pervasive, internal one, raggedly and shiftingly dividing *ra'īyatī* and *mawās*. On the one hand control of the main trade routes had to be followed through to their end. Stopping at a particular point, say half-way across the Deccan, would not only impair the use of such routes, which would then depend on what happened at the other end beyond the empire's control, but, what is more important, uncontrolled forces would find sanctuary there and be able to interfere with the route's traffic, even on the Mughal side. On the other hand, extending control along the trade routes made the extent of the interstitial areas grow pari passu. Both faces of the dilemma were amply demonstrated by Aurangzeb's experiences in conquering the Deccan, but by the same token it seems doubtful whether he had much of a real choice between continuing his costly campaigns or limiting his efforts to the areas conquered earlier.[41]

The problem showed its sharpest edge in Aurangzeb's campaigns, but we may doubt whether this was simply a matter of foreign conquest that one

[40] For these terms cf. Irfan Habib, *op.cit.*, p. 331, n. 5. According to Habib the term *mawās* is not found in the dictionaries. It is, however, given in J. Platts' *Dictionary of Urdū, classical Hindī and English* in the sense of "protection, refuge, asylum, shady grove or wood," which from the "rebel's" point of view, makes perfect sense.

[41] J.F. Richards (*op.cit.*, p. 310) suggests that Aurangzeb might have paused in 1687 to negotiate some form of tributary relationship with the Maratha king. This would have enabled the emperor to organize the newly conquered Deccan kingdoms of Bijapur and Golconda. Such a course of action might have alleviated, at least temporarily, the pressure, but it would not have changed the structural problem, since it is not clear what would have kept the Marathas from building up strength and renewing their inroads.

could decide for or against as one saw fit. The problem was essentially the same as that of the inner frontier. The inner frontier was not, of course, a more or less fixed line, but consisted of wide stretches of area weaving round the trade arteries. In these stretches competing groups of warriors, traders and landholders – categories which, as we saw, easily intertwined to the point of being indistinguishable – converged and struggled for control, while coming sometimes dangerously near to the main centres. To understand the nature of these areas, it may be useful to recall the classical Indian opposition between the areas – or patches – of settled agriculture and the wastes surrounding them, each of the two with its own way of life and institutions. While family and caste were at home in the agricultural village, the wastes were the home of the warrior and his war band. The two, though opposite and perpetually in conflict – latent or patent – with each other, were not mutually exclusive. People from the agricultural villages would join the warriors in the wastes, while the warrior and his retainers might be either called in for protection against other warriors or force their protection upon the village. Agriculturalists would try to extend their cultivation to the wastes, which on the other hand they needed for grazing their cattle, while warriors would strive for control of the settled agricultural areas and their productivity.[42] Most important, however, was the fact that the connections between the areas of settled agriculture and between them and the greater urban centres ran through the wastes.

Thus, for instance, an early Rajput chronicle of the great Rathor house relates how an ancestor, Vīrama, after joining two leading members of the inimical Johiyo clan, started a feud against his elder brother, was expelled, made attacks on the "imperial road," fought and dodged the troops of the sultan, and finally combining again with his two Johiyo allies "went and unyoked his carts at Vaderana. And the Johiyos gave Vīrama the fourth part [of the profits of] the road." Then, finding new allies through marriage, he "started to devastate the territory of the Johiyos and to seize the whole [profit of] the road," till Vīrama at last was killed with 140 of his men, as was the leading Johiyo, when the latter retaliated by devastating the villages controlled by Vīrama. And so the story of feuds, alliances, establishing and

---

[42] For the opposition between "nuclear areas" of settled agriculture and the wastes with their warriors, cf. B. Stein, "Agrarian Integration in South India," in: R.E. Frykenberg (ed.), *Land Control and Social Structure in Indian History*, Madison, 1969, pp. 175–216, esp. pp. 188, 192, 206. (Stein concentrates on the "nuclear areas" and their institutions, but their relationship with the "tribal" areas is made equally clear). Though the author deals with South India, there is no reason to assume that the opposition was limited to the South. In fact, it is not limited to India either, see, for instance, "Land" as against "Wald" (cf. O. Brunner, *Land und Herrschaft*, 6th ed., Darmstadt, 1970, pp. 185 ff.).

losing control over roads and villages, founding and attacking towns and principalities went on.[43] Though this particular episode relates to the fifteenth century, it may well serve as an epitome of the inner frontier under the Mughals.

As will be clear from the similarity with the small scale situation of the village and the surrounding wastes, the inner frontier was ubiquitous. But it was, of course, weightiest around the main through routes, which attracted the greatest density of interested parties, especially bands of warriors, and a correspondingly high level of competition and conflict. These areas amounted in many cases to what might be called "frontier marches,"[44] which included both revenue-paying regulation tracts around the market centres and uncontrolled areas in an inextricable but ever changing balance. Now cultivation and regulation were extended, then again sedition took over, whole tracts reverting to *mawās* status and giving shelter to "malefactors" and "non-chiefs."

The only thing that the Mughals could do to reduce these inner marches to a modicum of order was to involve themselves in their affairs and stake their power in the on-going tussle for their control – an activity that tallied particularly well with their origin and ideology of a war band. The time-honoured and, in fact, only way to do this succesfully was to make use of the pervasive conflict between the different participants and to enter into alliances with a number of them, so as to control the others. That is, in many ways they had to act not so much as powerful overlords, although this was certainly their intention, but rather as partners in the affairs of the inner marches.

The pattern for these arrangements was set from the start by the Mughal-Rajput alliance, which made the empire in effect a joint venture. This meant that the Mughals had to tie some of the great Rajput houses into their system by establishing asymmetric marriage alliances with them, which virtually made the Mughal into the highest ranking Rajput, and by giving them high *mansabdār* ranks with the corresponding remunerations and court privileges.

---

[43] Cf. L.P. Tessitori, "Bardic and Historical Survey of Rajputana, a Progress Report," *Journal of the Asiatic Society of Bengal*, NS. 15 (1919), pp. 33f and 39f.

[44] Rather than to the well-known Turner thesis of the American frontier, I feel indebted to P. Wittek's view of the frontier marches and their warriors (*The Rise of the Ottoman Empire*, London, 1938, pp. 16–32). Wittek sees the origins of the Ottoman empire in the warrior bands of *ghāzīs* ("warriors of the faith") with their distinct culture and institutions, operating in the marches – shared by them with the Byzantine *akritai* – between the Islamic and Byzantine worlds. In many ways the Mughal empire seems reminiscent of this situation. One might even say that the Mughals never quite overcame the frontier situation, or rather that they not only originated in it, but remained based on it in a way that the Ottoman empire did not. For "the Frontier in History," see also O. Lattimore, *Relazioni, X Congresso Internazionale di Scienze Storiche*, vol. I, pp. 103–38.

This particular alliance was a notable success. But the arrangement had as its corollary that many of the important roads running south from the Delhi-Agra area had to be left in the control of Rajput chiefs.

The direct route between Surat and Agra via Ahmadabad, which ran through the territories of tributary Rajput chiefs, was so much beset with dangers and exactions that usually the longer route via Burhanpur was preferred, although the latter was not free from considerable imposts and risks either. Moreover, the rules of the game, namely making use of and involving oneself in the existing factional alignments, implied that only a part of the Rajputs were effectively tied into the imperial system, while the Mughal had to content himself with, at best, tributary arrangements with the others. In fact, the situation was even more complicated, for factionalism did not stop at the level of the chiefs of the great Rajput houses. It was not unusual for their sons and relatives, when they felt they had been wronged, to "take to the fields" with their retainers and start harassing their chiefs till a settlement was reached.[45] The latter feature could, of course, work both against and in favour of the Mughals, but in order to exploit it they had to involve themselves in these dissensions, so as to maintain or restore the balance of forces. What is worse, involvement meant also that dissension could all too easily spread to the Mughal side as well. So the careful balance between the limited capacity to establish and keep up imperial regulation and the threatening forces of the *mawās* essentially depended on the exploitation of local dissension and making alliances with part of the other contenders – Rajputs, Marathas and others, as the case might be.

The constant rearticulation of the balance demanded that the Mughals most of the time had to commit their forces in local situations, sometimes becoming all but submerged in them to the point where imperial officers became enmeshed with "rebels" and vice-versa. Such was the pervasiveness of the inner frontier that they could often hardly do otherwise. In their *jāgīrs mawās* areas were often, and on purpose, included. Since the forces of the imperial or provincial centres were either already engaged in particular campaigns or otherwise dispersed in local involvements, extra support was mostly hard to get, so that the imperial officers both in their *jāgīrs* and in their posts were very much left to fend for themselves as best they could. They therefore had to adapt themselves to the ways of the "marches." There they had to tussle cheek-by-jowl with their opposite numbers, known in the imperial idiom as "malefactors," "rebels" and "non-chiefs" or as landhol-

---

[45] On the institution of *bhūmiyāwat* cf. W.H. Sleeman's *Rambles and Recollections* (rev. and ann. ed. by V.A. Smith, reprint, Karachi, 1973), pp. 245–52.

ders and officers if they had somehow obtained an imperial sanction.[46] In other words, they had to operate in the same way, intertwining their military and administrative functions with financial and landholding interests in a situation where imperial pretensions could easily become more of a burden than a support.

When viewed in this perspective it seems somewhat superfluous to look for specific internal reasons to explain the decline and fall of the Mughal empire. Even in its hey-day it rested on a precarious balancing of forces round the inner frontier. A break-down was always just round the corner, but the system could just as well continue indefinitely. It was, however, precisely this fluidity that gave the Mughal empire its remarkable resilience and durability, even under the pressure of overextension and adversity. For the working of the precarious balance and the corresponding diffusion of power meant that there was no single, readily definable point, where the imperial system could be attacked and definitively defeated. In fact it never was. It was simply overarched and finally replaced by a completely different dispensation.

7

After this lengthy disquisition it is time to return to the theme of expansion and reaction. But before we can speak about a reaction, or even before we can ask whether there was a clear-cut reaction at all, a few words must be said about the way expansion took place. In the first place it is important to note that there was no strategic level or centre where the expansionist forces could come to grips with the Mughal system in a decisive manner, even if they had wanted to do so. But except for a single and ill-prepared venture to start a diminutive empire of their own, the English, like their European competitors did not even want to do so. Instead they desperately tried to stick exclusively to their commercial role. When finally they were forced to give up this exclusive stance and started to intervene in India's politics, it was not because of the empire's weakness. Primarily it was a side-product of inter-European

---

[46] Perhaps the Mughal bureaucracy's dual alignment of military and financial offices can be viewed more as an adaptation to the factional structure, by putting in charge of each post at least two officers, than a purely rational division of tasks. Thus a provincial revenue officer could equally well intervene militarily, especially in the reserved crown domains. (For a differently formulated but not dissimilar dual alignment in the British Indian administration, see above, n. 2). The formation of semi-independent regional principalities, as in the case of Bengal or Hyderabad, started with a pulling together of both functions by the "proto-dynast" (cf. Ph.B. Calkins, "The Formation of a Regionally Oriented Ruling Group in Bengal, 1700–1740," *Journal of Asian Studies*, 29 (1969–70), pp. 799–806, esp. p. 802, on Murshid Quli Khan; J.F. Richards, *op.cit.* p. 277, on Mubariz Khan in Hyderabad).

competition for control of the sealanes. When this happened they had to combine their commercial operations with military activities and land control. In other words, the English – following the French lead – became partners in the classical game of the inner frontier, to the point where the Company Bahādur obtained, as provincial *dīwān*, the revenue rights of Bengal and Clive became a high ranking imperial noble with a resounding Persian title. Although this presented the somewhat jarring picture of a mercantile company going into agrarian land control, and on a dangerously large scale at that, this type of expansion hardly called for an Indian reaction. On the contrary, it was the English who reacted by adapting, not without enthusiasm, to Indian ways and circumstances. The game was played on Indian terms, even though the English generally could call the shots.

However, after what has been said about the precarious balance that the inner frontier implied, it is clear that the English venture in combining land control, finance, trade and military operations could all too easily lead to overextension and even a run-away process playing havoc with the Company's finances – as indeed happened during the first decade or so after Plassey. Essentially the choice before the English was either to involve themselves and their resources at the local level, to manipulate and arbitrate competition and conflict – as the Mughals had been forced to do – or to withdraw as far as possible from local conflict in order to pool and reserve the Company's power and resources. Since the first course of action – especially in the form of illegal private trade by Company servants using the Company's power and privileges – had proved disastrous, it was the second that imposed itself. This found its clearest expression in the Permanent Settlement of 1793. Whatever this momentous decree may have done for the introduction of full private ownership of land protected by law, its main thrust was the reservation of power and the use of force as well as the refusal to get involved in local affairs. This meant that now a public realm, the state, was decisively set apart from the web of competing social forces, which were left to cope with their local situations, as many new-style landowners found to their grief.

It took, of course, a considerable time before the policy could be fully effective. For some time the Company still had its own frontier areas such as the semi-independent Oudh kingdom, where British merchants and even official personnel together with their Indian partners continued to dabble profitably in trade and land control in the traditional way.[47] But when compared with the Mughal system the new dispensation was an unprecedented departure from tradition. Where the Mughals had been forced to

---

[47] Cf. P.J. Marshall, *art.cit.* (above, n. 24). Characteristically British commercial interests in the area strongly opposed the annexations of 1801.

involve themselves in local affairs and conflicts to the point of submergence, the English could extricate themselves from them and even pay the price of leaving a possible surplus in the hands of the landholders. Such a step the Mughals would never have been able to take, not because of indiscriminate greed, but because the undrained surplus would have strengthened the forces of dissension and aggravated the pervasive problem of the inner frontier. The English on the other hand could afford to do this, since theirs was not an exclusively agrarian empire but a world-wide trading network with its power centre safely outside India and soon to be backed by the industrial revolution.

On the other hand the British Indian regime was far from being a laissez-faire proposition. It had to and did pursue vigorous policies of pacification, regulation, education and public works. Apart from that, even while following a policy of reservation and withdrawal, the government could not ignore Indian society. The British Raj, like any colonial regime, was perpetually pulled in opposite directions by the need to leave the ruled-over society alone and the equally pressing need to deal with it in an effective way. However, not only the rules of the game, but the game itself had changed. By way of metaphor one might say that the traditional game was the balance of the inner frontier, which demanded "horizontal" involvement and disper-sion; the new one, on the other hand, was that of an equally precarious balance, but now between "vertical" involvement and withdrawal. Or, in less metaphorical terms, where the Mughal was concerned with nobles, chiefs, "malefactors" and even "non-chiefs" in their comprehensive capacities as leaders of men controlling local influence networks, the British Indian government only recognized them as isolated individuals holding narrowly defined legal rights of land ownership. With the Mughals they had been little kings and partners in empire, in the eyes of the English they were simply landowners, albeit sometimes big ones. Even when the great rebellion of 1857 – in fact not a reaction but a chaotic resurgence of the sprawling inner frontier – had dramatically demonstrated the need to give them special consideration, the English could do no better than to classify them for the purpose as the arbitrary category of landholders, whose estates paid 5000 rupees and upward per year in land revenue, and the modern type association that was meant to give substance to this category never came really to life.[48]

This, however, did in no way mean that Indian society was destroyed as the English, taken aback at their own innovative daring, were often prone to think. The fact is that their own mode of operation, however striking a departure from tradition it was, precluded such drastic results. The new

[48] Cf. T.R. Metcalf, "From Raja to Landlord," and "Social Effects of British Land Policy in Oudh," in R.E. Frykenberg (ed.), *Land Control . . .* (see above, n. 42), pp. 123–62.

dispensation implied that in order to preserve itself from the run-away effects of involvement in society the government refused to work with influence networks and their leaders, but only dealt with categories and legal abstractions. The British Indian government could only view society in terms of census categories and of nested territorial units from the revenue village upward – incidentally creating considerable misunderstanding about the concepts of caste and village. In other words British rule was a thoroughly bureaucratic one, – the ideal of the Mughals, who had, however, been betrayed by the circumstances. Now bureaucracies may be utterly irritating and deeply disturbing, but they can not by themselves change society. Although the British Indian government increasingly widened and deepened its dealings with Indian society, they only did so by reducing total situations to abstract models, which were amenable to impersonal rules and regulations. For instance, shifts of rights in land from indebted landlords to their creditors – a disturbing phenomenon to the administration which feared that it might result in sedition and violence, or rather, more deeply, felt this to be a threat to its static view of society – led to the construction of agricultural as against non-agricultural castes, so that legislation, preventing alienation of land from one category to the other could be devised and applied. That such categories are not too well-founded in reality is, of course, clear from what we have already seen of the unavoidable interlocking of landholding, commerce, finance and, as modern additions, journalism and law practice. Local society could, of course, find its way towards accommodations with the bureaucratic heaven and its less heavenly minions. But the important point is that government action was directed at specific, abstractly defined cases, not at the fluid, multidimensional web of relations that is the substance of society and was for the same reason studiously avoided by the administration. Actual influence networks could sometimes be destroyed by bureaucratic action, but then there were others to take their place without a change in the social system being effected. Thus, for instance, in a study of the social consequences of extensive land transfers in the Benares region, B.S. Cohn, answering the question what happened to the dispossessed, concluded that "the overall answer may well be that nothing happened."[49] On the other hand the bureaucratic grid and procedures may have added a new but hardly innovative way for fighting the old fights.[50]

[49] Cf. B.S. Cohn, "Structural Change in Rural Society, 1596–1885," in R.E. Frykenberg (ed.), *Land Control* ... (see above, n. 42), pp. 53–121, esp. p. 113.

[50] A case in point is the one, analysed by Frykenberg (*Guntur District*, see above, n. 2), of a district chief clerk, who, combining various interests, managed to build up a tightly controlled network. In other words, he had used the bureaucratic facilities to build his own "dependency" in much the classical way. Interestingly the conspiracy was broken by the efficient co-operation of an

It seems then that the respective modes of operation of the British Indian government and of Indian society were not only different but worlds apart from each other. They could and did impinge on each other, the government by specifically directed actions and groups from society by claiming government support. But they had their being in different worlds. Encounters remained incidental, limited to specific activities and only for the duration of the activity. For persistent contacts, and a broadly based confrontation there was no room. And this may well be the reason for the impression of "a Dasehra duel between two hollow statues locked in motionless and simulated combat," life entering into the duel only when at last the forces within Indian society itself came to grips with each other.

It would seem then that the episode of European expansion did not evoke a consistent and directly related reaction – except for the reception of yet another classical medium, the English language, in India's impressive range of literary idioms. Should we then resign ourselves to the mockingly hollow echoes of Forster's Malabar Caves? They might seem a fitting epitaph to the era of expansion, but it is not what happned.

8

What happened is, briefly and prosaically, this. Instead of obtuse stagnation, or the equally popular notion of a vulnerable arcadia, Indian society showed once again its remarkable resilience. The public domain of the state had been taken out and set apart from society. But this equally set Indian society free to develop new potentialities. The withdrawal of power and resources which had fed and strengthened the interaction and overlap of society's innumerable local and regional segments meant at first that Indian society lost much of its diffuse but effective coherence. It became more parochial and fragmented, even though the government covered all of the subcontient. However, the corollary of the government's aloofness was that society was left with more resources than before, which moreover increased considerably over the nineteenth century,[51] and these resources stimulated the development of new

English administrator and his Indian chief clerk, the latter belonging to the same background and community as the conspiring head of the district bureaucracy. Probably it was his particular knowledge and understanding of the utterly tangled particularistic situation that made the enquiry a resounding success. It almost looks as if the English had to use – albeit unknowingly – the potentialities of intra-communal factionalism in order to break the conspiracy, that is they acted in the "traditional" way.

[51] For the increase of resources, cf. M.D. Morris, "Towards a Reinterpretation of Nineteenth Century Indian Economic History," *Journal of Economic History*, 33, 4 (Dec. 1963), reprinted

linkages.[52] The government, by creating channels for its actions and allocations, set certain cadres for these developments. The most conspicuous of such cadres was the rigid hierarchy of territorial units. Present day "regionalism" may owe as much to this circumstance as to India's variegated cultural history. But the government could not contain, let alone guide, these developments and was rather prone to panic when confronted with their unforeseen results when they threatened to overflow the neat bureaucratic grid of units, categories and rules.[53] The important question was, however, not whether the government could contain the growing impetus of new developments and supra-local linkages, but whether Indian society, left in this respect largely to itself, could devise the means to regulate itself on a wider scale than the local community. Briefly, the main problem was that of supra-local, universalistic authority. For authority on an all-India scale had been reserved by the government and was administered in bureaucratic fashion, impinging on but not guiding society.

Now universalistic authority transcending local society – or any actual society for that matter – had always been there in its specifically Indian form of the renouncer, who stood outside society and therefore was the ideal arbiter and consensus-maker.[54] When the increased possibilities and resources in society tended to uncontrollable wild growth and pervasive conflict passed far beyond local society, India naturally had to fall back on the institution and transcendent values of renunciation for guidance. It is hardly surprising then that, when developments had gained momentum in the interbellum period, the acknowledged leader should have been a Gandhi, who saw himself and was acknowledged as a classical exemplar of renunciation – however enigmatic and contradictory the Gandhi phenomenon may have appeared, first of all to his own compatriots. Paradoxically, the fact that he could so easily be entombed in the halls of rhetoric fame and all but forgotten, may be considered a measure of his real achievement. This achievement had

with critical comments in *Indian Economic and Social History Review*, 5 (1968), pp. 1–100, and Morris' rejoinder, *ibid.* pp. 319–88.

[52] For the development of local positions of strength and their supra-local connections, cf. e.g. D. Washbrook, "Country Politics: Madras, 1880–1930," in: J. Gallagher – G. Jonhson – A. Seal, *Locality, Province and Nation*, Cambridge, 1973, pp. 155–211; C.A. Bayly, "Patrons and Politics in Northern India," *ibid.*, pp. 29–68.

[53] An illustration is provided by the unrest in the Punjab canal colonies, where wealthy peasants had built up their strength and, using their rural-urban networks, undermined the neat grid of bureaucratic rule. See N.G. Barrier, "The Punjab Disturbances of 1907," *Modern Asian Studies*, 1 (1967), pp. 353–383.

[54] For the institution of world renunciation, cf. L. Dumont, "World Renunciation in Indian Religions," *Contributions to Indian Sociology*, 4 (April 1960) pp. 33–62; for a different view, cf. author, "India and the Inner Conflict of Tradition," *Daedalus*, Winter 1973, pp. 97–113.

little to do with his usual image of a not too decisive social worker. His aim was nothing less than the reorganization of Indian society on the universalistic basis of the renunciatory ideal. His spectacular non-cooperation and civil disobedience actions were not so much directed against the British regime, as aiming at the founding of national unity under the aegis of the renouncer's ultimate authority. This meant that national unity was to be realized by an ultramundane "renunciatory" society which required its adherents to give up en masse their state supported positions and distinctions. For all its dramatic expressiveness this was hardly a viable proposition. Nor could it aim at overthrowing the government. In so far as it could be viewed as open rebellion it could only be so in the way of a temporary "secessio in montem sacrum," leaving state and government in their place and ready to arrive at a negotiated reconciliation – as time and again happened. It is therefore perhaps not fortuitous that Gandhi's actions had the same specificity as bureaucratic state action. As bureaucratic action was geared to apply specific rules, so Gandhi's actions were aimed at breaking specific rules, for instance the government salt monopoly. But all the same they remained within the overall conventions of the government. They were not meant to be formally "seditious" and the road to negotiated settlement was expressly left open. Here then, it would seem, was the real issue, namely to develop a workable relationship between state and society. This could obviously not be achieved by the dramatic but ephemeral non-cooperation and civil disobedience actions. What was needed was a lasting organizational framework for supra-local, national unity, a framework that could function as an effective counterpart to the state. To this end Gandhi reorganized the Indian National Congress in successive stages during the interbellum period so as to keep it attuned to the devolutional reforms of the state.[55] Though this organizational work was totally unspectacular and therefore easily overlooked, it may well be that this was the field where Gandhi's leadership showed its most important and lasting results.

This Congress was not a movement, still less a party, but an all-India arena for handling the pervasive conflicts of particularistic society. It did not aim at eliminating particularism – anyhow an impossible task – but at accommodating it in a universalistic setting. While it accommodated conflict, it took care of national consensus as well. Now Congress had since its beginnings in the eighties of the last century laid great stress on producing unanimous

[55] Notwithstanding Gandhi's professed disregard for constitutional niceties, the Congress constitutions of the interbellum period clearly bear the inprint of his considerable organizational talent and ideas. For these Congress constitutions, cf. D. Rothermund, "Constitutional Reform versus National Agitation," *Journal of Asian Studies*, 21 (Aug. 1962), pp. 505–22.

resolutions, to the point of simply skipping important but controversial points. But consensus enforced by the renouncer's transcendent authority was altogether a different matter, as the concerned Indian parties found to their discomfort, for instance, in the heated controversy over the separate vote for untouchables, when Gandhi started on a fast unto death to force consensus. But even more important was the fact that Gandhi practically transferred his authority to the consensus-making centre of the Congress, which therefore during the last decade of the British regime came to be journalistically known as "the high command." With that Gandhi's role virtually ended and could be safely enshrined in India's rich mythology.

In this way the dual system of post-independence India came into being. On the one hand there is the government with its wide-spread professional and rigidly hierarchical bureaucracy administering impersonal laws and regulations; on the other hand the essentially horizontal arena of Congress – the low degree of professionalization of its organization is significant – taking care of interest groups and their intensely personal conflicts, while at the same time handling national consensus. Though its form was only developed in the interbellum period it is strangely reminiscent of the horizontal, factional system of management by conflict that was both the bane and the blessing of the Mughal dispensation. The dual structure was comparatively easy to maintain as long as the English were there and Congress was barred from the government apex. When Congress had to take over the central government the precarious balance between state and society became intensely problematic.[56] The horizontal arena increasingly encroached on the vertical organization and process of government, whose bureaucracy had already before independence lost much of its celebrated "steel frame" character. It may well be that new formulas will have to be developed to handle the balance.[57]

The point I want to stress is that the new dimension added as a result of western expansion enabled Indian society seriously to attempt the realization, however partial and ephemeral, of long-standing universalistic ideals that so far had been beyond the grasp of reality, such as Gandhi's attempt to realize the old ideal of outerworldly harmony in the modern political terms of national unity. That ideals, when brought to earth from the safety of their

[56] On the friction over the relationship between the governmental apex and the Congress centre, cf. S. Kochanek, "The Indian National Congress: The Distribution of Power, between Party and Government," *Journal of Asian Studies*, 29 (1965–66), pp. 681–97.

[57] It is, of course, too early, to view the recent developments in their proper perspective. However, it may well be that in the end it is not so much the state that will have eliminated society's encroachment on its grounds, but, on the contrary, particularistic society and its turbid procedures that will turn out to have taken over the seat of government.

ultramundane haven, seldom make for happy endings, is, of course, all too
well known. Indeed the story given here in utter abbreviation is one of intense
conflict and unpleasant incidents. The most dramatic part was the break
between Hindus and Muslims. Whatever recent and future research on the
train of events leading up to the partition catastrophe will teach us,[58] it would
seem clear that the specific form of universal authority, as propounded by a
Gandhi, could not be easily acceptable to the conscientious Muslims, who
equally were forced out into the open to restate in modern terms the
implications of Islam for universalist authority. Whether the break was
unavoidable or merely the result of a series of quirks and accidents is hardly a
valid question. But the dramatic break does show that the introduction of
universalistic ideals into reality is beset with unforeseen and explosive risks.
Unhappily, these seem to be the price for grappling with new horizons.

To conclude: it would seem that the concept of a reaction to something
alien can better be replaced by that of a symbiosis within the relevant society –
a symbiosis between old-established particularistic and comparatively risk-
free modes of operation and organization on the one hand, and the risky
new dimension that promises the realization of equally old-established
universalistic ideals. The symbiosis is obviously an uneasy one, turning as it
does on incompatibility. The essential point is, however, that it steadily grows
and develops new forms. This symbiosis was brought about by Western
expansion, but the latter did not and could not share in it. Not because it was
Western, but because it would not involve itself in the problems of the
symbiosis.

Does this mean that there is only scope for ethnocentric history? The
answer would seem to be that the symbiosis is not a monopoly of ex-colonial
countries. It is a world-wide problem, which is usually and confusingly
known as "modernization." It was and is experienced in Europe as in other
parts of the world. Perhaps we may therefore expect that the comparative
perspective will overcome the barren fragmentation of ethnocentricity.

---

[58] See now F. Robinson, *Separation among Indian Muslims, The Politics of the United Provinces, 1860–1923*, Cambridge, 1974.

4. "WESTERN EXPANSION AND CHINESE REACTION" A THEME RECONSIDERED

by

E. ZÜRCHER

I. THE PREMODERN STATE AND SOCIETY: BALANCE, INTEGRATION AND TENSION

Pre-modern China[1] presents the picture of a cellular society, held together by the tenuous network of an official apparatus of government, which, on its part, was the executive arm of a theoretically autocrat imperial power. These three components functioned together in a subtle equilibrium established in the course of centuries – a precarious balance, disturbed by periodic crises, but always re-established again, primarily because each component needed both others to survive.

The imperial power, theoretically absolute, was actually limited as much by the practical irreplaceability of the official managerial class as by the traditional Confucian state ethos, by which imperial despotism was subject to very real (if primarily ethical) sanctions.

Moreover, the mandarin governmental apparatus had limited possibilities for the exercise of power, if only because of its small size and consequently restricted ability to impose its will throughout society: local state power could penetrate no deeper than to the district level – which was often still an area with several towns and many dozen villages.

In all its governmental activities, therefore, the mandarinate was forced to co-operate with the local leaders, and in particular with the literate upper

---

[1] The situation summarily related here is roughly relevant for the eighteenth century. To be sure, the consequences of Western expansion were marginal before 1860, and it would be possible to take a later cross-section. But this does not seem preferable, because in the decades before 1860, the traditional order was greatly disrupted by a number of endogenous factors, such as the disastrous financial consequences of the Emperor Ch'ien Lung's expansion policy in the second half of the eighteenth century, the growing agrarian distress in consequence of the population explosion (from 279 million in 1779) to 430 in 1850), and the chaos brought on by the T'aip'ing rebellion of the early 1850s. This sketch also only refers to China proper, and not the situation in the outer provinces, peopled mainly by non-Chinese.

stratum of "title-holders" (those who had passed at least the preliminary state examination), who are generally, and somewhat misleadingly,[2] called "gentry" and who, with their families, made up around 1–2% of the population. In all the essential functions pertaining to the state in the Confucian vision (the upholding of true ethical norms, indoctrination, the repression of deviant behaviour, the administration of justice, collection of taxes, "the recruitment of talent" through schools and state examinations, and welfare) the magistrate relied on analogous gentry activities at the local level. This was even true for the task generally most closely associated with state power, namely the "maintainance of law and order" (in this case, the suppression of local revolts). In the last decades before Western penetration, when the official army (the Manchu "banners" and the Chinese "green batallions") was completely degenerate, this task was carried out at the local level by a militia led by the gentry themselves. Above all, the gentry were the exponents and conservers of the Confucian system of norms at the grass roots. With their literary and ideological schooling the notables were to influence and indoctrinate those beneath them, while, as graduates, they themselves constituted the reservoir from which future officials were recruited.

In spite of the intertwining of the government apparatus and the literate local elite, the two systems were fundamentally opposed. As a tractable instrument of the Emperor, the official was purposely uprooted and cut loose from his own local group. He could not serve in his province of origin (frequently an area as large as France); in principle he was transferred every three years during a virtually life-long service to the state, so that he had little opportunity to maintain contact with his home base. His position was almost that of a colonial officer, dependent on the co-operation of the local "native chiefs", whose language he sometimes scarcely understood. In other words, pre-modern China was characterised by the symbiosis of two opposing systems: the cellular, but in terms of culture and ideological training remarkably homogeneous, *particularist* sector of the gentry; and the basically *universalistic* system of the imperial bureaucracy, held together by a peculiar mixture of mutual dependence and reciprocal mistrust. Both formed part of a socio-political framework, whose rationalisation and ideological justification was given by Confucianism.

---

[2] If "gentry" is understood as "landlord" then the first half of that word is only partly suitable for the Chinese situation, and the second completely unsuitable. The income of the Chinese gentry in the late imperial period was only partially derived from the possession of land, as is shown by Chang Chung-li, *The Income of the Chinese Gentry* (Seattle, 1962). Also the word suggests an element of heredity, lacking in the Chinese situation. The Chinese term *shen-shih*, "gentlemen with silk belts," refers to the dress reserved for graduate *literati*, and is thus more neutral.

In theory, a third important sector – that of trade and industry – remained outside the symbiosis. In the Confucian vision of society the merchant is in principle under suspicion. Even as the leader of his guild or "regional association",[3] he was not a figure with whom to co-operate, but rather one to keep under control. In practice, however, the prosperous trader had close ties with the gentry, who, particularly in the towns, took a full part in commercial activities (just as in the country they monopolised usury). Even the officials, who were debarred by their status from any other profession, knew very well how to profit, either from secret investment or from their position as "official supervisors" in the state monopolies. In practice, the authorities co-operated as closely with prominent merchants, guild heads and bankers (who themselves often had a gentry background in their home base) as with "genuine" leaders of the gentry. And especially in times when the exchequer needed replenishing (the 19th century is a classic example) large-scale merchants were enabled, at exorbitant prices, to buy titles which conferred on them a sort of semi-gentry status. Incidentally, the role of the magnates in the great cities in no way resembled that of the rising urban bourgeoisie in the West. The trading community lacked not only concrete organs of power, but even the will to force the granting of privileges or to fight for urban independence. In fact, there was no clear town government; the magistrate who (perhaps) had his seat there ruled over a much larger area. The town itself was a walled conglomeration of groups and organisations with little mutual co-operation, and no common political aspirations.[4].

In principle, the mass of the population were mere subjects, the object of a paternalist government, which lost no opportunity to impress on the masses their basic norms of conduct: unceasing productive work, thrift, the meticulous fulfilling of all family duties and acquiescence to the supervision by family and clan elders, by leaders in the local community and the almost super-human authority of the magistrate. There was hardly any opposition to *these* elemental norms in traditional society. Popular uprisings, generally under charismatic leadership, were the consequence of concrete abuses which

[3] "Regional association" refers to the, sometimes very powerful, organisation (predominantly) of merchants, who were active in the large towns, but who generally came from the area outside the town and who maintained relations with their neighbourhood. Often this foreign element monopolised certain branches of trade and money dealings.

[4] A depoliticizing effect may have resulted from the relative ease with which powerful merchants in the late Imperial period could gain entry to the gentry through the examination system and the sale of titles. The system made possible a considerable degree of upward mobility for merchants within the established order, and thus gave no encouragement to deviant political aspirations. See P.T. Ho, *The Ladder of Success in Imperial China: Aspects of Social Mobility, 1368–1911* (New York, 1962) and L.S. Yang "Government Control of Urban Merchants in Traditional China," *Tsing Hua Journal of Chinese Studies*, VIII, (1970), pp. 186–210.

could be righted by an "enlightened prince". The ideologies associated with them were not revolutionary, but were rather variations of the established ideology:[5] they were aimed not so much at a fundamental alteration of social relationships, but at the re-establishment of the ideal order, not even necessarily under a new dynasty. On the threshold of the new era, the great exception was the T'ai'ping rebellion (1851–1864), inspired by Christian ideals, which turned against the traditional gentry ideals with its full force and which, as we shall see, brought the system to the edge of ruin.

During the Manchu (Ch'ing) dynasty (1644–1912), the empire had a continental orientation. Overseas trade was not stimulated, and was a source of immense wealth only for individual officials. Neither overseas trade nor the related emigration and settlement of Chinese communities throughout South East Asia gave rise to maritime expansion – anyone who left the empire was discounted.[6] The central government had little concern for insignificant Macao, for the very small-scale trade with the West in Canton, severely restricted and supervised, or for the scarcely appreciable smuggling along the China coast. The growing opium trade was irritating, but not much more. Even Japan was very largely ignored. As against this, there was intense concern for developments inland – and to this extent China's so-called isolation during the Ch'ing period is a myth. The government kept fully up to date with power shifts in Mongolia and Central Asia. Russian expansion in Siberia was closely watched (often thanks to intelligence given by the Jesuits) and, where necessary, was energetically countered. The enormous Chinese imperialist expansion on the continent, to which modern China actually owes its present boundaries – in 1792 Chinese armies pushed through as far as Nepal – presents a contrast to the passive attitude towards maritime affairs. Indeed, in spite of the "brute force" and "technical ingenuity" (both qualities lowly placed in the Confucian value system) of a few far-away barbarian princes, the Sino-centric world view was fully maintained: relations with the outside world were carried on unequally, as a matter of principle; they had to take the ritual form of tribute-plus-limited-trade, and even that as a favour.

In this very summary picture of pre-modern Chinese state and society, two qualities stand out, namely integration and equilibrium. Integration in this sense meant that, within the traditional policy, there was no consideration of any alternative, which would have been capable of affecting to the slightest

---

[5] See Vincent Shih, "Some Chinese Rebel Ideologies," *T'oung Pao*, XLIV (1956) pp. 150–226.

[6] On the extremely limited Chinese reaction to the massacre of Chinese in Batavia (1740), see Lo-shu Fu, *Documentary Chronicle of Sino-Western Relations 1644–1820*, Tucson, (1966), pp. 172–4.

extent the ruling pattern of values and the related social (Confucian) order. Buddhism and Taoism, always politically powerless, had lost all intellectual power of conviction by the late imperial period. After a promising beginning, the mission of the early Jesuits and their successors had completely failed – and anyway they had always deliberately sought to adjust to the existing order and had wisely refrained from preaching subversive ideas. Pre-modern China knew only one proponent of positive renovative action in the social and political field, namely the club or faction of "progressive" members of the government and literati who, while sometimes organised (or disguised) as a learned society, and sometimes openly as a pressure group, pressed for limited reforms by the court.[7] But even they were concerned with the elimination of particular abuses (corruption, imperial high-handedness, government by eunuchs) or with particular concrete measures (more concern for armaments or for copper mining), not with the presentation of genuine alternatives.

Contrasting with this aspect of integration was the precarious character of the balance between court, official government apparatus and local leadership. Traditional society knew a number of tensions that threatened to disturb this equilibrium. In the relationship between the court and the bureaucracy there had existed for centuries an unavoidable tension between the imperial autocratic desire for power (stemming from the Emperor himself or from the "strong men" in his entourage) and the interests of the top officials – a tension which could find an outlet either by massive purging of the bureaucracy or by a palace revolution. The mistrust of the court led traditionally to the diffusion of official competence (as little clarity as possible as to who was responsible for decisions, a preference for bodies with multiple leadership, a complex system of mutual control and supervision) and to the fear that the power of provincial governors and supra-provincial governors-general might lead to regionalism. The same anxiety that officials might develop roots in their districts through too close relationships with the local (gentry) networks of power, naturally led to the aforementioned rule requiring transfers every three years and forbidding service in native provinces.

[7] The classic example is the literati faction of the so-called Tung-lin Academy, which in the early seventeenth century protested against corruption and eunuch-power and was suppressed with force. See H. Busch, "The Tung-lin Shu-yüan and its political and philosophical significance," *Monumenta Serica*, 14 (1949–1955) pp. 1–163; Charles O. Hucker, "The Tung-lin movement of the Late Ming Period," in J.K. Fairbank (ed.), *Chinese Thought and Institutions* (Chicago, 1957), pp. 132–163; John Meskill, "Academies and Politics in the Ming Dynasty," in C.O. Hucker (ed.), *Chinese Government in the Ming Time* (New York, 1969), pp. 149–174. In many respects the reform party of 1898, which *i.a.* agitated for a constitutional monarchy, still bore this character; see below, note 10.

The danger of polarisation in the relationship between court and country was strengthened during the last dynasty because of the foreign origin of the Manchu imperial house and of the ambiguous policy adopted by this originally "barbarian" elite to maintain its position (on the one hand, extreme propagation of Chinese culturalism, "encapsulation" of the Chinese gentry and the incorporation of Chinese in the Manchu-Chinese diarchy; on the other the maintainance of a certain apartheid and of a large, albeit degenerate, military apparatus). In the lower strata, hate against the Manchu persisted, particularly in the subversive secret societies.

The relationship between the state apparatus and the gentry contained those forms of mistrust which probably always develop when a central authority and a particularist system are dependent on one another; apprehension among the gentry over official arbitrariness and censoriousness; anxiety in the centre over the growth of local foci of power which in special circumstances (chaos and economic distress, leading to rebellious movements among the masses) could grow to encompass a region. In particular, there was fear of the illegitimate use of the local militia in such a case, which always made discontented gentry a potential threat for the government.

The position of the commercial city "bourgeoisie" was ambivalent. In the light of Western history it may seem strange that a Confucian regime did not consider this class to be a particular source of political tension. It apparently took the line that the businessman, who naturally benefited from "law and order" was not likely to ally with movements of rebellion. In fact, commercial opportunism could take other, less loyal paths and, in times of great disorder, some merchants became indeed money-lenders and "contactmen" for these very movements.

This overview of pre-modern China would have been far too detailed, if it were not that the irruption of the West in the second half of the 19th and the early part of the 20th centuries must be placed definitely against this background, and that the Chinese reaction only becomes comprehensible in the context of these patterns of equilibrium of power, integration and tension. In very global terms it can be said that Western penetration in the 19th century increasingly upset this balance and intensified each of the tensions, until the point was reached (sometime between the Boxer rebellion of 1900 and the Revolution of 1911, or even earlier, with the debacle of 1898?), at which they became explosive and shattered the old structure. The abolition of the State examinations (1905) symbolises the break-up of the old order.

However, the same could be said for the Chinese reactions to Western expansion. Every reaction, every adjustment introduced in an attempt to cope with the new situation, threw the old polity further out of equilibrium and strengthened or re-activated a whole series of sometimes long-existing tensions: the isolation of the court and the growing anti-Manchu feelings, regionalism, the increasing irrelevance of the examination system, the activities of secret societies, the swelling anti-dynastic sentiment, and so on. Like some very sick organisms, the Empire was not killed just by external germs, but more, perhaps, by the effect of the antibodies which it manufactured to defend itself against them.

Finally, the West increasingly upset this state of "integration". The disruption of the old system, as much through external as through endogenous causes, was coupled with the proposal of alternatives, which were out of the question in the old society. In this lay the emancipatory force of Western expansion – a subject over which so many guilt-ridden sociologists have racked their brains. The old society knew few outlets – the single ideal of the official career, and the single road of Confucian study plus examinations leading to it, overshadowed all other perspectives. Moreover, anyone who could not adapt himself, within his own circle, to the Confucian system of norms, could only turn to the very fringes of society, such as the monastery, begging, the theatre, prostitution, or, (as an absolute last resort) the army. Even if initially only in a limited area, the coastal strip and the cities, Western penetration presented alternatives in virtually every field. Modern education finally broke through the Confucian monopoly. Intellectual status could be claimed by new professions, such as journalism, law, medicine and even technical specialisms that previously were considered as crafts. The professionalisation of an officer corps in the military academies (where the military were thought to acquire a modicum of knowledge and culture) made a military career an acceptable alternative. The generalising "amateur ideal"[8] of the Confucian "manager", with a wide literary and ideological education (who was thought to be able to do anything, because he had learned the right, that is to say the *ethical* way to think) gave way to a multiciply of specialist opportunities. The revolution of 1911 was thus revolutionary because it presented an alternative even for the Emperor – an alternative not derived from any autochtonous Chinese movement of rebellion, but from a distant echo of the French Revolution.

---

[8] Even the specialists who in practice were essential for the administration (in such fields as accounting, finance and public works), did not belong to the official apparatus proper; they were local "clerks," permanently attached to the magistrate's office and at a sub-official level. For the ideological background of this principle of generalism, see J.R. Levenson, "The Amateur Ideal in Ming and Early Ch'ing Society: Evidence from Painting," in *Confucian China and its Modern Fate*, vol. I (Berkeley, 1958), pp. 15–43.

II. PHASES OF WESTERN AND JAPANESE EXPANSION

The main lines of this process are well known and here only need to be sketched as a reminder.

After an initial phase, running from the treaty of Nanking (1842) to 1860, during which Western influence remained marginal (foreigners enjoyed extra-territorial rights in five ports while the interior was still closed to them), in the following two decades Western expansion became a torrent. The concessions extracted in 1860 led to the opening of the whole interior for trade and proselytization, to posting of Western diplomats in Peking, to Western control over Chinese import duties and to the rapid expansion of concessionary quarters in the big cities, through which Shanghai became bastion and centre for the diffusion of Western influence. The seventies were notable for the nibbling away at the fringes of China's territory, with Russian expansion in Turkestan and continuing colonisation by the French in Annam and the British in Burma, while only a few years after the Meiji restoration, Japan seemed to have learned its first lessons. A Japanese punitive expedition went to Formosa in 1874, and in 1876 Korea – a Chinese vassal state for centuries – was forced to conclude an "unequal treaty" on the Western model with Japan. Meanwhile relations with the Westerners were relatively undisturbed; these were the golden days of the "Old China Hands" in the treaty ports, where also developed a hybrid "Treaty Port Culture" among the Chinese. The threat from Japan became progressively clearer, culminating in the total defeat of China and the destruction of the modern military apparatus, built up with much difficulty, during the Sino-Japanese war (1894–95). By combined intervention Russia, Germany and France, each of them afraid of too great a Japanese supremacy, managed to moderate the extreme Japanese demands. However, China's impotence had become evident and the Western powers, who had till then been afraid of the eventual awakening of the "sleeping dragon", prepared for the "mad scramble for concessions": Russia in Manchuria and Liaotung, Germany and England in Shantung, France in the southern provinces. China was partitioned into spheres of influence; it was clearly on the way to becoming (in Sun Yat-sen's words) a "hypocolony", ruled by a club of great powers. The Boxer rising, an anti-western popular movement supported by the Manchu court, ended in failure and bloodshed in 1900. The very heavy Western and Japanese sanctions imposed in the Peking Protocol of 1900 meant the moral and financial bankruptcy of the Ch'ing regime. In opposition to the Western powers, little inclined to revolution anyway, Japan meanwhile made political use of the Chinese dissidents and revolutionary (i.e. anti-Manchu) groups which had sought sanctuary in Japan. Since the failure of the Movement for Constitutional Reform in China, in 1898, Tokyo was not only the most important channel by which Western know-how reached the new Chinese intelligentsia in a form more accessible to the Chinese public, but also the leading centre of Chinese revolutionary activity. "Republican China went to school in Tokyo."[9] An analogous role had been played since the late nineteenth century by Hong Kong and the Western concessionary quarters, particularly in Shanghai, which moreover kept their role as refuges for dissidents and breeding grounds for illegal organisations until well into the twentieth century.

III. THE CHINESE REACTION: LEVELS OF RESPONSE

It is tempting to bring the Chinese response to Western and Japanese expansion into this pattern, and to correlate it with these phases of penetration. Tempting perhaps, but shortsighted, because such a pattern would be practically limited to reactions and decisions of a political nature. Certainly, a clear correlation can be found in this limited sector between the phases of Western expansion and Chinese and Manchu attempts either to protect China from total disintegration or to keep the dynasty in the saddle.

So, on that level, during the seventies the beginning of a programme of "enlightened conservatism" can be recognised, based on the idea (in reality untenable) that it was possible to strengthen China technically and militarily while maintaining the "substance" of all traditional norms and institutions. In the period between 1875 and 1885 the intrusion of the powers into the border areas led to heightened military activity, combined with the beginning of diplomatic intercourse with the West and Japan. In the following decade there was growing fear of Japan and increasing insecurity and frustration in reform-minded circles, in both cases as a consequence of the limited success of the Self-Strengthening Movement The shock of the 1895 defeat brought a group of *literati* (still organised on the old pattern as a faction or pressure group,[10] but very strongly influenced by Western political ideas and by the

[9] J.K. Fairbank and E.O. Reischauer, *East Asia, the Modern Transformation* (London, 1957), p. 631.
[10] The movement led by K'ang Yu-wei had such traditional features as the personal network of K'ang who had a master-disciple relationship with his most important assistants (Liang Ch'i-ch'ao, Chang Chih-tung); or the classical "scriptural" basis for his reforming ideology, which was based on a singular, very shaky re-interpretation of the Confucian canon, and the influencing of gentry opinion though examination candidates, and of the court and the top levels of

example of the Meiji emperor in Japan) to desperate radical struggle for reform, with the support of the young Emperor (1898). After some three months of chaos came the conservative reaction, led by the Manchu court, which felt threatened; this culminated in the Boxer movement. In a period when, throughout China, people were fully alive to the acute menace to the country (the "mad scramble for concessions" after 1895), this purblind policy was fatal to the dynasty. The emphasis on specifically dynastic (and therefore Manchu) concerns increased anti-Manchu feelings, both traditional (the activities of the secret societies) and modern (the nationalist republican movement). After 1900, the court attempted to save the situation with a series of last-minute reforms, namely modern-style ministries, modern schools following Japan's example and the abolition of Confucian state examinations, the reform of criminal law and government finance, and – in an attempt to win back the gentry, who were rejecting the monarchy – the establishment of provincial councils as a first step towards a constitutional government. This late attempt to realise the ideas of 1898 failed for various reasons, such as the lack of able leadership, the wavering and ambiguous attitude of the court, the impatience of the provincial gentry to take more influence via the new institutions, and the growing suspicion that the Manchus were prepared to "sell China" in exchange for the maintainance of their own position of power. The revolution of 1911 was supported by all sections of the Chinese population and so the Empire fell (on 12 February 1912) virtually without a blow being struck.

These are the main outlines of the accepted picture. However, this periodisation is not tenable as soon as we consider the Chinese response as an articulated phenomenon, varying in form, content and intensity by sector, by section of the population and by region.

It is therefore clear that the general picture of a China allowing itself with the utmost difficulty and greatest opposition to be pushed along the road of modernisation (a picture that can be confidently propounded in a perspective limited to the political elite) is completely invalid for such an important sector as trade and banking in the big cities. There, instead, we find an extraordinarily flexible transformation, a great deal of accomodation, a virtuosity in the combining of traditional and western techniques and methods of organisation and, in general, the capacity to maintain their own position and

government by individual and collective memoranda to the throne. See Lo jung-pang, *K'ang Yu-wei, A Biography and a Symposium* (Tucson, 1967); J.R. Levenson, *op. cit.*, pp. 79–85; Hsiao Kung-ch'üan, "K'ang Yu-wei and Confucianism," *Monumenta Serica*, 18 (1959), pp. 96–212, and *ibid.*, "The Philosophical Thought of K'ang Yu-wei," *ibid*, 21 (1962) pp. 129–193; L.G. Thompson (trans.) *Ta T'ung-shu, the One World Philosophy of K'ang Yu-wei*, (London, 1958).

influence as against a supreme Western business world.[11] Also, as soon as we leave the literate environment, we can recognise among the mass of the population a characteristic preoccupation with Christianity, the only element of Western culture with which these layers were directly confronted. The reaction could be positive and even dramatic (as, in the T'ai'ping rebellion, a crusade on "behalf of God" against "idol worshippers", the Manchus and Confucianism), or negative and destructive,[12] emphasising the "immoral" and disruptive influence of proselytization and missions, and turning to virulent anti-Christian sentiment: the Boxer rising. *Mutatis mutandis*, the same necessity to differentiate exists for the other sectors: the gentry outside the main towns, the military, and the new groups on the periphery (such as the new intelligentsia, the pupils at Western educational establishments, Chinese students in Japan and the Chinese in Hong Kong and the diaspora).

IV. THE PROBLEM OF THE INDIRECT REACTION

"The Chinese reaction" to Western and Japanese expansion is an abstraction; the Chinese response was an intricate, stratified phenomenon, complicated by overlapping and mutual influencing and by the fact that some reaction did not originate directly from external influence but had the character of "reactions to reactions." For example, the attitude of the court in the last years before the Boxer rising, panicky, shying away from any radical reform, was not a response to Western expansion, but a negative answer to the constitutional reform movement of 1898; and the beginning of the modern arming of China was not only a consequence of Western threats, but also an essential element in the struggle against native rebellion; the first army corps trained and equipped in the modern manner did not fight against England, but under the leadership of an American against the T'aip'ings![13]

[11] This is particularly true for the distribution process. In his classic study "Marketing and Social Structures in Rural China," *Journal of Asian Studies*, 24 (1964–5), G.W. Skinner argued that the whole native distribution net, with its system of local and regional markets, actually stayed intact into the 1950s.

[12] Paul A. Cohen, "The Anti-Christian Tradition in China," *Journal of Asian Studies*, 20 (1961), pp. 169–180, and *ibid., China and Christianity: The Missionary Movement and the Growth of Chinese Anti-foreignism, 1860–1870* (Cambridge, Mass. 1965).

[13] The famous "Ever-Victorious Army," commanded in a later phase by Charles Gordon, was started as a characteristic expression of the military activities of the gentry on the local level described in the introduction; it was a Free Corps, raised and armed by groups of prosperous Shanghai bourgeois, which later became a section of the government troups. See Stanley Spector, *Li Hung-chang and the Huai Army – A Study in Nineteenth Century Regionalism* (Seattle, 1964), pp. 29–31.

In some cases it is difficult to use the concept "reaction." When did the reaction in the literal sense of an opposition (conscious or unconscious) induced by an external stimulus, end, and when did autonomous action begin? Where was the border between a movement which arose, directly or indirectly, from the confrontation with the West, and an endogenous process which was touched, transformed and even reactivated – sometimes in the most casual manner – by Western ideas? The clearest illustration of the problem is the already-mentioned T'aip'ing movement (1851–1864).

The T'aip'ing Rebellion[14] was the greatest of a series of mass popular uprisings which more or less coincided with the first phase of Western expansion in China and which together brought the Empire to the edge of destruction. Apparently, this agrees with the accepted picture. The movement was founded and (at least in theory) headed until its end by a charismatic leader, Hung Hsiu-ch'üan, complete with visions, prophetic dreams, miracles and attacks of divine frenzy. It was sharply anti-Manchu, like many other subversive movements during the last dynasty. It proclaimed a number of utopian ideals of a very egalitarian nature, such as communal property, equality of man and woman, prohibition of slavery and so on; it preached a certain measure of abstinence, such as the prohibition of prostitution, opium and useless luxury, and it was directed towards the establishment of the Heavenly Kingdom of Peace (*T'ai-p'ing t'ien-kuo;* the term *T'ai-p'ing,* "peace" had been used in this context time and again in the past by rebellious movements). Was there nothing new under the sun?

---

[14] The Marxist re-interpretation of Chinese history, in which these kinds of popular risings are seen as the most concentrated expression of class struggle in pre-modern society, has led to the T'aip'ings receiving a great deal of attention, both in the form of source publications and of secondary literature and popularisations. From the Western side, there has since long been special consideration for the T'aip'ings, ever since the contemporary descriptions by Thomas T. Meadows, *The Chinese and the Rebellions* (London, 1853) and T. Hamberg, *The Visions of Hung Siu-tshuen* (Hong Kong, 1854). Detailed study is possible because the T'aip'ings are the only rebellious movement which left an extensive and generally surviving literature, which can now be obtained in full English translation (in vols. II and III of Franz Michael and Chung-li Chang, *The T'aip'ing Rebellion: History and Documents,* 3 vols., Seattle, 1966–1971). Some of the important Western language studies of recent decades are: Eugene P. Boardman, *Christian Influence upon the Ideology of the T'aiping Rebellion,* Madison, 1952; William J. Hail, *Tseng Kuo-fan and the Taiping Rebellion,* New York 1964; Jen Yu-wen, *The Taiping Revolutionary Movement,* New Haven, 1973; J. Reclus, *La révolte des Taï-ping* (1851–64), Paris 1972; Vincent Y.C. Shih, *The Taiping Ideology: Its Source, Interpretations and Influence,* Seattle 1967; So Kwan-wai, Eugene Boardman and Ch'in Ping, "Hung Jen-kan: Taiping Prime Minister," *Harvard Journal of Asiatic Studies,* 20 (1957), pp. 262–294; Teng Ssu- yü, *New Light on the History of the Taiping Rebellion,* Cambridge (Mass.), 1950; id., *Historiography of the Taiping Rebellion,* Cambridge (Mass.), 1962; Teng Yüan-chung, "The Failure of Hung Jen-kan's Foreign Policy," *Journal of Asian Studies,* 28 (1968), pp. 125–138; P.M. Yap, "The Mental Illness of Hung Hsiu-ch'üan, Leader of the Taiping Rebellion," *Far Eastern Quarterly,* 13 (1954) pp. 287–304.

However, this same Hung Hsiu-ch'üan, who in his birth-place (near Hong Kong) had come into the most casual and superficial contact with various protestant tracts, was also "the younger brother of Jesus." He had received from God the Father the commission of ridding China from these "Tartar devils" who had deceived the Chinese people with their diabolical heresy. Together with all other peoples, the Chinese had received the revelation, but they had become disloyal; Confucianism must be abjured and the classics burnt. When the T'aip'ings conquered Nanking this capital of the "Kingdom of Heaven" (because, in T'aip'ing usage the traditional *t'ien-kuo* took this meaning!) was expressly identified with the New Jerusalem of the Apocalyps. Moreover, in the T'aip'ing state examinations set up on the Imperial model (in which candidates had to write a kind of theological tract in the place of the traditional essay), there were only three basic texts: the Old and the New Testaments and the collected "Revelations" given by God through his youngest son. In contrast to earlier rebel ideologies (which, as has been said, generally consisted of a variant of the traditional ideology) that of the T'aip'ing was radically anti-Confucian, directed against the whole of the established order and based on the very un-traditional belief in one antrhopomorphic divinity, a true "Revenging God", who was actively involved in the struggle. It is no wonder that the T'aip'ing ideology was more strongly inspired by the Old than by the New Testament.[15]

However, even the apparently traditional components took on a new context. T'aip'ing universalism was not Sino-centric, but based on the universal power of God (and thus also of his youngest son). The egalitarian measures were justified by the tenet that everyone, men and women, were "children of one God." The prohibition of "sinful practices" was based on a sometimes extreme interpretation of Biblical instructions; and even the movement's very name, for all its traditional associations, was interpreted as "a new heaven and a new earth."[16]

This overturning of all values (Confucian contemporaries correctly saw the T'aip'ing rebellion as a threat to the whole social order) would easily bring us to consider the T'aip'ings as one of the most radical reactions to Western

[15] A remarkable fact, only expicable as a result of spontaneous selection in a situation of holy war, leading to emphases that elsewhere are peculiar to the Book of Judges." The parallelism is so pronounced that we observe in the T'aip'ing religious concepts and rituals which, albeit of Biblical origin, have never played a role in Christianity; such as the personal appearance of God as the leader in battle, the bringing of material offerings to God and the strict application of the prohibition on representations of men and animals.

[16] Immanuel C.Y. Hsü, *The Rise of Modern China* (New York, 1970), p. 281. I have not been able to trace this interpretation elsewhere, neither in the T'ai-p'ing documents published by Michael and Chang, nor in Vincent Y.C. Shi's study on T'ai-p'ing ideology.

penetration – in which case the remarkably early date of the reaction, in a period when Western influence on the Southern coast had scarcely gone beyond the stage of the Canton trade and smuggling, would remain a mystery. However, in fact, the link with the West was exceptionally limited. Two leading men in the T'aip'ings had undergone a certain amount of catechisation: most had never left China, nor had had any direct contact with missionaries. The sources of inspiration were limited to a few tracts and Gutzlaff's Bible translation (and the absence of any orthodox exegesis can be shown from Hung Hsiu-ch'üan's marginal commentary written in his own hand).[17] The West played scarcely a role in the T'aip'ing ideology, neither in a positive, nor in a negative sense, while, on the other side, the politicians and generals who fought against the T'aip'ings never associated Western (Christian) countries with this enemy of all civilisation. The T'aip'ing movement is thus the clearest example of an endogenous development which digested various elements of Western origin in an independent manner, and so took on a completely individual character, without *confrontation* with the West playing a significant role. As if by chance, Western elements turned up in an endogenous development, and had a "multiplier effect" there.

V. ACTIVATION AND REACTIVATION OF EXISTING PROCESSES

In other cases the picture is more obscure, because, in one perpective, the element of confrontation and conscious response can be seen, while, from another angle, the development was connected to long-existing processes, which it strengthened, and activated or reactivated. In this field, Chinese nationalism forms a very obscure and controversial problem.

A familiar opinion, repeated *ad nauseam*, argues that nationalistic sentiments had not developed in pre-modern China, and were even in opposition to the most fundamental traits of Chinese particularist thinking, which was only concerned with the small group (family, clan, local community, guild, club, faction and so on).[18] With hindsight, I believe that this Western vision (already eagerly propagated in the 19th century literature) should not be trusted. It lends itself far too easily to a justification – conscious or unconscious – of imperialist assertions, along the lines that "the Chinese

---

[17] English translation in Michael and Chang, *op. cit.*, vol. II, pp. 220–237.

[18] For an eloquent example from shortly after the turn of the century, see the argument of Otto Franke in "Der chinesische Staatsgedanke und seine Bedeutung für die abendländisch-chinesischen Beziehungen" (1904, reprinted in his *Ostasiatische Neubildungen*, Hamburg, 1911, pp. 1–19).

recognise no nation," *ergo* "it can not matter much to them what happens to their nation," *ergo* ...; and the blind spot shown in the same literature to expressions of pre-modern proto-nationalism only makes my suspicion stronger. In fact the whole debate between culturalism and nationalism deserves to be re-opened.

In any case it must be mentioned that this generalisation is only valid for one of the two components of traditional society described above as living in symbiosis, namely the "particularistic sector." The other component, the universalistic sector of the Confucian governmental apparatus, constituted a body which, in many respects, can be compared to a "nation politique," to an official elite identifying itself with the state (and not just with the ruling dynasty), and which had since long contained unmistakeable proto-nationalist sentiments, at least in times of external threat, as from the Mongols in the 13th, and the Manchu in the 17th centuries. This went much further than mere loyalty to an Imperial House, although this mostly played a part.

We find thoughts and slogans that seem familiar; the term "we Chinese" (*Han*, the name of a long-departed dynasty, which is still used today to denote Chinese identity), the "great men of the past", the communal inheritance which must be protected, the culture heroes from long ago, and so on. Anyone dealing with the enemy is not a disloyal servant of the dynasty, but a *Han-chien*, a "traitor to China," and, for centuries, alongside dynastic names, terms like *Chung-kuo* "the Middle Kingdom," *Hwa* and *Hwa-hsia*, "the Blossoming Hsia" (once again with a reference to a mythical empire in the distant past), have been used to indicate China as a state, as a country.[19]

Expressed in a less literary manner (although the role of folk literature and drama should not be underestimated) similar proto-nationalist feelings can be found among the mass of the people, even though at that level they are often confused by religious and magical elements. In particular this element can be found in the anti-Manchu propaganda of the secret societies (in which nationalist sentiment was sometimes expressed by a completely theoretical

[19] In contrast with the "ecumenical" concept *t'ien-hsia*, "Everything under the Heavens," indicating the absolute moral authority of the Chinese Emperor as the Son of Heaven. In actual political thought, a distinction was definitely made between the tributary states, which carried on ritual, diplomatic and commercial relations with the Chinese court on unequal footing, and the "ten thousand nations" beyond them. The status of vassal was in theory not imposed, but sought: tribute was not a duty but a favour. The famous edict of the Emperor Ch'ien-lung, to the King of England (1793) did not imply that England *per se* and from the beginning of time had been in principle subject to the universal lord – rather the arrival of Macartney in Peking meant, in Chinese eyes, that it aspired to that status from that moment.

call for the restoration of the Ming dynasty) and, above all, in the proclamation of the T'aip'ings, in which the element "We Chinese" was well to the fore.[20]

In this perspective, the modern nationalism of Sun Yat-Sen was much more (or much less) than a direct reaction to Western ideas plus Western threats. Three components were combined in it: first, the movements for reform, based on anxiety over China's fate, launched by Confucian "progressive conservatives" (with whom Sun originally tried to join forces); secondly, the undercurrent of anti-Manchu secret societies (with whom he closely co-operated in the first phase of the Revolution; for that matter, Mao Tse-tung would later sometimes do the same!); and, thirdly, a modern republicanism, put together from a jumble of half-understood books and tracts. Once again the impression is gained that this was both innovating on its own account and activating with regard to existing, in part centuries old, processes.

Turning to a completely different field, the modernisation of the military apparatus, we find the situation even more complicated. As was mentioned above, the beginning of modern arming was not directed against the West, but against the T'aip'ings; the successful restoration of the sixties, of which the strengthening and modernisation of the military was a part, was an indigenous consolidation of the empire after the total disruption caused by the great rebellions.

In the struggle against the T'aip'ings the traditional state armies, the Manchu banners and the Chinese "green batallions" were found to be totally useless. The essence of the military reform consisted in the formation of a new type of army, which nevertheless did not correspond to any Western example, despite its partially Western arming. It was a conglomeration of local forces, recruited by the gentry and led in the field by their own gentry leaders. The commander-in-chief managed these gentry leaders as his personal network; they swore personal loyalty to him and thus formed a sort of regional military faction on a provincial basis. This type of army turned out to be much more effective than the traditional banner troups, dispersed in garrisons throughout the Empire, and indeed succeeded in suppressing the great rebellions within a few years.

However, this very success led to the perpetuation of this type of army. In

[20] See, e.g., the proclamation of 1853 (Michael and Chang, vol. II, p. 179), the series of memorials as a reaction to an edict of 1854 (*ibid.* p. 276–294), the proclamation of 1858 (*ibid.* pp. 698–701) and the essay on monotheism (pp. 559–561). Han "China" is clearly posed over against the Manchu-occupier, frequent use is made of terms like "Our people," "Our glorious and great country," "the thousands years old birthright of the Chinese people" and even "let people know that China belongs to the Chinese." On T'aip'ing "Christian universalism," see J.R. Levenson, *op. cit.* vol. II (Berkeley, 1964) pp. 106–8.

the late 19th century, the first military academies were set up, complete with German instructors, language courses and translation bureaus, uniformed army and naval cadets, and programmes of dispatching students to the West or Japan for further training. In fact, however, the concept was maintained of a regional fighting force, composed of a conglomeration of lower leaders, each with his own following and each tied by personal loyalty to the commander, general or generalissimo, who thus made use of the army as a personal power base. That network of relations remained in existence, even after the leader took up positions in the civilian administration. This was how Li Hung-chang, the most powerful man in the eighties and nineties, managed the army of the Huai area, and this was how generalissimo and would-be emperor Yuan Shih-k'ai, the first president of the Republic, governed, using the network of the "northern" military academy. The model remained popular for a long time. Yüan Shih-k'ai has been rightly called the "father of the warlords": after him arose the genuine war-lords, each of whom relied on a regional apparatus of power, consisting of sub-cliques of professional soldiers. Although they were somewhat more substantial in ideological terms, both the reorganised Kuomintang of the twenties and the Chinese Communist Party in its earliest years fit into this picture: in both cases their roots lay in the military Academy of Whampoa (near Canton) and, at this stage, both were clearly based on a region.

Throughout this development it appears that the characteristic Western elements (Western technology, instructors, literature, terminology) were present continually, but that the typical end-product – the warlord with his parasitical, regional, military apparatus of power – actually seems scarcely to have been affected.[21] But, on the other hand, this is not a "traditional Chinese" type of army either: it is the consequence of an *indigenous* modernisation, developed in the struggle against internal rebellions and later strengthened and made more effective by the adoption of Western technology.

Within the economic sector too, no simple model of expansion and reaction seems satisfactory; here in particular we find a clear illustration of how existing structures and relationships continued and made use of new possibilities to strengthen themselves. Free participation of Chinese business in trading contacts with the West was the result of the abolition (forced by the Treaty of Nanking) of the old "Cohong" which operated under official control and had monopolised commercial contacts with the West during the period of the Canton trade. In its place developed the characteristic group of

[21] See Jerome Ch'en, "Defining Chinese Warlords and Their Factions," *Bulletin of the School of Oriental and African Studies*, 31 (1968), pp. 563–600.

"compradores," powerful merchants who acted as managers for all activities undertaken by foreign firms in China (including all dealings with the Chinese business community). So, early on – and exclusively in this section of society – there developed a partnership relation between Chinese and Westerners, based on mutual dependence and advantage. Compradores frequently turned their knowledge of Western skills and techniques to advantage by founding their own firms after some time, while, in the sixties, other, already established, Chinese business houses (which sometimes had an extended network of relations and distribution channels at their disposal through their guild organisation or their place in a regional association) independently began to import Western goods. Soon, they controlled the "interport trade," increasingly carried on with steamships, to such an extent that the largest Western firms consequently limited their operations to distribution centres in Hong Kong and Shanghai, because competition with Chinese trade made further expansion of a system of outlets unprofitable.

Willingness to make use of new opportunities was coupled with the continuation of traditional processes which sometimes had the chance to expand further, precisely through the new alternatives. Thus the "modern" local and provincial Chambers of Commerce, set up around the turn of the century, were virtually immediately monopolised by the old Chinese commercial establishment, those guild and regional association leaders who as of old commanded an extensive network of transport and distribution in the interior.[22] At each level, the family firm remained the obvious form of organisation, and, outside the People's Republic, has been so up to the present.

Another tendency had begun to make itself felt in pre-modern times but swelled to a torrent with modernisation. This was the commercialisation of the gentry in the large towns. As a class, the gentry preserved their bases in the countryside, but the old ideal of scholarly clan and village headship increasingly lost its appeal; after 1905, when the old class of "graduated notables" could no longer attain an official career throught the state examinations, all motivation for the maintainance of the traditional style of life in fact disappeared. More and more of the leaders of the gentry moved to the towns and invested in trade and industry there. Increasingly estranged from their traditional functions and from the political order ultimately based on them, they became susceptible to radical ideas, including Republicanism.

---

[22] For the role of the commercial establishment in these new organs, see Susan Mann Jones, "The Ningpo Pang and Financial Power at Shanghai," and Edward J.M. Rhoads, "Merchant Associations in Canton," both in M. Elvin and C.W. Skinner (eds.), *The Chinese City between Two Worlds*, Stanford 1974, resp. pp. 73–96 and pp. 97–118.

It is not by chance that the 1911 Revolution relied to a large extent (certainly financially) on the support of the increasingly indistinguishable groups of the "comprador-bourgeoisie" and the commercialised gentry.[23] As was mentioned above, the gentry's move to the towns and participation in trade and banking were themselves pre-modern tendencies. Western penetration strengthened them, sped them up and ultimately directed them differently, by offering modern alternatives. The result was never a replica of Western business life, even in a modern metropolis like Hong Kong.

As a summary (but what is the value of a summary of paragraphs each of which consists of generalisations about generalisations?) I can only conclude that the simple pattern of Western penetration plus Chinese reaction is lost, on further investigation, in a multiplicity of complete and partial influences, innovations, convergences, assimilations and adaptations, in which anything which seems genuinely to be new suddenly appears imbedded in traditional structures. There were as yet few real break-throughs in the nineteenth century. Only in the twentieth century – and even then on a very limited scale – would nationalism, individualism, liberalism, the ideals of "science and democracy" break free from their traditional associations and be fanatically professed.

The question remains as to whether the relatively short phase of Westernisation has had lasting consequences. Both the later Kuomintang ideology and the Maoist version of Marxism return, in the last instance, to a total ethical ordering of society, in which more elements of tradition can be recognised than are (at least in Peking) ever admitted.

---

[23] For the role of modernised commercial groups in the 1911 Revolution see Marie-Claire Bergère, *La bourgeoisie chinoise et la révolution de 1911*, Paris 1968; *id.*, "The Role of the Bourgeoisie" in Mary C. Wright (ed.), *China in Revolution: The First Phase, 1900[1913*, New Haven 1968, pp. 280–288; Mark Elvin, "The Gentry Democracy in Chinese Shanghai, 1905–1914." In: Jack Gray (ed.), *Modern China's Search for a Political Form*, London, 1969, pp. 41–65. Another expression of growing nationalist consciousness can be seen in the great anti-American boycott action of August 1905 to February 1906, led as much by the traditional guilds and trade associations as by the new Chambers of Commerce in the big cities, and directed against the limitation on Chinese immigration into the United States.

5. DUTCH "EXPANSION" AND INDONESIAN REACTIONS: SOME DILEMMAS OF MODERN COLONIAL RULE (1900-1942)[1]

by

I. Schöffer

I. CHANGES SINCE 1870

Dutch legislation in 1870 concerning the Dutch East Indies *(Nederlandsch Oost-Indië)* may be considered as a turning point in colonial development, though it took a long time before the consequences became fully apparent. In this year, the Dutch parliament introduced two laws concerning the future economic exploitation of the Indies. First, the so-called *sugar-law* abolished the obligation (since 1830) upon parts of the Javanese population to grow sugarcane in set quantities and prices under control of the colonial administration and for the direct profit of the Netherlands government. With this law the so-called Cultivation System came gradually to an end, the last obligatory production of sugar definitely being stopped in 1895, of coffee in 1917. The second, the so-called *agrarian law* regulated the landed property rights for the indigenous peoples in the Indies in such a way that cultivated land was declared inalienable to non-Indonesians, and uncultivated land *(woeste gronden)* could be leased by Europeans only for a period of 75 years. Such laws stimulated private European enterprise to open up and clear new land for modern agrarian exploitation without upsetting traditional indigenous society, and to look for this land partly outside the overpopulated and heavily cultivated island of Java: the so-called "outer islands" *(Buitengewesten)*, mainly Sumatra, Borneo and Celebes.

Just as had happened with the constitutional reform of 1848 in the Netherlands, which strengthened Dutch parliamentary control and allowed for increasing liberal influence of the bourgeoisie, the colonial legislation of 1870 preceded actual modernization in the colonies. Changes of opinion in Dutch political circles rather than economic and social pressures or political

---

[1] When the political situation in the past is to be stressed, the Indonesian archipelago is indicated according to the old-fashioned term "Dutch East Indies." Footnotes of this paper concentrate mainly on more recent Dutch publications, perhaps internationally less well-known.

and administrative needs were the causes of it.[2] And like the late industrial revolution in the Netherlands taking place a long time after the reform of 1848, changes in the Dutch East Indies as a consequence of the 1870-legislation needed time to become manifest. Undoubtedly there was a connection between such retarded industrialization in the mother-country (1890–1914) and the slow modernizing developments in the Indies. What colonial legislation had decided upon in principle, finally matured only after 1900. But in the end these changes would be important and drastic.

At first sight, Dutch colonial developments after 1900 towards what has been called imperialism, remind us of European colonialism in general. Take, for example, the actual Dutch territorial expansion and the establishment of the "Pax Neerlandica" in the whole Indonesian archipelago. There was, no doubt, a tendency to settle matters in this respect with more consistency than ever before. The protracted wars in Acheh, begun in 1871, finally came to an end in the first years of the new century.[3] Military expeditions into Borneo and Celebes in that same period brought Dutch law and order in the outer islands. The introduction of the "Short Declaration" (Korte Verklaring) in 1901 by the colonial government of Batavia – to be signed by almost all regional Indonesian rulers and princes – meant a legalized and uniformalized subjection to Dutch colonial rule, and seemed to confirm the picture of a rising Dutch imperialistic power. Military conquests, however, had been mainly caused by outside imperialistic pressures. Aggressive territorial expansion in the sense of purposeful enlargement of the colonial empire was lacking. And so was the supposed imperialistic urge by economic or social pressure from the mother country. Long before 1870 already the Dutch colonial government had been forced to take its territorial claims outside Java by the presence of colonial troops and colonial administrators in the formally recognized outer posts of the Indies. Punitive expeditions during the 1830's and '40's against "pirates" in the seas were followed by expeditions in the Moluccas, Borneo or Sumatra during the '50's and '60's. What happened after 1870 found its final consolidation after 1900 and was nothing more than a continuing rounding-off of much earlier colonial "internal expansion." Investments from the Netherlands were extremely hesitant in coming to the colonies and no need was felt for a search for colonial markets in order to relieve any sort of surplus-production at home.[4] Dutch territorial "expan-

---

[2] C. Fasseur, Kultuurstelsel en Koloniale Baten. De Nederlandse Exploitatie van Java 1840–1860 (Leiden 1975), pp. 204/5 in particular.

[3] P. Van 't Veer, De Atjeh-oorlog, Amsterdam 1969.

[4] A modern marxist approach underlines the non-imperialistic aspects of Dutch colonialism: F. Tichelman, Stagnatie en Beweging. Sociaal-historische Beschouwingen over Java en Indonesië in Aziatisch verband, Amsterdam 1975, pp. 135 ff..

sion" within the official Indies area was at the most a military or administrative demonstration of presence in those territories which had been
considered to be "Dutch" since 1815 or which were defined by later treaties
concluded with the English government.[5]

Dutch nationalism, moreover, was too weak to give strong support for
empire-building overseas. Since the successful Belgian Revolt (1830–1839)
the Kingdom of the Netherlands had dwindled into a small state with a "little
nation" mentality; the Dutch accepted their situation. They fostered at the
most a kind of self-satisfied patriotism, often looking back to former political
greatness. Real frustrations, like those that Italians, Germans, Czechs or
Hungarians felt about their lack of national unity, were absent. Resentful
aggressiveness caused by defeat or humiliation, like the French had suffered
in 1870–71, never vexed the Dutch. A Dutch government, helped by a
balanced constitution since 1848, and supported by a bourgeois establishment, could proceed in a gradual way of adaptation towards a more modern
society without the alarming social tensions such as could be found
elsewhere.[6] A stronger rise of nationalistic feeling had to wait for an outside
stimulus until 1899, when the Boer War in South Africa caused Dutch
sympathetic enthusiasm first, Dutch dismay later, for the fate of its *Afrikaans*-
speaking blood brothers. From then onwards, Dutch national feeling
underwent something of a revival, especially in circles of the *haute bourgeoisie*, and this carried with it a fuller and more conscious appreciation for
the Dutch colonial mission overseas as well.[7] Like the belated industrial
revolution, Dutch "imperialistic" ideology followed rather than preceded or
caused colonial "internal expansion" and the beginnings of modern exploitation in the colonies.

While causes and consequences in political, ideological or economic sense
for Dutch "imperialism" were the reverse of what was to be expected,
further developments in the relations between the Netherlands and the Indies
also had their own characteristics and traits. Modernization, both for
the mother country and the colonies, was in general a slow and gradual
process, before 1940 never developing into such a mature kind of capitalism

[5] A collection of papers on aspects of the Dutch East Indies during the period of imperialism
(among others W.F. Wertheim, J.M. Pluvier, S.L. van der Wal, R. Nieuwenhuys, The Siauw
Giap and Th. van Tijn) in *Bijdragen en Mededelingen Betreffende de Geschiedenis der Nederlanden*, Vol. 86 (1971) pp. 1–90.

[6] Social and political tension within the Netherlands reached a crisis situation only twice:
during the 1880's (agrarian crisis, a split in the great Dutch Reformed Church, labour-unrest and
a new socialist party, a parliamentary stalemate between confessionals and liberals) and once
again in 1903 with the Great Railway-Strike.

[7] No specific study has yet appeared concerning this upsurge of excited nationalism in the
Netherlands, temporarily provoked by the Second Boer War in South Africa.

and industrialism as one is accustomed to expect of other western colonialist states. Industrialization in the Netherlands, though because of its lateness technologically modern, never, prior to 1940, reached that level of significance of its industrialized neighbour-states. In the primary sector, mainly agriculture, a still substantial part of the Dutch population remained employed – the economic crisis of 1931 was therefore to be particularly severe for Dutch society and lasted until the German occupation in 1940.[8]

The same applies for the Dutch East Indies. The agrarian law of 1870 forestalled any rapid alienation of Indonesian land tenure to non-Indonesians and kept in this sense a greater part of indigenous society in the folds of traditionalism. Whatever criticism may be levelled against the economic theory of "dual economy" in the Indies, that term illustrates at least the actual continuity of traditional Indonesian society and economic ways of production side by side with European modern enterprise.[9] Private investments, Dutch or foreign, as has been said above, entered the Indies late and rather hesitantly. Industrialization in the colonies themselves remained marginal and insignificant. Colonial administration seemed at first sight to remain equally unchanged. Still, a comparatively small number of Dutch colonial officials tried to administer an immense area by indirect rule, with the help of the traditional Indonesian élite of the prijaji-class and local "heads" in the dessahs. Such "Internal Administration" *(Binnenlands Bestuur)* paid due respect to the existing indigenous customs and traditions with utmost caution and carefulness, as it had learned to do during the 19th centuy.[10]

Perhaps all this explains also why Indonesian reactions to Dutch colonial rule remained relatively weak and haphazard until 1942. Indonesian nationalism never reached such extent and depth, permanency or strength as was the case e.g. in British India. It started relatively late – in 1911 for the first time as a temporary mass movement with the Sarekat Islam. It suffered severe setbacks and internal weaknesses during several phases of its development and seemed to be severely handicapped from 1927 onwards. Traditionalism hampered deployment of strength. Wishes for modernizing westernization came up against older traditions of peasant-resistance. A new intellectual élite clashed with the older leadership of Islamic priests and prijaji-

[8] P.W. Klein, "Depression and Policy in the Thirties" in: *Acta Historiae Neerlandicae*, Vol. VIII (The Hague 1975) pp. 123–59.

[9] J.H. Boeke, *Indonesian Economics. The Concept of Dualism in Theory and Policy*, (The Hague 1961).

[10] W.F. Wertheim, "De geest van het Oostindisch Gouvernement, honderd jaar geleden" in *Bijdragen tot de Taal-, Land- en Volkenkunde*, Vol. 117 (1961) pp. 305–343 & 436–463, and R. Nieuwenhuys, "Tot de hoofdzaak van Lebak. Een antwoord aan prof. Wertheim" in *idem*, Vol. 118 (1962) pp. 271–76.

nobility. Still the Dutch colonial rulers proved to be extremely worried by the rise of nationalism and took several measures of repression by military force and severe policing. But they were able to ride the storms of revolt and opposition, notwithstanding their relative weakness of military strength and lack of strong support from certain indigenous groups.[11]

One may even get the impression that the Dutch East Indies remained up until 1942 what these colonies had been since the Dutch had reappeared on the scene after 1815, when they first started their strict but benevolent bureaucratic control and administration and soon developed their, often ruthless, economic exploitation, the Cultivation System. But such impression would be a false one. Initiated by the legislation of 1870, new developments exerted in the end their strong impact on Dutch colonial attitudes and governmental problems.

In the first place, the arrival of private enterprise on the colonial scene had its consequences and repercussions, however slow and gradual. The uncultivated land, especially in the outer islands, became exploited by European entrepreneurs engaging indigenous wage-earning labour. New products like tobacco, quinine and rubber, increasing quantities of raw material like oil and tin, made the Indies of the twentieth century a different exporting area in the world economy from what it had been before, when Java produced mainly sugar and coffee for the world market. The number of Europeans settling in the colonies grew impressively. Soon the private settlers outnumbered the officials, who had been the main group of Europeans before 1870. Whilst in 1870 not more than 40,000 Europeans were counted, this number had risen by 1940 to about 250,000.[12] And with this growth in numbers an even more important change took place in European attitude and style of living in the colonies. A kind of "Europeanization" was discernible. In Java cities grew like Batavia, Surabaya and Bandung, on Sumatra Deli, with typical European quarters of more luxurious housing and gardens. European habits in cultural and social life were more easily kept alive. The rapid improvements of communication with the mother country (mail and

[11] There exists an understandable post-war tendency to overrate pre-war Indonesian nationalism in order to understand its strength and impact after 1942. Within a historial context, however, this author prefers to tone such appreciation down, without, of course, depreciating in any way the individual or intrinsic significance of nationalism as such, nor neglecting the overreaction of Dutch colonial administration against it, although it could be called technically successful.

[12] D.H. Burger, *Sociologisch-economische Geschiedenis van Indonesia*, 2 vols. (Wageningen 1975). A new statistical series will give more basis: W.M.F. Mansvelt & P. Creutzberg, *Changing Economy in Indonesia. A Selection of Statistical Source Material from the Early 19th Century up to 1940*. Three volumes have been published: *Indonesia's Export Crops 1816–1840* (1975), *Public Finance 1816–1939* (1976) and *Expenditure on Fixed Assets* (1977).

transport, radio and telegraph, regular leave to Europe) helped to link the European community more firmly with Europe than had been the case before. European wives came out in greater numbers and European family-life could be maintained thanks to the westernized technology of refrigerator, radio, bicycle and car, and also to the development of schools and colleges for the secondary level. Though never officially announced, an informal kind of social "apartheid" towards the Indonesians inevitably developed which had been lacking or at least less conspicuous in earlier periods when the European had to "Indianize" in dress and habits, by taking an Indonesian woman as concubine and sending the children to Holland as soon as they had to go to secondary school.[13] Club life, sporting events, balls, swimming pools, all remained exclusively European, notwithstanding a growing number of socially and intellectually "acceptable" Indonesians and Chinese.

In general, contacts and communications of the European colonial with the colonized Indonesian changed with it. On one hand, the European employer came into closer contact with the Indonesian employee, particularly in the home, but also at some levels in the office, the workshop or on the land. The colonial administration had to modernize and the administrator was forced to increase his dealings with the indigenous population, if only because of the necessity to fight epidemics, to cope with the problems of overpopulation and impoverishment, to foster the infrastructure of transport and services, to spread education and schooling. New sections of administration had to be introduced and kept going, like those for forestry, irrigation and land registry, health-service and loan-banking, road-building and port facilities. Even if one would prefer to typify Dutch colonial administration as primarily an accomplice of European private enterprise, such presumed exclusive Dutch self-interest inevitably helped to influence life and society of the Indonesian population. Even if one would suppose that any ideologically true belief in "the white man's burden" was missing, such Dutch interference by officialdom had inevitably some impact upon the indigenous peoples of the Indies.

Indonesian society changed also. The rapid increase in circulation of ·money, which was started earlier in Java with the Cultivation System, had important consequences after 1870. Salaries for the Indonesian officials within the system of indirect rule, had made these more dependent on colonial

---

[13] Cf. on developments from a colonial "Indian society" *(tempo doeloe)* before 1900 towards a modern, somewhat closed European society of colonials, R. Nieuwenhuys in his publications: *Tussen Twee Vaderlanden* (Amsterdam 1954) and *Oost-Indische Spiegel. Wat schrijvers en dichters over Indonesië hebben geschreven, vanaf de eerste jaren der Compagnie tot op heden* (Amsterdam 1972).

government and less careful for the interests of their Indonesian subjects. Possibilities for a more mobile labour-market increased migration within and without Java. Modern technology also penetrated into Indonesian communities with such items as the sewing-machine and the bicycle.[14] In two respects these general modernizing developments increased the problems of changing Indonesian society. They aided, or at least did not stop, the growth of population, particularly on Java, and they undermined in many ways the traditional structures of society.

The dramatic growth of the Javanese population began in the first half of the 19th century. The introduction in that period of a money economy may be one of the explanations, although not the only one.[15] But this growth certainly did not stop during the 20th century. "Overpopulation" of Java was to be one of the greatest worries of the colonial government. Underemployment at the least, unemployment during economic crises, was the cause of a discernable impoverishment of the Indonesian population in general. The population of Java and Madura rose from 30 million in 1905, to 42 millions in 1930. According to the last pre-war census of 1930 the whole population of the Dutch East Indies numbered 60 million in total.

Quite apart from the colonial modernization already discussed, traditional indigenous relationships changed through sheer weight of numbers. Modern Indonesian nationalism, its new intellectual leadership, and new modernistic political ideas about forms of Indonesian participation in government or even take-over of government, were clear symptoms and signs of such internal social and cultural change. Whatever has been said above about the relative weakness of this movement (as compared with developments elsewhere) Indonesian nationalism in itself was a thing of significance. We know now, through hindsight, that upon its apparently frail foundation, laid since 1911, something could be built which at the end (i.e. after 1942) gained such impetus that decolonisation of Indonesia became inevitable soon after the end of World War II.

It is impossible within the scope of this paper to do full justice to all aspects of the development in the Dutch East Indies here indicated. But it might be helpful to mention some developments and consequences in the actual relationships between the colonials and the colonized after 1900. It seems best

[14] Impoverishment may have had, on the other hand, isolating and internally complicating effects upon Javanese communities, according to a "shared poverty" principle, cf. C. Geertz, *Agricultural Involution. The Process of Ecological Change in Indonesia*, Berkeley 1963.

[15] Other factors may have had some impact: comparative slackening in frequency of internal civil wars, some infrastructural improvements (irrigation, roads) which may have eased transport in times of local famine, relief by emigration and mobility. Only after 1900 must general medical improvement have had influence.

to look further into this matter, with the inevitable knowledge of what happened after 1942, by dividing these aspects into two sets of what I like to call the dilemmas of that relationship. One set of problems will be seen from the colonizers' side, for the Dutch ruling presence in the East Indies was more important than the number of people involved and the size of the mother country. Another set of dilemmas will be treated from the Indonesian side, although this does not of course include the full internal development of Indonesian society with its own problems, often influenced only indirectly by the Dutch colonial presence. Since European expansion stands in the centre of the theme, a certain over-exposure of the Dutch aspects in the whole picture has to be accepted.

II. DUTCH COLONIAL DILEMMAS

In 1900, more than ever before, the Dutch East Indies seemed in popular imagination to "belong" to the Netherlands. It may be true that large sections of Dutch society remained outside the direct orbit of colonial interests. Only certain families, mostly from the liberal-minded bourgeoisie, had traditional links with the Indies. Already before 1870 some of their sons had gone to the Indies to make a colonial career as officials. Particularly in Amsterdam, some firms and companies had colonial relations and bought colonial products to sell and started, after 1870, a direct trade with private plantations. And finally there was always a trickle of young men of the poorer classes, who were recruited in the Netherlands to become colonial soldiers and lower-ranking officers in the colonial army. After 1870 more possibilities for enterprise and employment in the private sphere were opened and undoubtedly the group of "Indies-interested" Dutch families grew. But even then they remained a minority, recognizable often within the Dutch community as "Indië-gangers" or "oud-Indischgasten". Especially the cities of The Hague and Arnhem attracted those who came home on leave or returned permanently, creating a specific atmosphere of colonial "nabobs" and pensioners.[16]

But the existence of such a restricted group with direct interests did not exclude growing interest of a more general kind, among a greater majority of the Dutch population. Two factors played an important role in this. In the first place, one might mention primary education. This kind of education had a long (Protestant) tradition and already reached greater groups of the population in the 17th and 18th centuries than had been the case elsewhere. It

---

[16] Cf. novels by Holland's most gifted novelist Louis Couperus (1863–1923), describing the atmosphere of ex-colonial families living in The Hague.

expanded substantially during the 19th century, and then the introduction of compulsory education in 1900 guaranteed a steady development thereafter. Next to simple "reading, writing and arithmetic," at the turn of the century new disciplines of history and geography became part and parcel of the school program. Especially the discipline of geography could be directed towards the Dutch East Indies. Virtually all young Dutch citizens of all denominations had to learn topography, economy and ethnography of Indonesia. No child left school at the age of twelve without at least having a vague memory of Javanese volcanoes, Dutch plantations or Balinese dances.[17] In the second place, general notions of the Dutch East Indies were helped by the growing economic entertwinement between the Netherlands and the Indies, at least insofar these attracted attention in the schools or in the press. Gradually the idea that Dutch industry or Dutch trade were vitally dependent on the Indies spread and became an accepted myth in the mother-country. "Indië verloren, rampspoed geboren" ("When the Indies are gone, disasters will dawn") became an accepted slogan from the 1920's on.[18]

And within the establishment of the "*haute bourgeoisie*" such popular knowledge and feeling about the colonial possessions found their response in two mainstreams of thought and action, both originating in the 19th century but now finding their fullest expression. One was the tradition of liberal criticism levelled against the Cultivation System, which had finally brought it to its end. As it was formulated by C.Th. van Deventer, a colonial expert of liberal inclination, the Indies had been exploited for financial profit of the Dutch government at home, and for that very reason the Dutch owed a debt of honour *(eereschuld)* to the Indies as a whole. Whilst Van Deventer calculated this debt in a literal sense in an exact amount of millions of guilders (to be repaid out of the Dutch treasury into the treasury of the Dutch colonial governement), this helped also to stimulate in an immaterial sense a kind of missionary feeling in order to expiate a general guilt towards "the Indies" and its indigenous peoples.[19] This message fell in with another colonial tradition which had been fostered particularly within the ranks of colonial administration. When colonial bureaucracy appeared on Java in 1816 it brought with it certain ideals of the Enlightenment and the French Revolution, notwithstanding the dilution and pollution of these by colonial self-interest and arrogance. It was the duty of the Dutch colonial adminis-

[17] The educational development of the subject "geography" in Dutch primary schools deserves special study.

[18] H. Baudet, "Nederland en de rang van Denemarken" in: *Bijdragen en Mededelingen Betreffende de Geschiedenis der Nederlanden*, Vol. 90 (1975) pp. 430–43.

[19] H.T. Colenbrander & J.E. Stokvis, *Leven en Arbeid van Mr. C.Th. van Deventer*, 3 vols., Amsterdam 1916–1917.

trator "to look after the well-being of the indigenous peoples," as the governmental regulation *(Regeringsreglement)* for the Indies formulated the idea in 1854. And in order to gain such lofty purpose the colonial civil servant should protect the Indonesians against tyranny and corruption by the indigenous nobility, to forestall internecine dynastic wars, to teach and educate the "natives" to overcome primitivism and poverty. Such paternalistic ideology, often slumbering or even apparently dead, was revived by liberal opposition from the 1850's on, and, especially when a new generation of officials arrived who had read Multatuli's "*Max Havelaar*" (for the first time published in 1860) and felt it a duty to proceed according to the "spirit of Dutch-Indian government" *(de geest van het Nederlandsch-Indische gouvernement)*.[20]

It was of immense importance that both thoughts, of guilt and duty, became widely accepted by public opinion in the Netherlands, supported by party leaders and politicians, entrepreneurs and even traders. Two internal developments in the mother country stimulated the spread of these ideas of guilt and duty: the rise of the confessional parties from 1878 onwards and the economic revival of the Netherlands during the 1890's, ending in an economic boom in the beginning of the new century. The Protestant parties in particular gave a religious stress upon such ideas of duty and guilt. From their point of view the superior task of spreading the Gospel and impregnating society with Christian ethics supplemented, so to say, the more secularized ideas of the liberals giving it a more solid background and creating the word of an "ethical policy" towards the colonies. The great founder and leader of the first Protestant party *(Anti-revolutionaire Partij)*, Abraham Kuyper had formulated such thoughts of "ethical" colonialism in his party-program (1879) and one of his outstanding political pupils with colonial experience, A.W.F. Idenburg, entered the arena in 1901, soon became minister of colonial affairs and ended his career as governor general of the Dutch East Indies between 1909 and 1916.[21] The economic boom in the Netherlands made it possible to accept some of the consequences of such "ethical policy" in the material sense of the word. Idenburg was able to follow Van Deventer's thoughts of a "debt of honour" by granting the treasury of the Dutch colonial government in Batavia forty million guilders to stimulate infra-structural development in

---

[20] Influence of Multatuli's *Max Havelaar* (1860) required time to spread. A younger generation of Dutch colonial officials arriving in the Indies since 1870 seems to have been partly "Multatulian" by conviction.

[21] B.J. Brouwer, *De houding van Idenburg en Colijn tegenover de Indische Beweging*, Kampen 1958. Chapters I and II in particular.

the Indies.[22] Costly plans were formulated to be part of the special Dutch "mission" in the Indies like education, medication, irrigation and migration for the indigenous peoples (the four -*ations*). The apparatus of trained Dutch civil servants for such technical purposes grew apace. And the idea of a "white man's burden" found support even among those political parties in the mother-country whose electorate was not primarily identified with those groups who traditionally had direct relations with the Indies. The Roman Catholic Party *(Rooms-Katholieke Staatspartij)*, soon to become electorally the largest party of the country, and the strongest party of the left, the Social Democrats *(Sociaal-Democratische Arbeiders Partij)*, both supported the idea of a certain guardianship the Dutch had to fulfill over the Indonesian peoples.

The term "guardianship" itself illustrated the kind of dilemma or colonial paradox which was to be inherent of the colonial rule, in whatever ethical or enlightened form it assumed. The metaphor of a colonial "guardian" who had to educate the Indonesian "children" indicated the patronizing and paternalistic way in which the indigenous peoples were approached. It meant as such an (even very long) period in which such guardianship had to be maintained until the Indonesian peoples were "mature" enough to stand on their own feet. It included the strong conviction that western values, western technology and organisation were superior to the Indonesian ways of life and techniques. When Christian conviction formed the basis of this attitude, it could also mean religious superiority to existing beliefs of Islam or Buddhism. And, although the idea as such also implied that the Indonesians ultimately would be fully "grown-up," even here there was undoubtedly a kind of arrogance involved: not only the tendency to postpone such moment of "maturity" but even then, the thought that such maturity could not be fully enjoyed without the remaining presence of the Dutch as "teachers, advisors and mediators," frustrated the "children's excited hopes and expectations" that in the end they would be free and independent. It is with this dilemma in mind, that scholarly reactions to Dutch East Indian problems can be best understood. The academic studies of Indonesia and its pluriform cultures and societies were stimulated by the great stress laid upon the scholarly training of Dutch officials to be sent to the Indies (the so-called studies of "Indologie," first in Leiden, then later also in Utrecht) and by the general development of the new methods and ideas in the social sciences. Developments in linguistics, cultural anthropology, comparative religion and history modernized the studies of Indonesia and Indonesian society. But such studies were to be

[22] S.L. van der Wal, *Over de aktualiteit der koloniale geschiedenis*, Groningen 1968 (Inaugural lecture).

overlaid with a western system of values and attitudes, and found their base in the same idea of Dutch colonial "guardianship."[23]

Such attitudes could best be illustrated by the work of three Leiden professors, who each in their own discipline, made a deep impression upon Dutch colonial scholarship and Dutch colonial policy. The historian H.T. Colenbrander, (1871–1945) attempted to write Dutch colonial history along modern lines of historical criticism and with full use of direct source material. He strongly felt the Dutch "ethical" mission in the Indies and therefore traced back Dutch presence in the Indies from its beginnings in the 17th century. But as a younger critic of such approaches would write, he observed the Indies "from the deck of the ship, the ramparts of the fortress, the high gallery of the trading house."[24] Although Colenbrander could be highly critical about the way in which the Dutch looked after their own economic interests and rejected firmly such exploitation as the Cultivation System, his works are still filled with what he considered to be a justified Dutch national pride and a strong belief of the mission to be fulfilled by the Dutch in the Indies. His great biography of Jan Pieterszoon Coen, the founder of Dutch power in Java, was to be a mainly laudatory account. The Indonesian peoples in his histories were pushed into the background as virtually a silent part of the Indonesian scenery.[25]

The Arabist Chr. Snouck Hurgronje (1857–1936) gained a deep knowledge of Islam and of Indonesian Mohammedanism in particular. His famous reports to the Dutch government on colonial affairs were full of wisdom and humaneness.[26] But he had the strong conviction that a westernizing modernization would be a blessing for the Indonesians, if only their leaders of the noble class could be integrated into the Dutch colonial system, by "indianization" of the bureaucratic apparatus. His respect for traditional Indonesian society led him to believe that only the noble class of the prijajis would be able to strip their old beliefs to become equal partners of the Dutch

[23] A general survey of the development of "Indologie" at Dutch universities is lacking. Cf. a collection of reprinted biographies of twelve most famous Dutch scholars: Honderd Jaar Studie van Indonesië 1850–1950, Den Haag 1976.

[24] J.C. van Leur, Indonesian Trade and Society: Essays in Asian Social and Economic History, The Hague/Bandung 1955, quotation p. 261.

[25] Short biography of Colenbrander by A.J.C. Rüter in his Historische Studies over Mens en Samenleving, Assen 1967, pp. 450–58. M.A.P. Meilink-Roelofsz in her Asian Trade and European Influence in the Indonesian Archipelago between 1500 and about 1630 (The Hague 1962) pp. 3/4, drew attention to a shift in apprehension between early 19th century colonial historiography (De Jonge, van der Chys) and Dutch history-writing in the beginning of the 20th century (Colenbrander, Gerretson, Stapel).

[26] C. Snouck Hurgronje, Ambtelijke Adviezen. (Rijks Geschiedkundige Publicatiën, Kleine Serie. Nrs. 33, 34, 35). The Hague 1957–1965.

colonial rulers. Snouck considered Islamic religion and culture mainly as ideas of the past, to be overcome by such westernization.[27] On the other hand, the scholar of Indonesian law, C. van Vollenhoven (1874–1933) believed in the possibility of merging existing traditions with western modernism by fostering the respect for traditional Indonesian laws and customs (the so-called *adat*) and wished to leave tradition respectable and intact, particularly on the local and regional level, so that society could cope with modernizing influences in its own specific Indonesian ways.[28]

All three scholars, therefore, studied Indonesian facts and figures with a great deal of respect, and their knowledge in their different disciplines was great. But they never foresaw the possibilities of the creation of a nation-state led by a westernized new Indonesian intelligentsia of non-noble descent, without the support of Dutch "guardians" on the one hand, or the building upon Islamic traditions on the other hand. As intellectual Dutch "guardians" they could not imagine an Indonesia without Dutch presence and they tried to solve the problems of relationship between colonials and colonized by conservative notions and an unconscious prejudice about western superiority.

Such intellectual efforts on the part of the mother-country were paralleled by attitudes and measures taken by the Europeans in the Indies themselves. Here the practical necessities of modernization forced upon the colonial officials and their European counterparts in the private sector placed all "colonials" before the dilemma of a "guardianship". Education, among others, posed such problems. Was it to be nothing more than a very elementary introduction to social and economic problems and the simple teaching of reading and writing or should the more intelligent Indonesian be offered a westernized, more sophisticated school-organisation, which, however, would estrange him from his own society?[29] Governmental initiatives to draw some Indonesians into participation in administration and management on the local or regional level with the final purpose of political education for nation-wide tasks created problems of an equally difficult choice. Was modernization not harmful to indigenous communality? Would it not involve gradual ruin for indirect rule by which up till then the Dutch had held the reins of power with their relatively small number of Dutch officials?

---

[27] H.J. Benda, "Christiaan Snouck Hurgronje and the Foundation of Dutch Islamic Policy in Indonesia" in his *Continuity and Change in Southeast Asia*, New Haven 1972. pp. 83–92.

[28] H.L.T. De Beaufort, *Cornelis van Vollenhoven 1874–1933*, Haarlem 1954.

[29] P.L. Geschiere, "De meningsvorming over het onderwijsprobleem in de Nederlandsch-Indische samenleving van de 20e eeuw. De controverse 'westersch' of 'nationaal onderwijs'" in: *Bijdragen en Mededelingen Betreffende de Geschiedenis der Nederlanden*, Vol. XXII (1968/9) pp. 43–87.

Would not the loyal prijaji-class upon which colonial government had always built be left in the lurch by such social and political change?

The introduction of the "People's Council" *(Volksraad)* in 1917 illustrates the half-way attempts to modernize without upsetting existing relations too much, to foster gradual change, only avoiding radicalism or doctrinal consistency. This Council, to be filled by representatives of all three groups of the population in the Indies – Indonesians, Europeans and foreigners (Arabs and Chinese) – partly to be elected, partly to be appointed by the governor general, received only advising power to begin with.[30] But this administrative reform soon met with heavy criticism. On the one side there were severe complaints that such a *Volksraad* had no real power or even influence and therefore only frustrated and irritated the politically conscious intellectuals representing the Indonesians. A reform in 1922, granting the *Volksraad* co-legislative power, and one in 1928 increasing the relative representation of the Indonesians, did not, in the eyes of such critics, bring any change of substance. Final decision-making power was, after all, left in the hands of the governor general and his departments in Batavia and remained the ultimate responsibility of the Dutch government. And some hesitant beginning of "Indianization" within the colonial bureaucracy left the key positions to be occupied by Dutchmen. On the other hand, some colonial experts, within and without the Indies, rejected the idea of an "imported" parliamentarism for the Indies and considered such super-imposition of a parliamentary structure upon still traditionally organised bodies unnatural and contrived. In their conviction, political modernization could be developed only from "below," i.e. the local and regional level, with a possible federative structure gradually (and slowly) growing out of these beginnings at the grassroots.[31] In this way the *Volksraad*, although an important arena for public political discussion, remained halfway and problematic, causing by its existence feelings of discontent and frustration with Europeans and Indonesians alike.

Differences in attitude and opinion, moreover, grew between the Dutch colonial officers and the European private, temporary settlers. Even if traditions of "guardianship" and "ethical policy" had not played a role, the colonial official came to the Indies with other aims and ideals than the Dutch private immigrant, and also in a relatively different position of social and

---

[30] S.L. van der Wal (ed.), *De Volksraad en de Politieke Ontwikkeling in Nederlandsch Indië* [The Peoples Council and the Political Development of the Netherlands-Indies], 2 vols., The Hague 1964–5.

[31] B.J. Brouwer, *op. cit.* Chs. IV, IX, and X in particular. Also H. Colijn, *Staatkundige hervormingen in Nederlandsch Indië* (1918) and *Koloniale Vraagstukken van heden en morgen* (1928).

economic security. As an official, one had the express task to look after the indigenous society and indigenous interests, to protect the Indonesians against exploitation and humiliation. The European private citizen, economically often less secure – the economic crisis after 1931, for example, hit him hard – came to the Indies to find a living, to earn money, to improve his social standing. Frictions, accountable to such differences in attitude and views within the rather vulnerable and closed European community were often the results. And Dutch colonial officialdom was for this very reason placed in an ambivalent position: in social relationships, in ways of thought and behaviour, it felt one with the European community, but in its specific tasks of justice and fairness it had to protect the Indonesians against the often unlimited and inhumane self-interest of the Europeans. And more often than not, the officials tended to find an uncertain balance between their feelings of social solidarity with the European caste-like community and their direct "mission" as officials in favour of the interests of the Indonesians. Ideologically, favoritism towards the European minority could be defended along the lines that prosperity of the economically leading European entrepreneurs was in the interest of the Indies as a whole, whereas only excessive exploitation had to be fought. It cannot be denied that European capitalism often developed in this way at the cost of its Indonesian employees, profiting from low wages, abundant labour supply and virtually policed suppression of Indonesian trade-unionism. Fiscal measures were in general extremely lenient towards European concerns and plantations.[32] On the other hand, Dutch colonial government often took initiatives to protect interests of the Indonesians. One of the best examples of such endeavours was the way in which the Dutch colonial officers, who were trained economists, like J. van Gelderen and H.J. van Mook, tackled the economic crisis of the 1930's by inaugurating a kind of directed economic planning based in part on modern western theories but as much so on colonial experiences within the Indies. To grapple with such immense problems as immoderate population growth in Java, sudden collapse of prices and wages as the consequence of a severe slump of demand for raw material and colonial products, structural underemployment and malnutrition. Dutchmen attempted for the first time a kind of modern "économie dirigée" in an underdeveloped area which might well have some lasting value for later problems of economic development planning.[33]

[32] W.F. Wertheim, *Indonesian Society in Transition*, The Hague/Bandung 1959, pp. 96–117 and F. Tichelman, *op. cit.*, pp. 131–51 in particular.
[33] P. Creutzberg, (ed.), *Het ekonomisch beleid in Nederlandsch-Indië* [Economic Policy in the Netherlands Indies], *Capita Selecta*, 3 vols., The Hague 1972–75.

Looking at the whole situation and development of the Dutch East Indies during this century, it seems easy, by hindsight, to be highly critical – and a greater part of post-colonial history-writing has been like that. The basis of Dutch colonialism was the paradox of a government intending to keep a large area with millions of inhabitants under conditions of law and order while fostering economic, and, as a consequence, social and political changes through westernized modernization. It was also the paradox inherent in maintaining the traditional situation of indirect rule, whilst modernization brought forward a kind of centralizing parliamentarianism which gave a chance for a new class of more modern-oriented intellectuals and politicians to play their roles; it was the dilemma of being part of a larger closed community of "imported" Europeans who had direct interest in exploiting the economic possibilities of the colonies as against the "ethical" necessity to protect the indigenous "children," to educate them and to help them to profit from the economic development, which remained primarily in the interest of the happy European few. Even a comparatively enlightened and tolerant regime, weak in military force and numbers, like that of Dutch colonial rule, could not help becoming enmeshed in the great dilemma of a necessary quietening traditionalism and the inevitable pressure for change and modernization.

III. THE INDONESIAN DILEMMAS[34]

The Dutch "internal" expansion in the Indies – the spread of Dutch military and administrative presence in the whole area, intensification of contacts between Europeans and Indonesians, growth of an informal kind of "apartheid" of the European ruling community, increase of state-interference and westernizing technology – this "expansion" called forth Indonesian reactions, fully as mixed and paradoxical as those of the Dutch in the Netherlands and the Indies.

Seen from the outside, the larger part of the Indonesian population remained untouched by modernization and lived its traditional life in the countryside, protected, so it seemed, by such shields as indirect rule, conservatism of indigenous princes and "heads" and Dutch benevolent caution. The small peasantry remained the great majority and within the communal organisation of the *dessah* produced a meagre crop for its own

---

[34] This part of the paper has to be very short and even more superficial than the preceding parts. For two reasons: the author is not an expert in Indonesian History, and reactions to Dutch colonialism is only a small part of the general development of nationalism during the colonial period.

subsistance and payment of the levies due to its own Indonesian rulers and the Dutch colonial government. Even most signs of unrest and rebellion within this group seemed to remind one mostly of the traditional peasant-revolts protesting against excessive extortion or illegitimate rule, sometimes by Islamic "fanatics" or dynastic pretenders to some princely throne. Often these only indirectly intended to shake off Dutch foreign rule, which, if it was perceived at all, was mainly seen as an extension of social and regional tyranny.[35] It is understandable that most western observers were mainly struck by such outward traditionalism and conservatism and stressed the image of an unperturbed passive Indonesian "soul," which could and would not adapt to westernization.[36]

In reality, however, such a picture of "the" Indonesian was a wrong one, whatever Dutch colonials at that time might have wished and thought. After all, modernization, even in the technological sense only, could not remain unnoticed, even in the remotest *dessah*. The renewal and expansion of the system of transport by road, rail and sea increased mobility and opened the possibility of migration – internally in the overpopulated island of Java from the over-employed countryside to the rapidly growing cities, externally from Java to the outer islands. Governmental care for medication and measures of inoculation and quarantine penetrated into the inner lands, just as did modern technical improvements and new state-services like irrigation, forestry, postal service, telegraph and telephone. Educational expansion, with the introduction of the so-called dessah-school on the local level since 1906, helped to spread literacy and created the basis for a selected few who would in the future seek a more sophisticated primary and secondary schooling in nearby cities. In general, modernization seemed to be pressed forward by the very fact of the alarming increase of the Javanese population. That growth pushed Indonesian society willy-nilly over the verge of the existing traditional economic and social potentialities and forced it to look for other, sometimes new, solutions like migration, urbanization, employment with European private enterprise. It did not solve the ever-pressing population-problem – as we have seen, colonial government was alarmed by the consequences of impoverishment and social tensions within Javanese society – but it urged some changes which otherwise might not have been accepted with such good grace and eagerness. Economic and social change

[35] Sartono Kartodirdjo, *Protest Movements in Rural Java: A Study of Agrarian Unrest in the Nineteenth and Early Twentieth Centuries*, London etc. 1973.

[36] How strongly Dutch colonial expert and popular literature on Indonesian problems was based on the (positive and negative) prejudice about the "passive Indonesian soul" needs closer study, but is in general easily discernable.

could in the long run of fifty or sixty years be influential on all levels of Indonesian society. The increase in circulation of money in all islands opened possibilities for marketing and exchange in goods at a longer distance and with a consequentially greater variety of products to be bought and sold. The appearance of Chinese middlemen, penetrating more and more into small businesses like shopkeeping, small banking and lending, crafts and trades helped to bring about further developments in money-economy. The lending of small amounts of money, stimulated by the colonial government which created state-controlled pawnshops and credit-warehouses, (*dessah-loemboengs* and *dessah-banks*) finally provided humble folk with at least some chance of borrowing money at a reasonable price. Opportunities for wage-earning in the service of European private enterprise or in the lower ranks of colonial administration also offered some new kinds of employment.

Indonesian reactions to such all-pervasive modernization were in general adaptive and pliable. Traditional society proved to possess a great deal of resilience and elasticity in this respect. It often absorbed modernization in such a way that, to the outsider at least, change took place gradually and imperceptively. The great economic crisis during the '30's, moreover, helped to prolong the advantages of traditional society. To remain alive, most unemployed Indonesians fell back upon communal help and shared the meagre resources of a still seemingly self-sufficient production of primary needs. Traditionalism seemed in this way to put a brake upon the great dangers of famine and proletarianization. Such Indonesian adaptation kept many European observers from understanding the real significance of the more modern reactions of Indonesian active minority-groups. Indeed, even the Dutch colonial government preferred to look upon such reactions as being non-representative of what really was going on within Indonesian society. Only after 1945 such appreciation would prove to have been a wrong one.

Modernization, however, had more upsetting effects than the seemingly passive reactions of most Indonesians might indicate. The rise of a whole class of often underemployed or even unemployed Indonesian intelligentsia and the development of Indonesian nationalism were the apparent results. For the small élite of intellectuals, educated in the westernized schools or in the more traditional Moslem educational system, such modernization was either accepted with eagerness to support the new political nationalist aims, or rejected as a pernicious foreign import to be fought against in order to save Indonesian identity.[37] Both such reactions inevitably fostered a hostile, or at

[37] Cf. R. van Niel, *The Emergence of the Modern Indonesian Elite*, The Hague/Bandung 1960 and H.J. Benda, *The Crescent and the Rising Sun: Indonesian Islam and Japanese Occupation 1942–1945*, Bandung/The Hague 1958. pp. 9–103.

least highly suspicious attitude towards Dutch presence. Try as Dutch colonial administrators and theorists might have to win over these Indonesians as partners for a modern Dutch East Indies in which "white" and "brown" would live in a coexistence of equality, most of their active reactions to Dutch "expansion" were characterized by a principled and firm anticolonialism and a downright rejection of any prolonged Dutch tutelage or even in the last resort, Dutch partnership.

It is impossible to elaborate here on the full development of Indonesian nationalism during the last decades of Dutch colonial rule. Not all of it, of course, can be explained only as reactions to Dutch "expansion," although this became the rallying-point and the symbol for the bad forms of modernization. Such reactions helped Indonesians to close the ranks and to find a common negative goal. But within Indonesian society itself nationalism as such had to cope with its internal problems of "westernization," with or without Dutch presence. The measures of Dutch colonial rule against nationalism, however, scanned its rhythm of growth and decline as a political movement, and the most direct dilemma for Indonesian intellectuals was how to cope with these Dutch colonial attitudes and how to accept or to reject a kind of modernization, which had entered Indonesia along the channels of Dutch colonial administration and European private enterprise. Dutch colonial rule and power was to be, after all, the first reality. As a consequence, developments of Indonesian nationalism in many ways reflected Dutch colonial dilemmas.

Dutch colonial attitudes towards nationalism were varied and only in the end became more self-assured and therefore less subtle or flexible. If the idea of "guardianship" had to be taken seriously, then the "growing-up" of the Indonesian "child" had to be welcomed and even encouraged. There are several examples of the way in which the Dutch colonial rulers even tried to "educate" Indonesians politically, whatever must be conceded about the patronizing and paternalistic ways in which it was done. There were such endeavours as to introduce and expand the school-system for Indonesians, attempts also to push the most intelligent few to reach university-level and grant them scholarships for academic studies in Europe.[38] The creation of the *Volksraad* and local councils was intended to increase political participation of some of the Indonesians. Conscious "Indianization" of the lower strata of colonial administration proved not only handy means to economize in times of economic straits but also formed a deliberate policy

---

[38] I.J. Brugmans, *Geschiedenis van het Onderwijs in Nederlands-Indië*, Groningen 1938 and S.L. van der Wal (ed.), *Het onderwijsbeleid in Nederlandsch-Indië* [Education Policy in the Netherlands Indies], The Hague 1963.

of involving Indonesians in colonial responsibilities, although this was always done under the conditions set by Dutch colonial rulers and according to accepted Dutch values.

On the other hand, a "guardian" has to be severe and strict. Just because of the relatively small number of Dutch colonial officials and colonial force, the government in Batavia was extremely touchy about possible unrest and rebellion and observed the rules of law and order almost obsessively and often with a surprising lack of tact and leniency, although it had had such training with indirect rule. Indonesian nationalism passed in this way through several phases in which either Dutch relative permissiveness allowed for a more open development or Dutch repressive force pushed Indonesian nationalism underground and made it virtually powerless, through the arrest and internment of the political leaders. The first mass movement of the Sarekat Islam of 1913 was met by a prohibition of centralized party-leadership and the allowance of local committees. Socialist and communist union-movements were suppressed by strike prohibitions and severe police measures during and shortly after World War I. Communist revolts, though at first locally restricted to western Java (1926) and later to southern Sumatra (1927) and not approved by the Komintern, were not only themselves severely suppressed but started a series of policing measures which would remain exceedingly repressive during the '30's.[39] Although, compared with the kind of political persecution and destruction existing elsewhere, this colonial repression could be considered to have been relatively lenient and confined to small numbers only – an internment-camp in West Irian (Upper-Digul) comprised at the most 300 to 400 internees – even though within the limits of an originally principled "ethical policy" of guardianship granted by a mother country which enjoyed constitutional democracy herself, such repression had an extremely severe character. Dutch colonial rulers tended to interpret a radical anti-Dutch Indonesian nationalism as rebellious and dangerous and acted therefore as from 1926 on, accordingly.

Indonesian reactions to such ambivalent Dutch attitudes – the same colonial hand that reached out in token of partnership was used to punish – showed a comparable reaction of part-acceptance and part-rejection. On the level of tactics and opportunism the dilemma for them was clearly whether Indonesian political awakening would politically benefit by co-operation or by non-co-operation with the Dutch. On the level of fundamental principles the dilemma was in how far Indonesians would be wise to accept in-

[39] R.T. MacVey, *The Rise of Indonesian Communism*, Ithaca, N.Y. 1972. Also H.J. Benda, "The Communist Rebellions of 1926–1927 in Indonesia," in his *Continuity and Change in Southeast Asia*, New Haven 1972, pp. 23–37.

troduction of modernization out of colonial hands. Should the struggle against the Dutch also aim at maintaining traditional integrity of religion and culture, political system and social hierarchy within Indonesian society? What place should be left to European and Chinese minorities when at last Indonesia would become independent? Should capitalist exploitation be rejected only because of the fact that foreigners profited from it, or because of the system as such? Such fundamental questions were raised and often discussed but in the end neither was answered completely. The actual situation of coping with colonial reality kept them in the background. Moreover, whatever propaganda or ideology may have wished or expressed, Indonesian independence seemed to be far away. Therefore, confusion and discord were most often caused by actual problems of practical tactics towards Dutch colonial measures.

What strikes the observer of today is the relative weakness of Indonesian nationalism in general. The leading élite of political leadership was small and could be paralysed by relatively few arrests. The intellectual potentialities of the adherents remained limited, because of the relatively small numbers of those who had the chance to follow secondary schooling. Contacts between those small numbers of the intelligentsia and the Indonesian masses were often only temporary and never successful over a long period. Often the isolation of Indonesian nationalist leaders was not just physical, as when under arrest, but also spiritual, as when trying to win mass-support in vain. The gift of demagogic eloquence such as that possessed by Sukarno, helped to create occasionally large parties with an impressive and usually temporary financial support of no mean substance, but parties never developed into real permanency. In the opinion of many other leaders like Hatta or Sjahrir, Sukarno's actions proved to lack the support of a well-trained cadre and remained therefore too often flare-ups of enthusiasm and rather spasmodic activity.[40] The colonial situation, on the other hand, blocked possibilities of a more intense and fruitful contact and understanding between Indonesian and European intellectuals. The few exceptions like those of some Dutch law-professors and the lawschool in Bandung or of the author and critic Du Perron, who for a few years kept open house for his Indonesian friends, were remembered with gratitude, but only go to show how most unusual and uncommon such contacts were.[41] It is here that the inevitable and uncon-

[40] B. Dahm, *Sukarno and the Struggle for Indonesian Independence*, Ithaca, N.Y. 1969, Ch. III in particular. Also J.D. Legge, *Sukarno, A Political Biography*, London etc. 1973, pp. 109–30.

[41] G.J. Resink, "Rechtshoogeschool, Jongereneed, "Stuw" en Gestuwden." In: *Bijdragen tot de Taal-, Land- en Volkenkunde*, Vol. 130 (1974) pp. 428–50; E. Locher-Scholten, "De Stuw. Tijdstekening en teken des tijds." In: *Tijdschrift voor Geschiedenis*, 1971, pp. 36–65; J.H.W. Veenstra, *D'Artagnan tegen Jan Fuselier. E. Du Perron als Indisch polemist*, Amsterdam 1962.

scious development towards a society of informal "apartheid" hampered a more "natural" deployment of Indonesian political consciousness in exchange with European ideals and ideas, just as the administrative choice for firm repression and policing threw nationalism back upon its own resources and caused frustrated discontent and potential rebelliousness.

Thus new developments from 1900 onwards did not "solve" the problematic colonial situation. The mother-country became more closely linked to the Dutch East Indies both in economic interests and in general cultural and political consciousness. Colonial administration and economic exploitation were to be objects of deeper concern and often stronger responsibility both in Dutch circles at home and in the colonies. The actual expansion of Dutch power and influence, which was in part a material and physical spread in regions reached and penetrated, and in part a stronger impact on indigenous society, really began to embrace the Indonesian area as a whole. But consequences of such expansion were, to say the least, also the more problematic, the more its significance gained impetus. It helped to increase real European presence within Indonesia, in numbers and actual impact. It stimulated social and cultural separateness of the European community and helped to foster special European self-interests. It pushed Indonesian intelligentsia, often created by colonial influence and "ethical policy," into various kinds of anti-Dutch hostility. Unable to solve the pressing problems of overpopulation in Java and the general impoverishment of the Indonesian peasant-class, Dutch colonial rule gave the undeniable impression of serving its own interest first, although it pronounced such "ethical" ideals of enlightened guardianship. And modern Indonesian nationalism accused the Dutch of hypocrisy.

It is only when looking at such an accusation more closely that one may become convinced of the inevitability of a paradox inherent in all modernizing European expansions overseas. Even when one accepts the fact that any modernization in any traditional society will create serious problems like those of a self-interested exploitative entrepreneurship, a proletarianization of the traditional peasant-class, a creation of resistance of all groups of traditional values and customs, the fact that such modernization was to be introduced by foreign rulers created additional problems and dilemmas which remained insoluble as long as colonialism was present.

PART IV

EXPANSION AND REACTION IN AFRICA

6. FRENCH ACTION AND INDIGENOUS REACTIONS IN THE MAGHRIB, 1880-1914

by

J.L. Miège

I. THE DATA

1. French policy in North Africa and the reactions which it engendered among the local population occurred in territories very different not only in their ethnic and social composition, their economies and the strength of their native traditions, but also in their political position and their links with France. Morocco, an independent country undermined by the effects of European economic penetration and by internal disorders, was threatened by a conquest which began in 1907 but which was far from complete at the end of the period with which we are concerned.[1] Tunisia, which had just been occupied, saw the application of an attempt which began as, but quickly deviated from, indirect administration, namely the Protectorate.[2] Finally. Algeria, subjugated after 1871 and 1876, was a colony more and more considered as an extension of metropolitan France. Despite the courageous measures of certain governors, particularly Gambon, the stubborn action of Frenchmen in Algeria, who had the ear of Parliament, achieved the introduction of a system essentially constructed for the settlers (with the laws regarding landed property of 1878, the *indigénat* of 1881 and the laws of 1887 and 1897 etc....).[3] Thus, French governmental action in North Africa was essentially administration in Algeria, taking possession in Tunisia and the

[1] On Morocco at the end of the nineteenth and the beginning of the twentieth centuries, see J.L. Miège, *Le Maroc et l'Europe*, 4 vols. (Paris, 1961-1963); J.L. Miège, *Documents d'histoire économique et sociale sur le Maroc au XIXè siècle* (Paris, 1963); P. Guillen, *L'Allemagne et le Maroc, 1870-1905* (Paris, 1967).

[2] On Tunisia, see E. de Leone, *La colonizzazione dell'Africa del Nord*, Vol. I, *Algeria, Tunisia* (Padua, 1957).

[3] C.R. Ageron, *Les algériens musulmans et la France (1871-1919)*, 2 vols. (Paris, 1968); A. Nouschi, *Enquête sur le niveau de vie des populations rurales constantinoises de la conquête jusqu'en 1919* (Paris, 1961).

preparation for conquest in Morocco. It could not in any way be uniform.[4] Especially so, as it had to take account of wider pre-occupations. For the *Ministère des Affaires Etrangères*, for the French administration and for public opinion, North Africa was not a concern in itself, varied with regard to its different parts, but also in relation with France's general policy.

To the regional problems of administration and the military establishment should be added the wider geo-political views of France in Africa, with the plan, announced in the 1880's, of constructing a French Maghribian bloc and of uniting it with the French bloc in West Africa. The Maghrib was the jumping-off point for the conquest of the Chad region of the Sahara.[5] It was also seen within the complex whole of traditional French Mediterranean policy where financial, economic, and cultural interests were asserted along with concern for strategic equilibrium.[6] The Maghrib was an important factor in the totality of French relations with the Arabic-Islamic world. Finally, on the board of international politics, the North African pawn was part of the chancelries' game in the "diplomacy of imperialism" and the confrontations of the "Weltpolitik."[7]

Thus French policy is situated at several levels of pre-occupation and decision, as the points of view of Paris, of Algiers and later of Tunis and Rabat often interfered with each other.

2. Whatever may have been the pre-occupations, this policy was above all one of conquests and control; it clearly used military means but also, which will here concern us above all, the instruments of pacific conquest. The first characteristic to be noted is that, from the suppression of the 1871 rebellion to the march on Fez in 1911, including the expeditions to Tunisia and the campaigns in southern Algeria, North Africa never ceased, during all those years, to be a front, a terrain of military operations. This, by the way, is the essential fact of French colonisation, which distinguished it above all from that of the United Kingdom, namely its fundamentally military character. Not only because of the existence of a large army, as an expression of the

---

[4] On this diversity, see the descriptions by C.R. Ageron, *Politiques coloniales au Maghreb* (Paris, 1975); M. Brett, "Problems on the Interpretation of the History of the Maghreb in the Light of Some Recent Publications," *Journal of African History*, XIII (1972), no. 3, pp. 489–506. Also E. Hermassi, *Etat et société au Maghreb: étude comparative* (Paris, 1975).

[5] This is concerned with the immense question of the penetration of the Sahara, the railway projects and part of the interpretation of the scramble. See J.L. Miège, *L'expansion coloniale européenne et la décolonisation de 1870 à nos jours* (Paris, 1973).

[6] J. Bouvier, "Les intérêts financiers et la question d'Egypte," *Revue Historique*, 1 (1960), pp. 75ff; by the same author: "L'installation des groupes financiers au Moyen Orient" *Bulletin de la Société d'Histoire Moderne*, III (1959).

[7] Langer's works have well stressed these interferences.

nation and, in the climate of "revanche" an object of the Government's attention; but also, increasingly, there was the pre-occupation with maintaining a high total strength. The constantly aggravated demographic imbalance over against Germany led, at the turn of the nineteenth and twentieth centuries, to the overseas territories being considered as potential suppliers of recruits. The law of 17 July 1900, the "charter of the colonial army," no doubt did not directly apply to North Africa, for all that important levies of natives were raised. Conscription was finally inaugurated there by the decree of February 1912. Among the 600,000 men in the French army at the beginning of the century, there were more than a hundred thousand in the colonies, including about 60,000 natives. In 1910, 72,171 were quartered in Algeria and Tunisia, to which should be added the expeditionary force in Morocco; more than 100,000 men in all.[8]

This density of military *occupation* was contrasted with administrative understaffing. In this regard, the essential characteristic of the administration was its initial weakness, both in Algeria and in Tunisia. For all that the protectorate was "l'art de conduire les populations par l'intermédiaire de leur chef naturel,"[9] this personnel still had to be sufficiently numerous and adapted to the evolution of the societies. E. Etienne, a good judge of the situation, stated in 1898:

l'oeuvre poursuivie depuis 68 ans bientôt en Algérie est faite de contradictions sans cesse renouvelées: l'Etat français, usant tour à tour et du régime militaire et du régime civil, n'ayant aucune fixité dans ses conceptions, ni dans leur application, devait aboutir à l'incohérence et aussi à l'impuissance. Les pouvoirs publics ont expérimenté tous les systèmes d'administration sans pouvoir arrêter un régime définitif. Le point de départ, qui était de considérer l'Algérie comme le prolongement de la France a été funeste à tous égards. Diriger, gouverner, administrer directement de Paris un grand pays qui a sur son sol une population de 600.000 européens, de 3.750.000 indigènes.... est une aberration que le plus vulgaire bon sens répudie et condamne.[10]

Throughout this whole period and up to 1898, during which the assimilating tendencies were asserted, governor general de Chanzy's formulation of 1876 can be said to have remained valid: "l'initiative à Alger, la décision à Paris, l'exécution à Alger, le contrôle à Paris."

With the recourse on the one hand to minor civil servants of weak capacity and badly prepared for their jobs, and on the other to indigenous chiefs, there was frequently a gap in the middle ranks.

Thus administration essentially rested on those traditional elites who had

---

[8] Although it is essential, few studies have dealt with this problem.
[9] Following the formula by Vignon, *Une politique coloniale*, p. 37.
[10] E. Etienne, 29.4.1898.

been won over. With regard to motives, we can pass over the low politics of corruption, and the purchase of consciences with material advantages, pensions, honours and decorations, and the like. In this context, an analysis of the citation lists of the *Légion d'honneur* is instructive. Thus Sheik Si Amoud Sharif, Moqadem of the Zawiya of the Saouffa, was imprisoned on Corsica as an opponent in 1893, but rallied to the authorities and was soon decorated. This fact is a good example; it shows the general suspicions of the brotherhoods and the efforts to disarm and use them, by means of a chief won over to collaboration with the administration.[11]

French policy towards the brotherhoods and the marabouts was in fact marked, as in all other departments, by a deep ambiguity. Above all there was the fear of a concerted anti-French reaction by some of these brotherhoods, notably the Sanusiyya. Everywhere it was believed that there existed an Islamic plot and that, from Morocco to Tripoli, the insurrection was being organised by it. Watchfulness against this danger was constant. In 1882, Gambetta's journal, the *République Française*, claimed that "le désert entre en ébulliton et se précipite sur l'Algérie" and demanded preparations to combat in Africa the "plus redoutable soulèvement dont nous ayons été encore l'objet."[12] In 1885, the paper *Le Temps*, also multiplied appeals for vigilance against "l'union du sénoussi, du mahdisme et des ambitions turcs."[13]

This fear increased the latent hostility against Islam which had developed widely in Europe, from the campaign of 1875–6 against the Bulgarian atrocities and the Eastern Crisis of 1878 on.[14] Nevertheless, parallel to this, certain brotherhoods were used when they were considered moderate and when they could be used against other brotherhoods. In Morocco, the official protection accorded by the French legation to sharif Abdsellam, master of the Tayyibiyya order, tended to make the network of zawiyyas into an immense instrument of propaganda for France. The gliding of religious figures into politics and also into positions of economic power by means of the accumulation of land and the control over certain trading nets, particularly in the south, thus allowed an ensemble of forces hostile to the Sultan to be joined to the French camp.[15]

[11] Archives de la Guerre, Vincennes H. 192, Report on the political situation in the Bône subdivision, by general Rebilliard, Constantine, 6.12.1873, which concludes that "les Arabes (...) subissent impatiemment le joug."

[12] *La République Française*, May 4, 1882.

[13] *Le Temps*, Sept. 7, 1885.

[14] On this form of "racism," J.L. Miège, "Racisme et Expansion Outre-Mer," in *Colloque sur l'idée de race dans la politique française au XIXè siècle* (Marseille, 1975).

[15] *Ibid.;* see also L. Berrady, *Les chorfa d'Ouezzane, le Makhzen et la France*, (*Thèse*, Aix 1967).

Similarly, whether the "politique berbère" was a local factor in the dismemberment of social groupings tied to the regime, or whether it was a long-term means of action – as, notably, in Morocco with the "politique des tribus" opposed to a policy of agreement with the Makhzen – it was born of the conviction that these population groups were less tainted by Islam than the Arab tribes and less receptive to pan-Islamic propaganda.

3. The essential fact in the taking of control was the settlement of a considerable European population; according to the census of December 1881, in addition to 2,850,000 native Muslims, there were 423,881 Europeans in Algeria; while in 1891 the Europeans were 500,841 and the natives 3,459,000. The former had increased by 21.8% and the latter only by 14.4%. The European share of the population went up from 12% to 13.5%. This trend was maintained over the following decade so that the European proportion of the population was the highest that was ever attained.

ALGERIAN POPULATION

	1891	1901	% increase	1911	% increase
French	267,672	364,257	36.3	562,931	54.5
Foreign	233,169	245,833	5.1	283,111	23.1
European (total)	500,841	610,090	21.8	752,042	23.77
natives	3,559,687	4,072,089	14.4	4,740,526	16.41
total	4,060,528	4,682,179	15.5	5,492,568	17.3
% European	12.3%	13.03%		13.7%	

This demographic advance was also to be noted in Tunisia. There the number of Europeans grew from about 25,000 in 1881, to some 80,000 in 1896, to 130,000 in 1906 and to more than 150,000 in 1911, as against about 1,600,000 indigènes. In just 30 years, the non-native share of the population thus reached nearly 10% of the total.

This growth of population was accompanied by a seizure of land. The most immediate consequence of the suppression of the 1871 insurrection was the confiscation of 446,000 hectares of land, including much of the best. It "réduisit à une condition misérable les algériens des régions insurgés."[16] This appropriation went on increasing over the years, particularly in Algeria, especially between 1900 and 1914, during which time nearly 500,000 hectares were transferred from Muslim to European owners. Although less clear, the

[16] M. Emerit, "L'insurrection de 1871 en Algérie," Revue d'Histoire Moderne et Contemporaine, 2 (1972), pp. 261 ff.

development also occurred in Tunisia. In 1912, the European settlers – about 4,000 – occupied more than 854,000 hectares, while the 2,500 French settlers alone possessed 725,000.

LAND SALES IN ALGERIA BETWEEN NATIVES AND EUROPEANS
(annual average in hectares)

	Sales by natives	Sales by Europeans	Increase in European holdings	Five-year total
1900–1904	23,671	12,320	11,351	56,755
1905–1909	42,665	11,129	31,536	157,680
1910–1914	69,869	14,709	55,160	275,800
Total 1900–1914				490,235

Source: L'exposé annuel de la situation générale en Algérie," published yearly in Algiers.

This was associated with new agricultural investments, notably the growing of vines in Algeria. Thus a whole system of colonisation was built which relegated a large part of native agriculture to a marginal situation.[17]

This process was constantly encouraged. French policy in Algeria was developed in reaction to the liberal attempts of the Second Empire. The settlers imposed their desire for supremacy, with the willing or indifferent complicity of the central administration and of French public opinion. It was with a global system that, after 1891, the measures of reform had to contend.[18]

The policy of colonisation was aggravated by the deep crisis caused by the general depreciation of agricultural products which was rife between 1875 and 1900.[19] In addition to this stagnation, there occurred sharp conjunctural crises associated with climatic hazards, notably in 1878–79 in Algeria and in 1892–94 in Tunisia. To this was added the growing weight of taxation and the volume of indemnities and fines imposed on the defeated. These added up to more than 36 million *francs-or* from Algeria after 1871. Thus a collection of

[17] See the works of Zghal on Tunisia, of Lacheraf on Algeria and of Pascon on Morocco.

[18] On this consensus, see the articles in *L'Humanité* by Viviani or Jaurès. Also the latter's speech in the *Chambre*, Dec. 21, 1903, on Jonnart's actions. It was the general opinion that Algeria and Tunisia were the "terrain privilégié de la mission civilisatrice de la France." On the other hand, the conquest of Morocco was viewed with considerable reservations, even in those circles favourable, up till then, to colonial expansion. For example, see the warnings of P. Leroy-Beaulieu in January 1908 against an "opération d'un autre âge et d'un autre régime," *Revue des Deux Mondes*, Oct. 1, 1908, pp. 5–39.

[19] Ageron, *Les Algériens musulmans...*, and the review by A. Mouschi in *Annales, Economies, Sociétés, Civilisations* 1975, 5, pp. 867 ff.

demographic, economic and financial factors weighed on a more and more unbalanced agrarian economy.

However, still in the economic field, one whole sector was favoured by colonisation. It is undeniable that pacification, military provisioning and the introduction into wider monetary and economic circuits stimulated the activities of new sectors and above all brought about a great rise in commercial dealings. In Algeria, this unleashing occurred just after 1880, so that, between that date and 1903 external trade increased from 425 million francs to 675 million and, by 1913, had reached 1,168 million *francs-or*. In Tunisia, this evolution was even more rapid; dealings tripled within about thirty years.

EVOLUTION OF FOREIGN TRADE IN TUNISIA
(millions of *francs-or*)

	Exports	Imports	Total
1884–1885 (average)			45.51
1890–1891 (average)			81.93
1895	44	41	85
1896–1900 (average)	41.48	54.21	95.70
1901–1905 (average)	60.40	77.20	137.60
1913	178.66	144.25	322.91

Source: Yearly Customs returns.

(The yearly average has been taken for the years 1884–85 to make up for the effect of the great climatic disturbances at that time; for the years 1890–1891 in view of the customs law of 1890. For the years 1896–1900 the taking of an annual average counterbalances the otherwise disturbing effects of the first phosphate exports in the year 1897. The same goes for the years 1901–1905, where the great drought would have had the same unsettling effect.)

In the cultural domain, the policy of assimilation, propounded in principle in Algeria as well as Tunisia, remained, in fact, ambiguous and contradictory once again. It was only conceived as being brought about by language, and hence by the schools which were to propagate modern ideas and "refouler la barbarie islamique." However, due to budgetary difficulties, the problems of enlisting staff, the reserve of the local population and the fears of the settlers, this policy was only applied very slowly and inevitably had but an elitist character.

Schooling spread slowly following the reaction of the 1871 insurrection. In 1878, there were only 1,523 pupils in the Arabic-French schools in the territory of Algeria.

The decree of February 1883, which allowed the application, with adaptations, of the Ferry laws of 16 June and 28 March 1882, for the first time established "des bases d'un enseignement primaire et obligatoire ouvert aux

indigènes." However, the application of the law was slow and difficult. In
1891 there were still only 11,409 Islamic children in the primary schools, that
is to say less than 2% of those of school age. Moreover, there were no more
than 81 Muslims in the French lycées.

EDUCATION IN ALGERIA
(Muslims in French Schools)

	Boys	Girls	Total
1881–1882	......	.....	3,172
1886–1887	......	.....	9,064
1891–1892	10,277	1,132	11,409
1896–1897	20,387	1,876	22,263
1901–1902	23,956	1,696	25,652
1906–1907	29,615	2,540	32,155
1911–1912	39,180	3,508	42,688
1913–1914	43,271	3,992	47,263

In the following decade and particularly after 1901, the increase of education
grew and, in 1914, reached a figure of 47,000 Muslim children in the French
schools.[20] The number in the lycées reached 134 in 1907 and that of students
in French institutions of higher education about fifty. In 1914, the number of
lycéens was 386, indicating a limited but steady effort. Moreover, the effort
was purposeful.[21] In June 1910, Jonnart crudely stressed that "l'école primaire, qui est en France la pierre angulaire de la République, est en Algérie
le fondement de notre domination."

In the years before the war, these schools had already produced a
considerable number of educated persons: 240 schoolteachers, 24 lawyers
and doctors, 65 medical auxiliaries, in all, no doubt, significantly more than a
thousand persons.[22]

[20] For Algeria, the statistics are taken essentially from H. Desvages, "L'enseignement des
musulmans en Algérie (1888–1914), Le mouvement social (1970); for Tunisia, important parts in
P. Soumille, Européens de Tunisie et questions religieuses, 1892–1901 (Paris, 1975).

[21] Within the limits of this paper, the question of the content of this education cannot be
tackled. On the problem, see in particular F. Colonna "Le système d'enseignement de l'Algérie
coloniale," Revue Tunisienne de Sciences Sociales, XI (1974), pp. 175–197. On the general
question of acculturation in North Africa at the time of transition from pre-colonial to colonial
periods, J.L. Miège, "Probleme Kultureller Einflussnahme im Maghreb der vorkolonialen Zeit,"
Zeitschrift für Kulturaustausch (1975), pp. 7 ff.

[22] J. Corrieros, "De l'enseignement des indigènes en Algérie," Questions Diplomatiques et
Coloniales, I (1909), pp. 591 ff.

In Tunisia, the movement was at once slower and sharply reduced after 1898.

EDUCATION IN TUNISIA
(State Schools)

	French	Italians and Maltans	Jews	Muslims	Total	% Muslim
1889	1,064	2,674	3,704	1,765	9,207	19.1%
1897	2,683	2,832	4,241	4,656	14,412	32.4%

EDUCATION OF MUSLIMS IN STATE SCHOOLS
(1898–1903)

1898:	4,100	1901:	3,192
1899:	3,786	1902:	3,030
1900:	3,223	1903:	2,927

Together, these measures in the administrative, economic and cultural fields, the transformations that they induced in the traditional balances of life, the innovations and their effects, brought with them a series of reactions, favourable or unfavourable to the colonists.[23]

II. REACTIONS

1. The two main forms of French economic activity in North Africa, in rural matters and with regard to commerce, produced antagonistic local reactions. In the countryside, the seizure of the land and notably the confiscations after 1871 were the seed of terrible hatred, the quiverings of which were soon apparent to the most perceptive observers.[24] The reactions produced by the growing imbalance between the local population, the available land and employment; the "famine de la terre" became essential elements in the politico-social climate of the colonised Maghrib. Lacheraf has clearly shown

---

[23] Among the innumerable studies on these transformations, see H. Ṭimoumi, "La colonisation française et la sédentarisation de semi-nomades des steppes tunisiennes (1905–1925)," *Cahiers Méditerranée* n. 6 (1973) and X. Yacono, *La colonisation des plaines du Chelif (de Lavigerie au confluent de la Mina)*, 2 vols. (Algiers, 1955).

[24] Emerit, "L'insurrection...," p. 264.

its importance for the origins of the opposition movements.[25] First of all in Algeria and then in Tunisia there appeared in the countryside growing numbers "de paysans sans terre et sans travail régulier." The concentration of rural property enlarged "le décalage entre colons et fellahs d'une part, grands et petits propriétaires d'autre part."[26] Rural impoverishment increased parallel to the stages which A. Nouschi has discerned for the area around Constantine, namely the "temps de l'émiettement des sociétés rurales" up till 1881, the "triomphe des forts" from 1881 to 1901 and the "fin du monde rural" from 1901 to 1919.

Movements of agrarian unrest made themselves felt everywhere. As group revolt was impossible, they changed into individual brigandage with the complicity of the community. Particularly in the province of Constantine, native criminality reveals this deep crisis and its causes, by its character and extent. The agrarian civilisation of the Maghrib defended its own values by brigandage; the silent peasants saw these out-laws as their spokesmen. With each crisis breaking the old equilibrium, the ancient scourge of Mediterranean societies re-asserted itself with its retinue, such as stock thefts and burning of forests, characteristic of this kind of banditry.[27]

As against this, in the world of the new bourgeoisie and of certain new city-dwellers, the advantages of economic transformations were correctly considered valuable for enrichment and social advancement. Between the old networks and the new economic world, an intermediate native bourgeoisie was deployed which levied its fees on the two worlds. This "bourgeoisie conquérante" also appeared in Morocco, often allied with the governing administrative class. In all areas, this bourgeoisie reacted favourably to French actions in the initial phase. Thus, in the economic field, distinct contrary tendencies appeared between the rural world and that of the new towns.[28]

This rallying of the bourgeoisie to western values can be seen in Tunisia as well as Algeria, and also in Morocco. It was this group which sought the protection of the French consular authorities and which, from about 1898–1900 constituted a party favourable, in one way or another, to

[25] M. Lacheraf, "Constantes politiques et militaires dans les guerres coloniales d'Algérie," *Les Temps Modernes*, I (1961).

[26] J. Berque, *Le Maghreb entre deux guerres* (Paris, 1960); Zghal in *Revue Tunisienne de Sciences Sociales*, XII.

[27] Among the numerous items in the *Bulletin du Comité de l'Afrique française*, which was always quick to point out these infringements, see in particular, No. 9, (1910), p. 292, also J.P. Charnay, *La vie musulmane en Algérie d'après la jurisprudence de la première moitié du XXè siècle* (Paris, 1965).

[28] A. Berque, "La bourgeoisie algérienne," *Hesperis* I (1948).

European intervention; the only way, they thought, to give things a vigour which could not be found within the structures of traditional Morocco.[29]

2. A rather similar attitude was adopted by the modernist intellectuals for whom the rehabilitation of their new personality was achieved through assimilation. The attraction of this assimilation is clear, and perhaps even reinforced by the impediments erected against naturalisation. Here the reticence of the administration in face of the phenomenon of naturalisation should be noted. Of the 635 naturalisations in Algeria in 1881 there were only 30 instances of Algerian Muslims and in 1889 only 31 naturalisations of Algerian Muslims were registered, of 1881 cases.

The proponents of modernism who called themselves – or who are merged under the lable of – *Jeune Algérien* or *Jeune Tunisien* were only a minority. They were united in the same conviction that the future of their respective countries lay in the adoption of the main elements of Western technical civilisation, and in the same confidence in evolution and the hope that with it they would aquire equality of political rights with the Europeans.[30] They did not struggle for the breaking of the ties with France, nor for an independence which was unthinkable, given spirit of the times. Only between the two wars did the bitterness of waiting, which had been frustrated too long, lead to the envisagement of means of modernisation different from those offered by the colonial power.[31] On the contrary, between 1900 and 1914, a wish for assimilation marked the *Jeune Algérien* movement, and, albeit to a lesser degree, the *Jeune Tunisien* one.

However, this common position was accompanied by different attitudes to the methods of action and above all to the part of tradition in the desired evolution. Some of them, like the Tunisian Abd el Jelil Zaouch, thought that it was necessary to slough off the old skin and break completely with the past society. Others dreamed of simple mingling and often made the distinction between essentially Islamic private values and the public values derived from the guardian power. But this effort to open things up ran into systematic, and, as it were, visceral opposition, by those whom Charles André Julien has called the *prépondérants*. They were, to be sure, not only the owners of major economic power, but also those who owed to the colonial situation an influence to which they were all the more attached because it was slight and

---

[29] J.L. Miège, *Le Maroc*, vol. IV, pp. 380 ff.

[30] On all this, but too briefly, C.A. Julien, "Colons Français et Jeunes Tunisiens, 1882–1912," *Revue Française d'Histoire d'Outre-Mer*, n. 194–197 (1967) and C.R. Ageron, "Le mouvement Jeune-Algérien de 1900 à 1923," *Bulletin de la Société d'Histoire Moderne*, No. 2, (1962).

[31] The remarks of Hermassi, *Etat et Société...*, see note 4.

precarious. Their opposition, if not their hostility, to the native intelligentsia, was constant. It supplemented and re-inforced that of the administration. In the last instance, the administration preferred the marabouts and the traditional chiefs to the intellectuals nurtured on French culture.

Several years later, Zenati bitterly denounced this paradox, which, to the benefit of those old groups whom social and economic developments made less and less suitable for the job, held in suspicion the elite, which was oriented towards the future, and the most suitable to "servir de trait d'union, répandre un rôle médiateur entre la masse fruste et les représentants de la France."[32]

3. The modernist movement also awakened opposition on the part of the traditional literati and the adherents of strict Islamic culture. In Tunisia, this reaction fed the marabout movement and that of the brotherhoods. In this recourse to what was authentic, religious specificities culminated in local particularisms.

Recourse was also sought in millenarianism and Islamic universalism. The phenomena of "rogué" in Morocco and of Mahdism in Algeria, which has been analysed by Ageron, were moves in reaction to the cultural – and particularly spiritual – transformations introduced by the colonisers.[33] In Morocco, where Sharifism and the veneration of Saints had been one of the means of defense against foreigners especially since the Portugese efforts of the sixteenth century, the French threat re-inforced these brotherhoods. Sultan Moulay Hassan utilised them in his defense policy, just as he tried also, to check them through his policy of modernist reform. The French Government saw in these brotherhood movements one of the strongest obstacles to the maintainance or extension of its dominion.[34]

This extension – the policy of "pénétration pacifique" in Morocco and of military advance to the South – had many repercussions in the extraordinary "sounding-box" which is the Arabo-Islamic world. The effects of any event concerning one section were immediately felt by the others; thus French policy in Morocco played a part in instigating opposition movements in Algeria and Tunisia. It was the same with the French advance towards the South, in regard to which Etienne correctly noted that Algeria was the "clef de voûte de la politique africaine de la France et l'importance qu'y prenait tout acte vers le sud ou l'ouest."[35]

[32] R. Zenati, a muslim French citizen and director of the Constantine journal, *La Voix Indigène* (1929), in his study, "Le problème algérien vu par un indigène," in *Renseignements Coloniaux*, (April, 1938, and following).
[33] Ageron, *Les algériens musulmans...*, p. 921.
[34] J.L. Miège, "Moulay Hassan," *Jeune Afrique*, 1976.
[35] E. Etienne, *La Dépêche*, May 6, 1897. See also the *Bulletin du Comité de l'Afrique Française*, (1910), p. 290.

CONCLUSION

The ambiguities of French policy are disclosed in all fields. It wanted at the same time to assimilate and to conserve traditions. It offered its culture, if timidly, but refused the advantages of citizenship to those who adopted it. While seeming to be in favour of friendship with Islam, it was disquieted by movements of Muslim solidarity; quick to criticise Arabo-Islamic values and to denounce their character as irreconcilable with that of Western civilisation, it still played on the theme of Arab amity and evoked the spirit of its traditional relationship with the East. The French Government extolled peaceful penetration into Morocco, but pushed its troups all along the frontier between Algeria and Morocco to conquer Touat. So many contradictions and such pusillanimity left the field to the local "prépondérants", to the settlers and traditional chiefs who made a political virtue out of immobility.

It is not surprising that so many distortions between intention and action, so many *voltes face* of principle and so great a blockage at the local level produced very varied reactions. Their divergency, moreover, was increased by the complexity of economic and social developments and by the contradictory influences of the great stirring in Islam, wavering between refuge in tradition and modernity.

The contrast between the number of naturalisations requested by the population and those actually obtained on the one hand, the facility of naturalisation for foreigners and the extent of the protection bestowed on the Moroccans, on the other, underlines well the fundamental contradiction of French colonisation in the Maghrib; namely it brought with it human hopes, but was in the end full of disappointment for the very people who had been most fascinated by its promises.

7. FRENCH EXPANSION AND LOCAL REACTIONS IN BLACK AFRICA IN THE TIME OF IMPERIALISM (1880–1914)

by

HENRI BRUNSCHWIG

Strictly limited in time and space, this study is only a provisional report on research not as yet completed. Its intention is to specify how the contact between the white colonists and the black colonised operated on the ground. This contact had existed for a long time on the coast, where it had given rise to acculturated black groups who participated in the pre-colonial trade and often controlled it. It had not existed in the interior of the continent, where relations with the outside were ensured by the "commercial tribes" of the coastal region, who screened and limited them. The imperialist partition, by defining zones of influence, posed the problem of the organisation and occupation of immense regions, sometimes still unexplored, under the aegis of European governments. This establishment of colonisation between 1880 and the end of the First World War corresponds to the diffusion of Marxism in Europe, whose tenets would not gain ground in black Africa until after 1914.

This period is part of the developments in the middling term, the colonial "conjoncture," which ran from the "explosion impérialiste" of the 1880s to the decolonisation of the 1960s. This middling term, again, is situated within a long-term development characterised by the progressive integration of the black African world, isolated until the Islamic advance of the 9th century and the Portugese discoveries of the 15th, into the world civilisation represented by the great economic and cultural domains of Islam and Christianity. This took place at different paces, in different times and places. These variations in pace, their speeding up or slowing down, allow distinction, within the structural evolution over the millenium, of conjunctures dominated on the one hand by the introduction of techniques or new crops (the oriental plants – rice, cane sugar, bananas, coffee – or the American ones – manioc, maize or ground-nuts), on the other by the requirements of overseas trade (in slaves, ivory, palm oil, metals etc.) or by large scale internal African migrations, or by foreign conquests elsewhere.

The colonial "conjoncture" is distinguished within this long-term structure by a sharp acceleration of change. I am concerned with the beginnings of this acceleration, before it had reached cruising speed during the "mise en valeur" from 1920 to 1947, which was itself affected by the world economic crisis of 1930 to 1935. These beginnings present certain specific features in French Africa.

The research in progress is being carried out along three lines: into the impact in France of the doctrine of Paul Leroy-Beaulieu's *De la colonisation chez les peuples modernes;* into the contact between blacks and whites through the agency of the black interpreters in the centres of decision-making and of the black civil police on the level of enforcement; and into the local reactions of collaboration or of resistance.

On all these matters a scattered collection is being made of documents in the archives, essentially in the Series "Missions" III (Explorations, Missions, Journeys), XI (Police, Public Health, and Poor Relief), XIII (Agriculture and Trade), XIV (Labour and Manpower), XV (Private firms), and XVIII (Personnel), all in the *Archives Nationales, Section d'Outre-Mer.* The Yearbooks, the official *Gazettes* of the various colonies and the Administrative Bulletins have all been extensively used, as well as the books and articles cited in the notes.

The conditions under which imperialist domination was established were, on the African side, high population mobility, ended by colonisation, the fragility of the large empires, which were incapable, in the absence of bureaucracies and rapid communications, of imposing a lasting domination by a government on the numerous subjected peoples, the absence of a national sentiment or colour-based solidarity, which colonialism actually engendered, and lastly, the receptiveness of the animist societies to the religious and technical influences of the Islamic or Christian civilisations.

On the French side, a nationalism common to all elements of the population after the defeat of 1871 orientated towards colonial expansion governments which were confronted neither by demographic pressure nor by imperative needs for raw materials or for markets. It was a nationalism of the left. It asserted the right of peoples to self-determination, which Bismarck had violated by annexing Alsace-Lorraine to Germany. It condemned military conquests and criticised the distant expeditions of the Second Empire. It incorporated the humanitarian ideology of the philanthropists, and saw liberal democracy as the most advanced form of civilisation. But equally, it was anxious to show that, despite its defeat, France remained a "grande puissance," whose influence was indispensable to the Progress of Humanity.

I. THE WHITE PERSONNEL OF COLONISATION

The apparent contradiction between the right of peoples to self-determination and colonial expansion was reconciled by Paul Leroy-Beaulieu's book *De la colonisation chez les peuples modernes*, the first edition of which passed virtually unnoticed in 1874 but whose second, published in 1882, became authoritative. To brutal conquest and occupation of foreign countries, it contrasted a colonialism of staff and of capital which was perfectly adapted to the situation of the Third Republic: civilian, economic and liberal. The French did not emigrate. But they were rich, and, in the manner of the great Ferdinand de Lesseps, their engineers were in a position to offer the benefits of industrial civilisation to backward populations. This sort of peaceful colonisation would assure a universal diffusion of the French language and culture, and France, more liberal and more disinterested than its rivals, would guide those peoples that accepted its tutelage to some system of assimilation or association which would respect liberty, equality and fraternity.

Leroy-Beaulieu's call was adressed essentially to French capitalists. It is known that they did not answer it. In his recent study on *L'investissement français dans l'Empire colonial*,[1] M. Jacques Marseille estimates that by 1914 the French had invested 45 thousand millions *francs-or* abroad, of which only four thousand million, that is 9%, was invested in their colonial empire. Of these four thousand million, 1600 had gone to the A.O.F. and the A.E.F., but three quarters of this sum, 1200 million, originated in the public funds, on which interest was to be repaid out of the colonial budgets.[2] These investments had allowed the undertaking of great public works improving the infrastructure, from which the private sector, which had only invested 400 million, profited greatly.

French capitalists did not respond to the call of modern colonisation, But others heard it; Leopold II first of all, then the Belgian state, whose Congo colony was for a long time regarded as a model. And without doubt they would have completely realised the programme of Leroy-Beaulieu if the colonisers had been able, in good time, to emancipate their pupils and guide them towards political independence.

In France, those to whom Leroy-Beaulieu did not adress himself, because

---

[1] Jacques Marseille, "L'investissement français dans l'Empire colonial," *Revue historique*, Oct-Dec. 1974, pp. 409–432.

[2] Jean Suret-Canale, *Afrique Noire, II, L'ère coloniale* (Paris, Editions Sociales, 1964), p. 206. A.O.F. and A.E.F. are, respectively, French West Africa and French Equatorial Africa.

they possessed neither capital nor technical skills, responded to his call with much more enthusiasm than has hitherto been noticed. They laid claim to commissions, to free passages, to subsidies and to territorial concessions, whether from the Ministry or from the governors of the colonies as they were set up.

Originally, this caused no disquiet at the Ministry. Concessions had always been the affair of the authorities on the spot. In Senegal, Governor Genouille laid down regulations for them by the decree of 5 January 1887, without consulting Paris. However, the sudden expansion, which endowed France with immense protectorates and zones of influence between 1880 and 1898, forced it, like the other colonising countries, to envisage costly measures of control and organisation.

Initially, the British and German Governments evaded the matter by favouring chartered companies, which they guaranteed against foreign meddling and to which they handed over the administration and exploitation of the territories, under more or less defined conditions. Eugène Etienne, as Under-Secretary of State for the Colonies, would have liked to imitate them, but the project he submitted to the Senate in 1891 was voted down. Delcassé, Under-Secretary in 1893 and Minister the following year, decreed rights to seven concessionary companies, of which three, Verdier's on the Ivory Coast, Daumas's on the Upper Ogoué and Le Chatelier's at Fernan Vaz (Gabon) were set up. Their concessions were revoked between 1895 and 1897, not without substantial indemnities. Nevertheless, Etienne's projects were re-suscitated in 1895 by Senator Lavertujon and once again encountered parliamentary mistrust. Giving up hope of having the law passed, on 6 July 1898, the Minister for the Colonies, Trouillot, founded a "Commission des concessions coloniales et du domaine," chaired by a *Conseiller d'Etat*. It was to establish a sample roster of charges, to examine the requests and to advise the Minister on the granting of concessions. The history of this commission, which examined all the proposals for concessions in the A.E.F. and, from 1904 those for large concessions in the A.O.F., has yet to be written. Its first decisions resulted in the sharing out, in 1899, of two thirds of the French Congo between 40 companies. Thirty were effectively set up, with a nominal capital of around 51 million francs in all. At the expiration of these thirty-year concessions in 1928, only six remained. Their history and an analysis of the predatory economy which they developed has been described by Mme. Coquery-Vidrovitch.[3] Practically speaking, however, between 1880 and 1899, during the period of expansion and of the progressive creation of the

[3] Catherine Coquery-Vidrovitch, *Le Congo au temps des grandes compagnies concessionnaires, 1898–1930* (Paris, Mouton, 1972), chs. 1 & 2.

colonies, only the authorities on the spot possessed competence in this matter. An examination of the requests adressed either to the Governors or to the Ministry, which forwarded the requests to them, allows the following remarks to be made, subject to corrections which might be imposed by research, as yet uncompleted:

1. The documentation does not allow a totally accurate assessment, because the various dossiers often mention concessions not found in the *Bulletins* or *Journaux Officiels*, and because it is not always possible to find out what replies were given to certain requests or to establish if a provisional concession was withdrawn or made into a definite one.

2. The rush which the authorities expected – Paris wanting to encourage it and the governors trying to limit the streams of emigration – did not materialise. The healthy districts, like Futa Jallon, praised by many explorers (such as Sanderval, Bayol, Noirot and so on), were not "empty", and the administrators were concerned to avoid conflicts with the inhabitants.

3. Up to 1899, the Governors adopted various solutions to all the problems of colonisation. Thus in Senegal, in Guinea, in the Ivory Coast and in the Sudan they acted on their own initiative with regard to building land. In Dahomey and in the Sudan, in cases of concessions over 500 ha, they asked for ministerial ratification. While, in all the other colonies, concessions were provisional for periods varying from 1 to 3 years, in the Ivory Coast they were immediately definite.

4. The requests were concentrated at the time of the foundation of the towns, especially of Conakry and Cotonou. Speculators squabbled over ground which the governors had difficulty in surveying. The case was the same, in the Ivory Coast and the Sudan, as regards permission to prospect for or to exploit mines. The regulations, painfully worked out for Senegal and the Sudan and promulgated on 14 August 1896, were complicated; if anyone had indeed found profitable goldmines there, the conflicts would have been numerous. The Ivory Coast and the A.E.F., perhaps excluding Gabon, interested primarily the large companies. Individual candidates were not numerous.

5. It is surprising just how carefully the requests were investigated, even when they stemmed from men who were clearly bereft of both competence and fortune; nevertheless they were the subjects of enquiries by the police prefectures, of long reports from the Public Works and Agriculture Departments and of considered advice from administrators. The decree of 23 Ocotber 1904, for the A.O.F., left the decision about concessions of less than 200 ha. to the Governors, about those between 200 and 2000 ha. to the Governor-General and about larger ones to the Minister.

In addition to the major commercial companies – *Société Commerciale de l'Ouest Africain (S.C.O.A.)*, *Compagnie française d'Afrique occidentale (C.F.A.O.)*, *Maurel et Prom*, *Mante frères et Borelli*, *Fabre, Verdier* (Cie de Kong), *Daumas* (Société du Haut Ogoué) etc., the applicants came from below the higher ranks of society, like Pierre Caquereau, a commercial traveller from Bordeaux whose wife was a housekeeper in Paris, or the writer, Laumann, who laid claim to 90 hectares in Guinea to set up a plantation of kola trees. He intended to invest 142,000 fr. in ten years, of which 50,000 would be subsidy from the state, and claimed that after ten years the annual revenue would be 3,608,000 frs. His proposal, forwarded from the ministry to the governor, Noël Ballay, was refuted point by point and turned down by him on Nov. 19, 1894. It was the same with the "jeune homme" warmly recommended by the vice-president of the Senate, to the Minister of Trade and Industry: Guillaume Vacca wanted to set up a cotton industry in Guinea. The investigation of the Ministry of the Colonies showed that Vacca was not conversant with the problems of cotton production and the requirements of spinning and weaving. Prudently, the Minister, Gaston Doumergue, rejected the proposal, asserting that his department had already sent out several commissions to look into this matter.[4] Ex-soldiers, labourers who had worked laying down railroads, explorers and medical officers all requested the help of the government. I have investigated elsewhere the attempts of the doctor Paul Colin in Bambuk, of Paul Soleillet in Obock[5] and of Aimé Olivier de Sanderval in Futa Jallon. Examples of colonial applications could be infinitely multiplied. All of them, every time, referred to the ideas of Leroy-Beaulieu, exuded patriotism and lacked capital. Always again, there is proof of the readiness of incompetent politicians to receive these proposals in Paris; and then the very thorough investigation by the specialist departments and the reserve of the colonial authorities rejected them. Once they had arrived in Africa, these righteous little colonisers, convinced, of course, of their superiority as whites, found themselves virtually at the mercy of the official authorities, who did not receive them without qualms and wearied of their unreasonable demands and meddling in African politics. As late as 1894, Delcassé sent to the governor a "Circulaire Ministérielle au sujet des bonnes relations que doivent entretenir les fonctionnaires et officiers avec les colons

---

[4] ANSOM, Missions 17, Guinée XV, 8, Guinée XIII, 7.
[5] Henri Brunschwig, "Le Docteur Colin, l'Or du Bambouk et la colonisation moderne," *Cahiers d'Etudes Africaines*, XIV (1975) pp. 166–188; *id.*, "Une colonie inutile; Obock (1862–1888)," *Cahiers d Etudes Africaines*, VIII (1968), pp. 32–47.

qui viennent s'établir au Sénégal." In it, he summed up the doctrine of modern colonialism.[6]

It is difficult to know the number of these colonists, because the censuses did not classify them separately. However, a statistic of the Ministry of the Colonies regarding the A.E.F. estimated the "commerçants ou colons" at 532 Frenchmen and 230 foreigners.[7] I have not found such precise figures for the A.O.F., but 2932 French reservists figured on the roster of the recruiting agency on August 1, 1914. Of these, 1754 were called up. The black French citizens are included here along with the colonists and the administration. A reasonable estimate of the number of non-official Frenchmen settled in the A.O.F. would thus be less than 3000.[8] It is relatively easier to know the number of officials and agents, French and African, who served the colonial expansion and profited from it. Relatively so, because the Year books change their presentation of the figures from one year to the next, because the boundaries of the colonies changed, because the ranks of the officials changed, and, finally because often, in one and the same yearbook of one colony, the figures presented for each district do not tally with those given in the table surveying the whole colony. Without pretending to rigorous precision, the following figures are probably accurate within 5 or 6%.[9]

TABLE I

Year	A.O.F. (French West Africa)		A.E.F. (French Equatiorial Africa)	
	Administrative Services (general services, admin. of colonies, Native Affairs)	Other Services	Administrative Services	Other Services
1900	256	–	–	–
1906	566	296	–	–
1913	1085	1090	358	175
Totals in 1913	2175		533	

6 "Circulaire ministérielle au sujet des bonnes relations que doivent entretenir les fonction-naires et officiers avec les colons qui viennent s'établir au Sénégal," 23 June 1894, *Bulletin administratif du Sénégal*, 1894.

7 ANSOM, A.E.F. XX.[1]

8 Lieutenant-Colonels Weithas, Rémy and Charbonneau, *La conquête du Cameroun et du Togo* (Paris, Impr. Nat. 1931), 601 pp. 81, (Exposition coloniale de Paris, Collection Armées françaises d'Outre-mer), p. 35.

9 Figures culled from the Yearbooks of the A.O.F., 1900–1914 and of the A.E.F., 1912–1913, which give lists of the names of the various agents.

Examination of it shows, first, the rapid growth in personnel, leaping from 862 to 2708 employees between 1906 and 1913. Then there is the later growth of the "other services," which were only organised after 1906, but finally caught up the administrative branch. Finally, an investigation of these other services shows that the most developed were those that were most useful, not to the colonised but to the colonists. The following table is revealing:

TABLE 2

Services	AOF	AEF
Public Works	250	33
Customs	222	51
Post & Telegraphs	218	48
Education	140	4
Judicial services	70	26
Printing	60	7
Agriculture	57	2
Public Health	56	–
Registry, Public property, Treasury	17	4
Total 1913	1090	175

It can be seen that Public Works, Posts and Customs take up two thirds of the staff in the A.O.F. and three-quarters in the A.E.F. The moral side of colonisation was neglected. Education was in fourth place in the A.O.F. and had hardly begun to be organised in the A.E.F., where a Public Health service did not exist at all.

A comparison of the number of French merchants and colonists censused in the A.E.F. in 1914 with that of officials and staff, that is to say 532 to 533, recalls Bismarck's ironical definition put forward during his speech in the Reichstag of 27 June, 1884, which Delcassé rebutted in his circular of 1894: "On a dit fréquemment que la France n'avait que des colonies de fonctionnaires et de soldats...." And one might wonder whether those primarily interested in the colonisation of black Africa before 1914 were not these last.

Stemming from this, the question I would pose is this: In the absence of a genuine system of colonisation, systematically put into practice by governments equipped with the necessary wherewithal – and in the absence of private investments operated by substantial capitalists with the assistance of competent technicians – how in daily practice was contact established between colonists and colonised?

II. THE INTERPRETERS

The first contacts were established through the medium of interpreters. The interpreter in question was an African who spoke French and one or several African languages. The quality of their French was often, in the beginning, extremely mediocre. The interpreters, recruited from among the discharged *tirailleurs* (riflemen), were frequently illiterate. Mr. Hampaté Bâ has sketched some of their careers in his remarkable account.[10] Explorers like Brazza or administrators like Noirot often mention these interpreters, used more or less regularly. Boubou Penda, a boy (1885), cook and then advisor to Noirot followed his master from Sine-Saloun to Futa Jallon and was finally incorporated in 1901 into the ranks of the interpreters.[11] No doubt the great majority of these indispensable auxiliaries of the administration were merely casual, in the beginning, and little differentiated from domestic servants. Thus it is not possible to count them, nor to gauge their influence, nor, even by studying the reasons for their being decorated,[12] to appreciate their services.

However, the Colonial Governors very quickly experienced the necessity of supervising and regulating these henchmen. Hence the creation of a staff of regularly paid interpreters. The first was inaugurated by order of Jauréguiberry on December 1st, 1862;

Nous, gouverneur du Sénégal et dépendances,

Vu les services chaque jour plus importants que sont appelés à rendre les interprètes des diverses langues que parlent les populations placées sous notre autorité ou avec lesquelles nous entretenons des relations politiques et commerciales d'un haut intérêt.

Considérant que l'administration ne peut apporter aujourd'hui dans le choix de ces agents toute la sévérité nécessaire parce que leur organisation ne leur donne ni des garanties, ni une solde susceptibles de les attacher à leur fonction en rémunérant convenablement leurs services;

Avons arrêté et arrêtons....

the creation of a special corps of established and auxiliary interpreters under the control of the director of Native Affairs, of the *commandants d'arrondissement* and of the *chefs de poste*; that is to say twenty permanent

---

[10] Amadou Hampaté Bâ, *L'étrange destin de Wangrin ou les roueries d'un interprète africain* (Paris, Union générale d'Editions, Coll 10/18), pp. 15 ff., 44, 118.

[11] J. Lemaire, "En Guinée....", *Annales Coloniales,* 23 Jan. 1908; Personal dossier of Noirot, ANSOM E.E. 1160¹. Note by the Inspector of the colonies Frezouls on Noirot in 1905, E.E. 1160²; deposition of Cousturier before the Inspector of the Colonies Reinhardt, 3 Sept. 1906, Interpellation at the Chambre by Pelletan, *J.O.,* 19 Nov. 1907; 2e séance, p. 2343, col. 2; Deposition of the Almamy Baba Alémou, 2 June 1905, p. 209, Arch. Dakar, 7 G 85.

[12] ANSOM, A.O.F. XVIII¹, Personnel, Decorations 1896–1907.

staff ranked in four grades, recruited by an examining board and paid from 600 to 3000 francs a year.[13]

This staff was in force in Senegal till the decree of 27 Nov. 1893, which reduced the number of permanent staff to 17, and increased the salary to 800 francs for an *auxiliaire de 2e classe* up to 3600 for an *interprète principal*.[14] The various other colonies equipped themselves with an interpreter corps which met with local requirements; Dahomey by decree of June 15, 1897,[15] Sudan on Nov. 18, 1895,[16] Ivory Coast on July 31, 1897,[17] Guinea on Sept. 14, 1901,[18] Mauretania on Sept. 26, 1906.[19] In A.E.F. there was an attempt to fix the rate paid to competent private individuals for the required translations, but then the decree of April 29, 1914, set up the corps of writer-interpreters appointed as was needed by the governors of the colonies of the federation (Gabon, Middle Congo, Ubangi-Shari, Chad).[20]

If all these, frequently modified decrees are compared, the differences in the ordinances from one colony to the next are striking; salaries, ranks, recruiting examinations, all varied. Up till 1914 there was no uniform regulation in the A.O.F.

This can doubtless be explained on the one hand by the particularism of the governors or lieutenant-governors, on the other hand by local circumstances. Thus General Dodds was led in 1894 to increase the salaries in Dahomey, where there were numerous polyglot indigenous merchants. The first draft of the decree, of February 24, 1894 stated:

Nous nous trouvons en relations directes avec des populations auxquelles il importe d'inspirer confiance pour les attirer à nous d'une façon définitive. Il nous faut, pour nous aider dans cette tâche, des agents zélés, connaissant suffisamment notre langue, et en qui nous puissions avoir une confiance absolue. La première condition pour

---

[13] *Feuille officielle du Sénégal et Dépendances*, 9 Dec. 1862, p. 441.

[14] *J.O.*, *Sénégal*, 27 Nov. 1893 and *Bulletin administratif du Sénégal*, 1893, p. 475.

[15] *J.O.*, *Bénin*, 1 July 1892, modified (wages), 1 Mar. 1894, then *J.O. de la Colonie de Dahomey et dépendances*, 15 Mar, 1899. Decree of 6 March, with names, then *J.O. de l'A.O.F.*, 25 Feb. 1914, Decree of Governor General W. Ponty, lists of 13 names in *Decision*, 14 Aug 1984, in *J.O. Dahomey*, 1 Sept. 1894, and of 43 names in the *Annuaire du Gouvernement Général de l'A.O.F.*, 1904, p. 289.

[16] *J.O. de l'A.O.F.*, 4 Jan. 1896, Decree of 18 Nov. 1895. Cf. ANSOM Soudan VII[5], Budget of 1897, Cahier 8, art. 3, 4.

[17] *J.O. Côte d'Ivoire*, Decree of 31 July 1897, and ANSOM, Côte d'Ivoire VII[6]; Conseil d'administration, meeting 31 July, 1897.

[18] *J.O.*, *Guinée française*, 1 Oct. 1901, Decree of 14 Sept.; cf. *id. Note sur les indemnités*, 27 July 1901, *J.O.*, 1 Sept....

[19] *J.P.A.O.F.*, 29 Sept. 1906, Decree of 26 Sept.

[20] *J.O.*, *Gabon-Congo*, 23 July 1887, Decree of 7 July. *Annuaire du Gouv. 't. Général de l'A.E.F.*, *Supplément à la partie documentaire de l'annuaire de 1912*, Decree of 29 Apr. 1914 (Brazzaville, 1914), pp. 428–431. *Id. Annuaire* 1912, 2nd partie, pp. 397–402.

TABLE 3. STATUTES ON INTERPRETERS EMPLOY

	Senegal	Sudan	Dahomey	Ivory Coas
Sources	Journal Officiel Sénégal 2 Dec. 1893 Decree of 23 Nov. 1893	J.O., A.O.F. 4 Jan. 1896 Decree of 18 Nov. 1895	J.O., Dahomey 15 March, 1899 Decree of 6 March 1899	J.O Côte d'Iv 1897 Decree of 31 July 189
Interprète Principal hors classe		6000		
en Chef 1e classe			5000	
2e classe			4000	
Interprète Principal 1e classe	3600	3600	3600	1800
2e classe	3000	3000	3000	1500
3e classe			2400	
4e classe				
Interprète Titulaire 1e classe	2600	2400	1800	1200
2e classe	2000	1800	1500	1000
3e classe	1500	1200	1200	800
4e classe	1200		1000	600
5e classe				
Interprète Auxiliaire 1e classe	1000	900		
2e classe	800			
Interprète Stagiaire			600	
Elève interprète				
Total number employed in 1904	5	29 (19)[1]	43	56

[1] The summary table gives 19, but counting by *cercles* and *postes* amounts to 29.
[2] On "promotion", 100 frs. more for the *titulaires*, 50 frs. for the others.
[3] Wages in Europe were half of this.

arriver à recruter ces agents est de leur faire une situation sortable et de leur allouer un traitement supérieur à celui qu'ils pourraient trouver dans le commerce.[21]

The best paid of the established staff were to receive 3600 frs. instead of 2400.

The table above, based on official sources, allows the situation of the interpreters and officials in the various colonies of the A.O.F. to be compared between 1895 and 1906. This table would not survive heavy criticism. It is not always possible to check from the budgets that these salaries have actually been paid. It is absolutely impossible to ascertain the number of interpreters. The indicative figure of 156, given for 1904, would have been 127 for 1903 and 163 for 1905, 221 for 1910 and 228 for 1914. Most of the decrees, fixing salaries, did not

[21] ANSOM, Dahomey VII[5], minutes of the *Conseil d'administration des Etablissements français du Bénin*, meeting 24 Feb. 1894.

A.O.F. BETWEEN 1895 AND 1906

Guinée	Mauretania	A.E.F.	Wages of Administrateurs des Colonies[3]
J.O., Guinée	J.O., A.O.F.	Annuaire, A.E.F.	Bulletin officiel du Ministère des Colonies
1 Oct. 1901	29 Sept. 1906	1914	
Decree of	Decree of	Decree of	Decree of 4 July, 1906
14 Sept. 1901	26 Sept. 1906	29 April 1914	
			16500–17000 administrateur en chef
			15000–16000
			13000–14000 administrateur
	3600	4000	11000–12000
	3000	3500	9000–10500
		3000	
		2500	8000– 9000 administrateur adjoint
	2500	2200	6500– 7500
1900–2100	2000	1800	5000– 6000
1600–1800	1500	1500	
1300–1500	1200	1200	
1000–1200			
600– 900	1000		
	800		
		800	4000– 4500 administrateur stagiaire
450– 550[2]			
21	2		

lay down the number of these agents, who were recruited as needed. And most of the "interprètes" were not on the permanent staff. The *chefs de poste* or *de mission*, the administrators, nominated their most resourceful boy or rifleman and paid them out of the petty cash, and then discharged them or appointed them elsewhere when they failed to present themselves to the examining boards set up by the decree. What is important is the mobility of the African staff who passed easily from one job to another, from rifleman, instructor, superintendant of customs, merchant and so on to interpreter, or in the reverse direction. However, a decree of February 20, 1897 gives some insight in the importance of the official interpreters. It fixed at between 1800 and 3000 francs the salaries of the "commis indigènes du cadre auxiliaire," which consisted of four ranks.[22] The interpreters could earn even more. They seem to have been the best paid of the African staff, and generally, they could augment their income considerably with the perks of their job. Again the importance of the interpreter can be appreciated by comparing his

[22] J.O., A.O.F., 1897, p. 71.

position with that of the administrator, whose salary in Europe was half of that in the colonies: thus an *interprète principal de première classe* in Senegal, Sudan, Dahomey, Mauretania and in the A.E.F. received about the same as an *administrateur-adjoint des colonies de 2e classe* in France and nearly twice the salary of an *administrateur* at the beginning of his career in Europe. Moreover, the great favourites, at the top, the *interprète principal* in Sudan or the *interprète en chef* in Dahomey were as well rewarded as the *administrateurs des colonies de 2e ou 3e classe* in France.

The salaries of the various civilian policemen, who were generally recruited from among the ex-riflemen, were in this period 480 frs, for the *gendarmes* in Senegal, 456 frs.25 for the *gardes de police de 2e classe* in Guinea, 360 frs for the *gardes indigènes de 2e classe* in the Ivory Coast and the *gardes de cercle de 2e classe* in Niger, and 180 frs for the *gardes régionaux de 4e classe* in the Congo.[23]

Was the confidence that the numerous "commandants" showed in their indispensable interpreters justified? Did they assist, or betray the colonisers? The research that is in progress on the origins, the level of education and the career of these men will perhaps allow judgement on this. At the moment, I have no more than a few dozen examples. From this it is apparent that there was no uniform behaviour among the interpreters. They seem to have been guided essentially by their individual interests. Most of them never considered the problem of a choice between assimilation or loyalty to their traditions. No doubt Xavier Béraud, *interprète en chef de 1ère classe* and his twenty colleagues who were listed on the first page of the *Journal Officiel* of Dahomey on March 15, 1899 had made their choice. They belonged to the acculturated bourgeois élite; the administration looked after them and could rely on their services, as it could on that of the interpreters in the courts in Senegal. Later on, many like Mr. Moukouri, a Douala from the Cameroon, who was born in 1909 and entered the service as a scribe and interpreter in 1926, knew genuine conflicts of conscience. He admirably described the false situation an interpreter found himself in when he was not a member of the local aristocracy and the son of an Elder. A counsellor and a conciliator, easily scorned by the whites, who called him "tu," and by the blacks who suspected him, he felt himself to be continually threatened with unmerited sanctions. As opposed to Mr. Hampaté Bâ's Wangrin, he was not solely ruled by his personal interests.[24] The main model for Wangrin might have been Diaman

---

[23] *J.O.*, *Sénégal*, 28 Apr. 1894, Decree of 21 Apr.; *J.O. Guinée*, 1 June 1901, Decree of 2 May; *J.O.*, *Côte d'Ivoire*, 1 Jan. 1895, Decree of 29 Dec. 1894; ANSOM, Niger VII², Decree of Governor General W. Ponty, 3 Febr. 1913; *J.O.*, *A.E.F.*, 6 Dec. 1902, Decree of 2 Dec.

[24] Jacques Kuoh Moukouri, *Doigts Noirs* (Montréal, Les Editions à la page, 1963).

Demba Bathily. A native of Kayes, a marine in the campaigns against Dahomey and Samori, *commissaire de police* in 1894, *interprète titulaire de 2e classe* in 1896 and promoted to *1ère classe* next year, transferred to Bobo Dioulasso in 1903, well known and decorated with the *Légion d'Honneur* and with other medals, he was suspected of plotting against the French during the revolts against conscription in 1916–17 and was summoned to Bamako, where, in 1918, sufficient proof of his guilt could not be established. He died of an acute haemoptysis, as the autopsy showed.[25]

His case is paralleled by that of Ousman Fall, *interprète principal* at Medina in 1889 and *chef de canton* in Sanié. He was decorated with the *médaille d'honneur*, with the rank of *chevalier de la Légion d'Honneur* and with the crosses of Cambodia and Nicham Iftikar, and was well known. Following numerous complaints, he was arrested in 1890. The enquiry revealed that he was associated with a gang of plunderers who were terrorising Bambuk. Accused of insubordination towards the *commandant du cercle*, Lieutenant Baudot, and towards the "regular authorities," by "pretending to the right of administering justice," of having raised taxes for his own profit and of having taken prisoner and sold free men and women living in Medina, he was saved by the enormity of his crimes. The governors of Senegal, Clément-Thomas and de la Mothe, agreed with the commander-in-chief in the Sudan, Archinard, whose report requested that Ousman Fall should not be brought before a civilian court "to avoid complications in these over-excited times." The matter was covered up. Ousman Fall was dismissed, struck from the *Légion d'Honneur* and banished from the Sudan.[26] He is another possible model for Wangrin. In both cases those truly responsible were the administrators who put too much trust in their interpreters.

The interpreters, who were a necessary evil, did service or disservice to the colonising process, depending on the time and the place, depending on the administrators they worked for and depending on their own interests and ideals. The "commandants" who would have been paralysed without them, often realised their dependance. A decree on the staff of the Native Affairs department in the Sudan stated in 1897 that "tout employé européen du cadre des Affaires Indigènes pouvant justifier devant un jury d'examen de la connaissance parfaite d'une des langues ou idiomes parlés au Soudan: arabe, peulh, bambara, malinké, sarakolé, sera de droit promu immédiatement à la classe supérieure et conservera dans son nouvel emploi l'ancienneté qu'il possédait dans la classe à laquelle il appartenait."[27]

[25] ANSOM, A.O.F., XVIII¹ (decorations), and Arch. Dakar 15 G 202, 203, 204.
[26] ANSOM, Soudan XVI b.a.
[27] *J.O.*, *A.O.F.*, 20 Feb. 1897, p. 71, art 8.

In 1912, governor-general Merlin said of the interpreters:

Ils ne sont pas recommandables; beaucoup d'entre eux ne désirent pas qu'un Européen entre en contact direct avec des indigènes susceptibles de révéler des faits qu'ils entendent dissimuler. Ils s'efforcent alors de troubler les investigations et d'écarter des témoignages gênants. C'est pourquoi, lorsqu'on le peut, (sic) c'est de se priver de leur services, d'apprendre une langue de communication parlée par plusieurs tribus et de s'en servir pour converser directement avec les indigènes.[28]

III. THE AFRICAN POLICE

Decisions, more or less inspired by the interpreters, were in the end put into effect by the police. Their officers had different names, *gardes de sûreté*, *gendarmes*, *miliciens*, *gardes régionaux*, *gardes civils*, *gardes indigènes* or *gardes de cercle*. Their specific character was that they depended totally on the civilian authorities (governors or administrators) who gave them civilian tasks: police work, the transmission of orders from the administration, escorting, guarding convoys or, in case of troubles, safeguarding the lives and, if possible, the property of the Europeans and their African protegés, until the arrival of troups to re-establish order.[29]

They were recruited essentially from among the ex-riflemen, and never conscripted. The candidates were attracted by the wages, which were relatively higher than those of a "boy" or a porter, by the additional profits derived from abusing their position, and by the prestige that it gave them. Fily Dabo Sissoko recounts a meeting in 1916 in Dori with a slave who had fled to Saint-Louis to enlist as a rifleman, and who, after forming part of the Fashoda column and completing fifteen years of service, re-engaged as a *garde-cercle*; he was free and had been happily settled for eight years at Dori, where he had two wives and numerous children.[30]

The Governor of French Guinea, Cousturier, on June 29, 1901, wrote in his circular to the administrators that:

Les gardes ne sont pas des militaires. Les agents locaux conservent leur établissement dans le pays, y ont leur champ, leur bétail et tous leurs biens. . . . Il ne saurait s'agir que de mercenaires complètement civils. . . . et susceptibles d'être employés à des corvées auxquelles on n'astreindrait pas des soldats. Il est notamment de principe dans

---

[28] A.E.F., XVIII³.

[29] *J.O.*, *A.O.F.*, 1910, p. 458, Decree on reorganisation of the *gardes de cercles* in Ivory Coast, 11 Oct. 1910. The tasks, more or less detailed (Prison wardening, arrests of criminals etc.) are nearly identical in all the regulations for the *gardes civils*.

[30] Fily Dabo Sissoko, *La Savane rouge* (Avignon, Presses universelles, 1962), p. 75; and on the abuses on those *gardes* charged with levying taxes, pp. 96–8.

diverses colonies que la garde de police construit ses casernements par ses propres moyens, comme tout indigène. Il en est d'ailleurs de ce personnel particulier comme de tous les personnels indigènes. Il importe donc de ne pas se faire d'illusions sur la valeur très relative des gens qui le composent et qui sont toujours aisément remplaçables par d'autres d'égale valeur.... Jamais nous ne risquerons de manquer de personnel dans aucune des catégories.[31]

From 1862 there existed a "corps indigène de gardes de sûreté" in Senegal; three *brigadiers* and thirty *gendarmes*, mounted, armed, charged with policing the districts and paid from 25 to 35 frs. per month; the policing of Saint-Louis was insured by twelve *agents* and two *brigadiers*, paid from 40 to 50 frs. a month.[32] The extension of French domination and of the area of the Protectorate finally required the placing at the disposal of the "*administrateurs des cercles* où il n'existe aucune force militaire, d'un groupe de quatre ou cinq indigènes spécialement affectés à toutes les missions de police." As an economy measure, an attempt was made to replace quantity with quality. "Or le premier élément de qualité que puissent avoir les réprésentants de la force publique en pays indigènes, c'est leur armement. Si nos gardes de police ou gendarmes indigènes sont armés avec des armes à tir rapide, avec des fusils modèle 1874 par exemple, ils deviendront de suite un élément sérieux de force."[33]

In 1893 and 1894, three decrees created forces of *gendarmes* on horseback and on foot, who were finally described as *gardes régionaux*. The decree of April 21, 1894, fixed the number of those serving at 72, in twelve ranks, with the *garde régional* to be paid 720 francs a year and the *garde principal* 1200. The urban and regional police forces were finally reorganised on July 6, 1911, as the *gardes de cercle* and the *agents de police*.[34]

Initially the various posts and offices, which grew into autonomous colonies, depended on Senegal;[35] it might be expected that their governors

---

[31] *J.O., Guinée*, 1 Aug. 1901.

[32] *Feuille officielle du Sénégal et Dépendances*, 16 Dec. 1862, Decree of 8 Dec; *ibid.*, 3 May 1864; decision, 15 Apr.

[33] ANSOM XI 1a, Lamothe, governor of Senegal and Dependances to the Under-Secretary of State for the Colonies, 13 Dec. 1891.

[34] *Bulletin administratif du Sénégal*, 23 Nov. 1893, pp. 469–470; *J.O., Sénégal*, Decrees of 21 Dec. 1893, 21 Apr. 1894 and 6 July 1911.

[35] Guinée française et dépend. Decree, 17 Dec. 1891; Guinée, Decree 10 Mar. 1893; Guinée, Côte d'Ivoire et Bénin, Decree 10 Mar. 1893; Sudan, Decree 16 June 1895; Dahomey, Decree 17 Oct. 1899. The *Soudan*, suppressed by decree of 17 Oct. 1899, reappeared as *Territoire de Sénégambie et Niger* under the control of the Governor General, then, with a Lieutenant-Governor, under the name of *Haut-Sénégal et Niger* (decree 18 Oct. 1904). Mauretania was administered as a *Territoire* by a commissioner of the Governor General (18 Oct. 1904). Details in *Sources de*

would follow the Senegalese pattern in the organisation of their police. Nothing of the sort took place. As with the interpreters, the governors reacted to the pressure of local circumstances and made a clear effort to communicate with the ministry, even when Senegal was involved. The same tendency can be seen after the creation of the post of Governor General, who had a great deal of trouble for over fifteen years before he could impose his control over the subordinate governors. Everyone wanted to be his own boss and was particularly jealous of "his" troups. This resulted in another, long, rivalry with the military, which claimed control over the African police. It only succeeded completely in 1917.[36] In the mean time, the governors had increased the *gardes de cercles*, which remained under their exclusive control, and whose ordinances the governor-general did not succeed in unifying before the eve of the First World War.

The beginnings of the police were often quaint. In the Ivory Coast, where the French positions had been evacuated in 1871, the French resident in Grand Bassam, Arthur Verdier, who came from La Rochelle, asked the Ministry of the Navy for a free supply of 25 muzzle-loaders and the same number of belts, bayonets and cartridge pouches for "la petite troupe de police indigène chargée de maintenir l'ordre dans nos établissements de la Côte d'or" (August 1886). It was very difficult to find this obsolete material, which the War Ministry would only give up for money. From January 1, 1887, Verdier received a subsidy of 6000 frs. a year, paid out in La Rochelle, for the organisation of an African police force, which then consisted of ten men. By March, there were twenty in Grand Bassam and Assinie, and they received uniforms, weapons and ammunition paid for by the local budget of Senegal. This militia of 20 men was re-equipped,[37] when the expedition of Treich-Laplène, a local officer of Verdier's, was organised in 1888 against Kong, to link up with Binger, who had come from Senegal. When Binger, who had been appointed governor in March 1893, organised the colony, he issued two decrees on December 29, 1894, with regard to the police and the *Garde Indigène*.[38] It was not until 1910 that this force was re-organised under the title *Gardes de Cercles*, along the lines of the African *Gardes* in the other colonies of the A.O.F.[39]

l'Histoire de l'Afrique au sud du Sahara.... I. Archives.... (Zug, Inter Documentation Company, 1971) pp. 872 ff.

[36] ANSOM, Affaires politiques 2803, (Contribution de l'A.O.F., aux dépenses de la Metropole, Brigades indigènes transformées en régiments de tirailleurs) August 1917.

[37] ANSOM, Sénégal XVI, 32.

[38] ANSOM, Côte d'Ivoire XI, 1a, and *J.O. Côte d'Ivoire*, No. 1, Jan. 1895, Decree of 29 Dec. 1894.

[39] *J.O., A.O.F.*, 11 Oct, 1910, Decree of Governor General (Ponty) on the reorganisation of the *Gardes des Cercles* in Ivory Coast, pp. 658–662.

In Guinea, from which Senegal withdrew its riflemen when the colony became autonomous, the interim lieutenant-governor, Cérisier, created a body of 51 *gardes civils indigènes*, distributed among the stations as a matter of urgency "en attendant la réglementation définitive, actuellement à l'étude et concernant l'organisation policière et militaire générale des Rivières du Sud de Senegal et de nos Etablissements de Grand Bassam et Assinie." The 36 *gardes de première* and *deuxième classe* were paid 1.35 and 1.25 fr. a day, while the five *sergeants* and the ten *caporaux* received 40 and 50 francs a month, respectively. However, they were not armed.

Governor Ballay, sent on a special assignment called this to the immediate attention of the Under-Secretary of State for the Colonies. On October 21, 1890, he wrote to Etienne from Conakry:

Le poste de Benty n'a pas un seul fusil, une seule cartouche, Boffa a deux fusils, Dubreka et Boké chacun dix. A Conakry même, les indigènes sonts des plus inoffensifs, mais dans le cas où j'aurais à imposer ma volonté, les moyens me feraient absolutement défaut.

Mais c'est surtout au point de vue de notre influence que cette situation pourrait amener à la longue les résultats les plus déplorables, car dans l'esprit des indigènes, c'est la force seule qui est respectable. Le nombre actuel des miliciens étant de cinquante et un, il y en a par conséquent trente et un qui ne sont pas armés. L'année prochaine le personnel de la milice sera augmenté. En outre des miliciens, il y aurait d'ailleurs intérêt à armer les agents européens des douanes, leur canotiers et certains laptots,

that is to say, 12 white men and 57 blacks.[40]

A comprehensive regulation did not come about until 1901. Then it specified the policemen's tasks, salaries, hierarchy and discipline, but did not impose conditions on recruitment by the administrators in the districts or the Police Commissioner in Conakry and allowed the manpower to vary "selon les circonscriptions, les besoins du moment et les prévisions budgétaires." According to the 1904 Yearbook of the A.O.F., the strength was one *commissaire de police*, two *brigadiers* and thirty *gardes de police* in Conakry, and 36 *brigadiers* and 260 *gardes* in the districts.[41] The mediocre quality of the force can no doubt be explained by the fact of local recruitment.

At the time of Dahomey's separation from Senegal, the *Lieutenant-Gouverneur des Rivières du Sud* in Porto Novo decreed on November 9, 1889 the creation, on his own initiative, of "une force armée comprenant une compagnie de gardes civils indigènes pour la protection des Etablissements du Golfe du Bénin," consisting of 114 *gardes* and two Europeans. After the

[40] ANSOM, Guinée XVI, 2.
[41] *J.O., Guinée française*, 1 June 1901, Decree of 2 May; *Annuaire, A.O.F.*, 1904.

conquest of Dahomey, General Dodds organised this civilian force on the lines of a military organisation: 355 men including 9 Europeans divided into three companies.[42] As in the Ivory Coast, in 1909 the Governor-General, William Ponty, promulgated a general ordinance regarding the *gardes de cercle*: the 1910 Yearbook of the A.O.F. distinguished these last from the *gardes indigènes*; there were seven *gardes de cercles* and 133 *agents* and *gradés de police*, including one white, on the one hand, and 540 *gardes indigènes* (including two white *inspecteurs*), on the other.[43]

A circular from the Governor General to all the Governors of the A.O.F. on October 21, 1910, attempted to standardise the police *(gardes de cercle)*. It insisted on recruitment from among ex-soldiers with a certificate of good conduct, on training and on a common hierarchy *(brigadiers-chefs, brigadiers, gardes de 1ère* and *2e classe)*, and on a standard uniform. These plans were followed by the decree of February 3, 1913, on the organisation of the *gardes de cercle* in Niger.

At this time a distinction was made between the *gardes de cercle* and the *garde indigène*, the latter a military force charged against the local budgets of the colonies and commanded jointly by the commander-in-chief and the Governor. The former had control over recruitment, training and discipline, and the latter over stationing and the maintainance of internal security. "Son personnel est interchangeable avec le personnel des troupes régulières."[44] The militarisation of the *gardes indigènes*, originally a civilian police force, was completed in 1917 by their fusion with the riflemen in Senegal. However, the civilian police survived and, as *gardes de cercles* or *agents de police urbaine*, were under the exclusive control of the administrators.[45]

In the Congo and the A.E.F. the *milices indigènes*, who were militarised and, so it would seem, had been locally recruited since 1891,[46] were replaced by the *gardes régionaux*, whose sections carried out the tasks of the civilian police under the orders of the administrators. However, their training, in a "portion centrale" and their hierarchy of ten ranks running from the *garde de 4e classe* to the *adjudant* made them like lower-paid soldiers. Nevertheless, their military value was small. In March 1914, the report of Inspector Sabatier concluded that: "Il faut se borner à l'envisager comme une force de police et de gendarmerie destinée à seconder les administrateurs dans leur

[42] *J.O., Etablissements et Protectorats français du Golfe du Bénin*, 1 Jan. 1890, Decree of 9 Nov. 1889; *J.O., Dahomey*, 10 Aug. 1894, Decree of 23 June.

[43] *J.O., A.O.F.*, 2 Feb. 1909, Decree of 2 Feb.; *Annuaire, A.O.F.*, 1910.

[44] *J.O., A.O.F.*, 1910, pp. 663–664, Circular of 21 Oct. 1910; ANSOM Niger VII 2, Decree No. 174 on the organisation of the *gardes de cercle* in the *territoire militaire du Niger*.

[45] *J.O., A.O.F.*, 1911, Decree no. 672, pp. 385–388.

[46] ANSOM, Gabon – Congo IX, 14a, Budget 1891.

action de tous les jours vis-à-vis des indigènes." It was to be hoped that they would be transformed "et qu'elle réponde le plus tôt possible au voeu de la loi qui voit en elle l'auxiliaire éventuelle de l'armée régulière."[47]

As with the interpreters, a table of the position of the *gardes* at comparable dates shows great difference from one colony to the next.

TABLE 5

	Sénégal	*Guinée*	*Ivory Coast*	*Benin Dahomey*	*A.E.F.*
Dates and Sources	J.O. Sénégal Arr. 21.4. 1894	J.O. Guinée Arr. 1.VI. 1901 Annuaire AOF 1904	J.O. Côte d'Iv. Jan. 1895 Arr. 29. XII 1894	J.O. Dahomey Arr. 23. VI. 1894	J.O. Congo Arr. 16. VII. 1909 ANSOM AEF XVI 3
Names	Gardes Régionaux	Gardes de Police	Garde Indigène	Gardes Civils	Gardes régionaux
Number of Gardes	72	329	72	355	1821
Number of ranks	4	4	6	7	10
Wages for Natives	720 to 1200 frs	480 to 720 frs	360 to 1080 frs	456.25 to 1000 frs	180 to 1200 frs

These differences were also present in the matter of recruitment and show the absence of thought out and regularly applied policy and system.

Indications of the numbers of the various *agents de police* or *gardes* given in the Yearbooks for 1900 to 1914 do not allow detailed interpretation, because of the deficiencies of the sources. Nevertheless, they do reveal a continuous increase in the number of Africans serving: 314 in 1900, 369 in 1902, 930 in 1903, 1375 in 1904, 1650 the next year, then from 2365 in 1906 and 3413 in 1909 to 3832 in 1910, decreasing to 3658 the year after. In the A.E.F., there were 700 *gardes régionaux* in 1902, and 2441 in 1911, according to the report of an inspection. This means that on the eve of the First World War there were in total some 3658 African police in the A.O.F. and 2331 in the A.E.F.

[47] *J.O., Congo français*, 15 Aug. 1909, Decree of 16 July; *Annuaire du Gouvernement Général*, *A.E.F.*, 1912, Pt. 2, pp. 423–446; A.E.F. XVI₃, Report of *Inspecteur adjoint* Sabatier, of the Frézouls *mission*. As can be seen above, the inspector's report, in ANSOM, A.E.F., XVI₃, indicates a number of 2331 Gardes Régionaux for 1911 – the Commission for the *Budget de la Chambre des Députés* indicates an effective police force of 1865 men; A.E.F. XIX 4: Observations au rapport de M. Violette, p. 6.

However, these 5989 Africans were officered by rather few Europeans. The highest proportion that I have discovered concerns the *commissaires de police urbaine* in the A.E.F., where there were five for sixty *agents*, that is to say 8.3%. In 1902, eighteen Europeans commanded 700 *gardes régionaux*, which means they provided 2.57% of the force. In the A.O.F. the proportion fell from 4.10% in 1900 to 1.03% in 1911. The black *gardes* were not strictly controlled.

What use were they? They had a bad press, but policemen are never liked. Their very tasks led them into temptations. Scattered in small detachments, without the continuous control of a *garde principal*, of a *commissaire* or an officer, they considered it normal to accept little gifts, to live on the land when they were escorting a convoy, to threaten in order to collect taxes more quickly, or to resort sometimes to abominable acts of violence. In the extreme cases, to be found in the literature, they yielded nothing to interpreters like Ousman Fall. Fily Dabo Sissoko describes the torturing of peasants around Dori in 1910–11. However, he also gave a description of an honest *garde*, that ex-slave who had originally signed up as a rifleman and served in the Fashoda expedition.[48] With or without the knowledge of their commanding officers, militiamen rampaged in Guinea, in the Congo,[49] and so on. The list of abuses was long and would appear to be confirmed by official reports.

In fact, the inspectors of the colonies were severe on the police forces recruited by the governors. For example, Inspector Hoarau-Desruisseaux stated in 1895 that the militiamen hastily engaged in Guinea had no military instruction at all. The Governor, Cousturier, pointed out that local recruitment did not permit the organisation of a force, which would eventually be capable of replacing the soldiers who had been sent back to Senegal in 1890. He insisted on the "manque absolu d'esprit de discipline chez les Sousous" and on "la tendance de tous les indigènes revêtus d'un semblant d'autorité à en abuser immédiatement, et le peu de confiance que l'on peut avoir en ces miliciens dès qu'ils sont livrés à aux-mêmes. Il serait impossible, à l'heure actuelle de détourner ces miliciens de la modeste tâche d'agents de police dont ils s'acquittent de manière assez satisfaisante."[50]

In the A.E.F., the inspectors of the Frézouls commission of 1910–11 supported the efforts of the military to control the *garde régionale* and deplored the fact that the latter were only a "force de police et de gendarmerie

[48] Fily Dabo Sissoko, *La Savane Rouge*, pp. 97–98 and 75.
[49] E.g. Arch. Dakar 7G⁸⁵. Enquête Stahl, Frézouls' report to the Governor General on the political situation in Futa Jallon (July 10, 1905); see also Coquery-Vidrovitch, *Le Congo*, p. 93 etc.
[50] ANSOM, Guinée XVI 2a, Conseil d'administration, 18 May 1895 and Letter to the Minister of the Colonies, 24 May.

destinée a seconder les administrateurs dans leur action de tous les jours vis-à-vis des indigènes." Frézouls stated that, when they were sent out on detachment, the *gardes* were solely under the control of the officials commanding in the district. They quickly lost their military qualities and, for example, in Libreville they had been assigned "pendant une quinzaine, sur l'ordre du lieutenant-gouverneur, à la reconstruction du Lazaret, érigé en maison de campagne du chef de la colonie." Lieutenant Lasserre, who was charged with the organisation of a transport convoy in the Central Logone, described the *gardes* as "brutes dangereuses, paresseuses et indisciplinées," and criticised local recruitment; the natives were, he said, "des isolés qui cherchent un moyen, soit d'assurer leur existence matérielle, soit de disposer d'une parcelle d'autorité permettant de pressurer leurs compatriotes."[51]

Nevertheless the picture should not be painted too black. The most severe authors also recognise that there were good *gardes*. Like Fily Dabo Sissiko, M. Hampaté Bâ has come across *gardes* who became interpreters and were honest. The citations for the *médaille d'honneur* relate careers of numerous riflemen who were re-engaged as gardes and sometimes became interpreters. This was the case with Moussa Diakité, who was a spahi from 1890 to 1899, was discharged with the rank of sergeant, joined up again as a *garde* and was decorated in 1903; or with Mamadou Ba, who was born in 1875, was a spahi from 1895 to 1901 and became a *garde régional* in the Kaedi district. Wounded while pursuing a group of Moors who had lifted sheep belonging to Gattaga district, he could not be promoted to *brigadier* because he was illiterate, but he was decorated.[52] It would be easy to multiply these examples.

The quality of the *gardes* no doubt tended to improve as the process of expansion ended and that of training began. Nevertheless, the general impression gained of these enforcement officers, as of the interpreters, is that the extreme vulnerability of the staff, who were too few, too little fixed, too unfamiliar with local life, hindered the full exercise of colonial authority. Similar observations would be arrived at from a study of the low-ranking African staff of the other services – *laptots*, canoers or boatmen working for the Customs or the public works, labourers and mechanics on the railways, postmen, male nurses, orderlies and so on. They are not easy to reach, because the Yearbooks do not mention them and the level of staff provided for by the decrees was not always reached. Their careers can be seen in the citations for decorations. Their total number cannot have exceded that of the militia, and

---

[51] ANSOM, A.E.F., XVI 3, Reports by Sabatier, Frézouls, Lasserre.
[52] Hampaté Bâ, *L'étrange destin*, p. 118; on the interpreter Romo, see ANSOM, A.O.F., XVIII 1, decorations, 1896–1907, Paris 1 Sept. 1903, 25 July 1903.

many of them were only employed for the duration of the work with which they helped.

French penetration in black Africa was still very superficial in 1914. In fact, from this research it would seem that, in a country of seven million square kilometres – that is fourteen times the size of the motherland – with a population of around sixteen million, France made its presence felt through some 2708 white officers assisted by 230 black interpreters of various ranks and some 5989 black, armed *gardes civils*.

It should be repeated that these figures are rather uncertain; but if account is taken of officials on leave, of staff provided for by the ordinances but not appointed, and of money claimed and then not paid out, they are rather higher than the true figure.

The colonisers could also count on the support of the soldiers, who, in August 1914, numbered 14,142 black troups, with white officers, in the A.O.F. The only white troups were the colonial infantry batallion stationed in Dakar. As against this, 150,000 black troups were serving in North Africa.[53] Moreover, France had invested 1600 million *francs-or* in black Africa, of which three quarters had come from national funds destined for public works.

A consideration of these figures, on the one hand, and of the extent and relative depth of French influence in modern black Africa, on the other, shows first of all that the cultural and economic expansion was essentially accomplished after the First World War, after the period of establishment between 1870 and 1914, with which this study is concerned.

Furthermore, looking out from the African bush, it can be seen that there was no colonial system before 1914. Rather there was a kind of anarchy. On the one hand the process of decay of the indigenous social structure was speeded up, a process which was already more or less advanced depending on the length of the contact with the West, on the distance from the coast and on the progress of the lines of communication. On the other hand, the new social structures brought in by the colonisers were so frail and so inconsistant that they failed to create stable conditions and even to attract those Africans who desired to adopt them and to adapt them to their ways.

This relative anarchy, with the people solicited by two types of equally feeble – or weakened – structures appears as the alternative to the civil war which threatened the organised states and the prime example of which was given by the Ashante confederation.[54]

---

[53] Weithas *et. al.*, *op. cit.* (n. 8), pp. 25 ff.
[54] Ivor Wilks, *Asante in the Nineteenth Century: The Structure and Evolution of a Political Order* (Cambridge, U.P., 1975), pp. 549 ff.

IV. COLLABORATION AND RESISTANCE

Native reactions during the course of this period of establishing colonisation are only intelligible if a long-term view is taken. For thousands of years, black Africans had lived isolated from the world civilisation of either the east or west Mediterranean. They were isolated, not isolationist. Those tribes which have long been described by anthropologists as models of traditionalism have always given witness to a rare degree of receptiveness and of aptitude for syncretism. "Assimiler, non être assimilé," said Senghor. These two terms are not opposed to each other; rather it is a question of rhythm. One assimilates when one is not pressured. The orientation remains the same. Over the course of the centuries, Africans have assimilated elements from Islam or Christianity, as place and circumstances required; they collaborated with the merchants, the slave dealers and the marabouts of the East, as well as with the tax-collectors of the West, and the coastal peoples or the commercial tribes have often controlled or competed with the Europeans, whose language they had learned. [55]

On the other hand, the political and military history of Africa did not begin in the 19th century. The rival tribes always fought with one another, never hesitated to call in foreigners, and often suffered the domination of mighty potentates, whose empires grew weaker as they grew larger, and disintegrated after a generation or two; Ahmadu Seku, Al-Haji Umar, Samori, Gallieni.... Peoples passed from one sovereignty to another, suffering, tricking, profiting.

When the foreigner made contact with the African at the level of the tribe, he entered more or less cleverly into the political game between the tribes. When he met organised states, he acted likewise toward their rulers, who were more or less flexible and were always worried about the possible connections between this foreigner and the tribes that they had subordinated. Moreover, princes threatened by their neighbours called in foreigners – and this had gone on for centuries. Their was no fundamental difference between the diplomatic and military action of Al-Haji Umar or Samori in the Western Sudan and that of Gallieni. All three smashed *resistances* of the same order, which were rather *revolts* to conserve customary or monopolistic rights to hunting, to pasture, to trade. This has nothing to do with the "Resistance" of differing peoples united within the framework of defined frontiers, by a common national consciousness, and strongly tainted with xenophobia. Such frontiers were created, in the ignorance of the Africans, by the divisions between

---

[55] Richard Gray and David Birmingham (eds.), *Pre-colonial African Trade: Essays on Trade in Central and Eastern Africa before 1900* (London, Oxford U.P., 1970), p. 8.

Europeans. They were neither more nor less unjust than those of the pre-colonial African states, but they have lasted longer, because the administrators possessed the telegraph.

The collaboration of the Africans, without which the whites would not have been able either to conquer or to administer their colonies, had nothing in common with that of the "traitors" in the European nations. An African could only have "betrayed" his tribe, something he never did; often he collaborated to serve it. Resistance and collaboration do not designate two contrary reactions during this period of colonial expansion. Rather they describe successive dominant attitudes of the resisters, which gradually emerged between 1920 and 1940. The resisters of decolonisation are the sons of the collaborators of colonisation.

8. EUROPEAN IMPERIALISM AND INDIGENOUS REACTIONS IN BRITISH WEST AFRICA, 1880–1914

by

RONALD ROBINSON

From experience of an empire on which the sun never set the Victorians had learned long before 1880 to distinguish sharply between the extension of rule and the expansion of the nation. Tropical Africa seemed no place for either. They looked upon colonial commitments as an unmitigated burden on their domestic state which a representative constitution kept deliberately short of finance and land forces. [1] Scarcely could these be wheedled out of Parliament for such purposes in dribs and drabs in an age when twopence extra on income tax might decide the fate of ministries. On the other hand, expansion to the Victorians meant the proliferation abroad of their domestic society at private expense – colonists reproducing new Englands overseas, merchants and investors replenishing the world's bank and workshop – private enterprises from which the nation as a whole prospered. Most of the outstanding successes of their expanding economy were being won indeed, without the aid of imperial rule, in independent ex-colonial North and South America or self-governing Canada, South Africa and Australasia. [2]

As in these new European worlds the Victorians were achieving expansion without empire, so in the non-European world they had found that imperial intervention rarely achieved expansion. For all their earlier meddling in Chinese politics, Lancashire was still waiting for its four hundred million customers; for all their earlier efforts to regenerate tropical Africa with gunboat and Bible, the region remained unreconstructed and unsaved. Far from following the flag, their trade on the west coast often fled from its exactions. India was always the great exception. There, from the rotted dragons' teeth of the former Moghul regime, they had raised up a terrible empire of the sword which secured their interests around half the globe. More

---

[1] The expenditure of the British government was £81 millions in 1879–80 and rose to £100 millions in 1884–85.

[2] See Ronald Robinson and John Gallagher with Alice Denny: *Africa and the Victorians*, (London, 1961), 6.

recently, they had gone on to divert part of the indigenous economy to produce for their home industries. Yet, but a fraction of the wealth and power required for this spectacular empire was imported from the British Isles. Sepoy armies[3] largely conquered and enforced it; indigenous elites and institutions carried out its decrees; and with their indigenous land taxes, the Indian peasant paid. Through the mediation of involuntary Indian collaborators, the financial sinew, the military and administrative muscle was drawn from the sub-continent itself.

If in the new European world the late Victorians were achieving expansion without empire, in India they seemed to achieve empire almost without expansion. It was a feat which they feared after the great mutiny might prove as unsubstantial as the Indian rope trick. They never forgot that the circumstances which made it possible were unique. No such indigenous collaborators or institutions had been found among the culturally unified mandarins of China or the revolutionary, nationalist samurai of Japan. In India alone the British had discovered native organisations strong enough to deliver large armies, taxes and authorities into their hands, yet weak enough to be cajoled into doing so, rather than unite and resist the invaders. Nevertheless the risks involved kept statesmen in London awake in their beds, resolving not to chance such luck elsewhere.

By 1880, therefore, the Victorians had left the simplicities of empire building for empire's sake far behind them. Certain Treasury tests had been established to decide whether a territory was worth ruling for purposes of expansion or not. Firstly, if it was both necessary and profitable to do so, the country should be able to pay for its own acquisition and government out of its own local revenue. Secondly, once acquired, its administration ought not to extend or intensify any further or faster than local revenue could be raised to meet the extra expenditure. Thirdly, the burden on the British taxpayer must be diminished, not increased. These fiscal principles were the acid test of the necessity of empire. They defined the direction and form of Victorian colonialism. In effect, the rules of the Treasury ensured that the empire of Downing Street behaved as the occasional hired servant of expansion, not the master. They insisted that the imperial pro-consuls must live off the country, arming and feeding themselves on local profits of British enterprise or native sources of wealth and power. A country where this was impossible was by definition a liability to the expanding economy and world power of the British Isles. Colonial rule, if it was to replenish and not to drain the greatness of

---

[3] In the Indian armies of the 'eighties there were 130,000 Indian troops, 350,000 of princely states, and 66,000 British soldiers, (R. Temple: *India in 1880*, (3rd ed. 1881), 392; Sir C. Dilke: *Problems of Greater Britain*, (London, 1890), 2, 66).

Britain must draw its strength, not from the metropolis but from the peripheries.

The Victorians knew therefore what Eurocentric theorists of imperialism later forgot: colonialism is not simply a function of the expansion of Europe. To serve that end effectively it must be converted into a major function of indigenous structures and resources. In the new European world where the inputs of men and money from Britain were comparatively heavy, the conversion into local resources had been so successful that imperial rule contracted into independence or colonial self-government. But in non-European countries where the inputs of expansion were tiny and the indigenous framework uncongenial, the possibilities of imperialism depended on the vulnerability of indigenous organisation. According to their calculus of empire on the cheap the Victorians summed up the possibilities of ruling these countries in three ways. Firstly, would a small, initial investment of force win sufficient native allies to suppress opposition to their flag cheaply? When the cost of prolonged subjugation with British forces was politically prohibitive, the degree of resistance met was critical. Secondly, were there enough effective as well as cooperative native authorities at hand to be manipulated into a *pax Britannica* economically? Thirdly, if so, would it lead to a significant expansion of trade? The possibilities of imperial dominion were calculated in terms of indigenous collaboration and resistance.

Leaders of communities in the polymorphic societies of Africa and Asia worked out the same equations in reverse, when they strove to rescue what they could of independence from British invasion. Was it wiser to fight or come to terms? The high velocity guns of the white man were not easy to beat, but trading and borrowing from him was profitable; to learn his knowledge and technology was power. If he could not be excluded, he could be persuaded to collaborate with indigenous leaders in securing their particular communal interests. The prestige of the British imported into indigenous politics an alien source of wealth and power which attracted allies from every internal division and rivalry like a magnet. But for indigenous elites no less than for the British, the balance of advantage between fighting or cooperating depended on the terms of the bargains on offer. If British demands damaged too many native interests, non-European leaders had no choice but to repel them. Otherwise they would lose control of their own followers. On the other hand, if resistance spread the British would defeat their own object. The more exacting their demands, the more their allies' authority to impose the forced contracts on their indignant people dwindled. Where each side needed the help of the other so badly, they both inclined to accomodate rather than confront each other's interests.

The terms of these so-called bargains made up the systems of local cooperation through which in tropical Africa as in India, Victorian imperialism worked. At the outset they provided the means of informal, commercial penetration. Only when an informal system broke down did the British usually turn to the question of colonial rule, and then as a means of reconstructing the system. Thereafter the type of collaborative system attainable largely determined the form and depth of colonial administration. At every stage the type and degree of imperial intervention was tailored to fit local disunities and local resources, to head off resistance and win compliance. Indigenous reaction governed British imperialism just as much as British imperialism provoked indigenous reaction. Each was an integral working part of the other. The inter-action of the two in west Africa may therefore be defined in a study of the equations of collaboration as they were calculated in the official mind of imperialism and as they changed from the pre-colonial into the colonial era.[4]

There were three critical shifts in the terms for Anglo-African association in this region. The first of them took place in the first half of the nineteenth century during the Victorian crusade against the slave trade along the west coasts. The second shift occurred toward the end of the European scramble for the region. From 1894 to 1905 the terms for colonial intervention in the interior were beaten out. The third alteration, which lies outside the scope of this essay, took place between 1947 and 1956 when the new bargains with the nationalists that led to decolonisation were struck. Each crisis saw old understandings disrupted by intensified conflict between erstwhile associates. Each was followed by renewed cooperation under revised contracts. At the peak of the first two crises a revolution in the terms for partnership seemed imminent. But such was the strength of indigenous reaction that the terms which eventually proved acceptable to west Africans and therefore practicable for the British swung back towards the *status quo ante*. In spite of the apparent one-sidedness and discontinuity introduced by colonial rule, the collaborative equations on which the new regime rested proved not so very different from those embodied in the pre-colonial trading arrangements on the coast.

---

[4] For a further explanation of this approach, see Ronald Robinson: "Non-European Foundations of European Imperialism" in R. Owen and B. Sutcliffe, (eds.): *Studies in the Theory of Imperialism*, (London, 1971); W.R. Lovis, Imperialism: the Robinson and Gallagher Controversy, (New York, 1976).

PRE-COLONIAL COLLABORATION ON THE WEST COAST[5]

The original understandings for Afro-British cooperation, reached in the long age of the Atlantic slave trade were defined fairly equally in the partnership of horror. Africans monopolised production and supply on land; the English supplied the capital and bartered in gin and muskets at the water's edge. From 1807 the British attempted to sell less equal but more humane contracts to their African partners. No longer slaves but vegetable oil was wanted and the white man offered the blessings of peace and free trade if the black would give up his slave raiding and his monopolies of supply. By the eighteen sixties the navy's stormy vigilance had helped drive the slave ships from the sea, but colonial intervention and moral suasion on land had failed to elicit African agreement. As the Victorians refused to exert the necessary force on such an unpromising region, the revised terms could rarely be imposed; but indigenous authorities of their own free will would not agree to them. Few of them were to be found desperate enough to cut their own throats for the glory of God and the profit of Liverpool.

Among the myriad ethnic groups and authorities in the area, the British found allies in plenty for other purposes. The difficulty however was this: after four centuries of dealing with the white man, African leaders on the coast were apt to manipulate him for their own ends, rather than be manipulated for his. On the Gold Coast, for example, after 1821 governors of the colonial forts found ready clients in the petty, middlemen chiefs of the Denkyras, Wassaws, Akims, Assims, Fantes and Accras. As they needed British help against the invasions of the dominant, highly-centralised Ashanti empire, they submitted trade disputes to British arbitration. But the little colony paid more for this grudging alliance than it was worth. The Fanti refused to unite or pay tax for the common defence, while the brunt of Ashanti drives to sweep them aside and trade directly with the ports, fell upon the colony. A series of Ashanti wars checked its trade and piled up its debt. Exasperated, the British annexed their allies' territory in 1874. This did nothing to bring them to heel, but the Victorians felt morally obliged as administrators to free their new subjects' domestic slaves who supplied the labour for carriage and tillage. This only imported British ethics to the detriment of British trade. Nor was that the end of the misfortunes of colonial intervention. In 1874 an expensive expedition came from England to chasten the Ashanti into peaceable cooperation and then to withdraw, leaving their

---

[5] For an extended account see Robinson and Gallagher, *op. cit.*, 27–52.

political organisation intact. This rare exercise of the mailed fist also defeated its own object. As a result of the blow the Asantehene's control of his own people bordering the colony fell to pieces, so that anarchy spread into the colony. For the next quarter of a century the attempt to construct a collaborative system in the Gold Coast hinterland lapsed into frustrated quiescence.

African institutions proved no more amenable north of the colonial base at Lagos, which had been established in the mid-century to woo the Yoruba-speaking peoples west of the Niger River into an orderly zone for free trade. These peoples had once been united in the empire of Oyo. By the time the Victorians came in search of palm oil the trade paths ran through a number of successor states – Ibadan, Ijaye, Ijebu-Ode, Oyo and Abeokuta – fighting each other for hegemony or survival. Abeokuta in the 'forties and 'fifties seemed a ready-made spearhead for British influence over the interior. The hundred and fifty thousand inhabitants of its walled capital stemmed from refugees of different ethnic groups, and answered to numberless different ritual, military and merchant chiefs under an Alake. Like the Fante they needed help against the invasion of more powerful neighbours. In exchange for canon-layers from Lagos to defend them from Dahomey, they opened their gates to missionaries, Sierra Leoneans and other agents of British firms. They even began growing cotton for Lancashire. To the Victorians this seemed the very hallmark of enlightenment. Yet the promised day of Christianity and free trade never broke over Yorubaland from Abeokuta. After 1862 the strain of unequal bargains on the quasi-democratic politics of the Egba became intolerable. The missions were driven away and the gates closed to save the entrepreneurial profits of their own chiefs from the grasp of British firms. Disappointed, the governors of the colony mounted yet another abortive effort to break through the Yoruba middlemen states to the palm-oil producers up-country, with Abeokuta and Ijebu-Ode as their enemies and Ibadan and Ijebu-Remo for their friends. For thirty years to come, the civil wars between the Yoruba states interrupted the trade and baffled the influence of Lagos.

These and many other endeavours to sell the revised contracts through colonial intervention inland ended in fiasco, as the colonial balance sheets showed. "In Lagos," officials in London complained, "we have assumed a government without a revenue... there is not yet one self-supporting colony in West Africa."[6] Lagos, Gold Coast, Gambia and Sierra Leone altogether contributed a mere half-million pounds worth of export annually to British

---

[6] Elliott, Minute, 30 Nov. 1861, on F.O. to C.O., 28 Nov. 1861, C.O. 147/2.

trade in the 'sixties and 'seventies.[7] Liverpool traders were striking much better bargains with Africans privately on the Congo and lower Niger, with no more imperial help than an occasional visit from a consul on a gunboat. The Congo trade equalled in value that of the colonies combined. The Niger trade fell little short of it. Stage by stage these regions had been linked to the British economy without the expense of linking them with the British crown.

The delta and hinterlands east of the lower Niger offered traders two advantages which the regions west of it denied them: a navigable river for sea-power to invade the land; and palm forests undefended by highly-organised territorial states. Up-river the Ibo and Ibibio-speaking peoples lived in segmented villages and clans without centralised authority, though in part of the area the Aro priests controlled ritual, disputes and long distance trade. A congeries of city states however guarded the entrances to the river. Being essentially associations of African merchant "Houses," each with a hierarchy of domestic slaves, the Calabars, Bonny, Duke Town and the rest pursued trade monopoly rather than territorial dominion. On the lower Niger black and white traders could do business with each other free of imbroglios in the territorial rivalry of great states. So long as the Liverpool traders drew palm oil from the river through the indigenous monopolists, the commercial partnership remained comparatively harmonious. But when in the 'sixties and 'seventies a few of the more adventurous firms broke through the African ring to trade up-river, commercial competition jerked the miniscule politics of the area into uproar. Some Afro-British partnerships embargoed and assaulted others, and from the mid-seventies dropping palm oil prices on European markets spiked the turmoil with quarrels over the share-out of dwindling profits and rising losses. If to the west of the Niger the Victorian search for African collaborators was frustrated in the politics of the powerful forest states, to the east it was baffled in the end by the economics of trade depression.

After sixty years of questing, the Victorians by 1880 had abolished slave exports and rigged up a trade in palm oil. They had found a few African commercial partners but no effective political allies on their terms. Though the African economy had responded a little to the lure of profit, the African polities rejected Christianity and free trade. As a result their monopoly of production and supply remained invincible, while the anarchic free play of their politics strangled economic growth. A thousand miles of riverine and oceanic coasts yielded in tiny parcels a mere million pounds of export annually. Wherever the British had tried to break through native monopolies,

---

[7] See Table, Robinson and Gallagher, *op. cit.*, 32, f.n. 2.

Africans had cut off commerce with the coast. Colonial intervention as a result disrupted indigenous authorities without curing disorder or improving trade. The hinterlands stayed virtually shut to European merchants. Wherever the British had found a free trading ally, neighbouring states cancelled the contract in effect. Those African rulers who could be induced to cooperate proved ineffective; those who might have been effective refused to cooperate. Yet when force was applied to bend them into compliance, their authority seemed to turn fragile and snapped in pieces. It was too diffuse in some areas, too fragmented or resistant in others to be conscripted for purposes of informal sway. Indigenous revenue seemed as inaccessible as indigenous authority. Africans paid tribute to their rulers, either in the way of social obligation, which could hardly be transferred to aliens, or through monopolistic charges on trade, which the British were intent on sweeping away. On all these counts the rulers of India, used to seizing great provinces by the head, knew that nothing of the kind was possible in tropical Africa. They concluded that African institutions were too numerous, petty and divided to serve as levers of informal suasion and too poor to be worth conquering. Further intervention seemed to them so hopeless that it was reined back. The balance point of terms for Anglo-African cooperation had hardly moved from where it had been in the era of the slave traffic. The late-Victorians who had achieved expansion without empire in North America, empire without expansion in India, were sure that neither expansion nor empire could be achieved in tropical Africa.

PARTITION AND PACIFICATION[8]

During the last twenty years of the century, with the imperial flag to tropical Africa they went nevertheless. Confronted with the French and the Germans scrambling for territory, they were compelled to stake their claims also. By 1891, after a flurry of treaty-making and cartography in the chanceries of Paris, Berlin and London, the diplomats had divided the entire region between the empires of Europe; but they had left some highly controversial details to be settled in a race of expeditions to claim actual occupation in the 'nineties. It was the advances of the French that drove the British at last to invest a modicum of force in west Africa and elsewhere.

At first the outburst of African enthusiasm in Paris and Berlin astonished the old imperial hands in London. Salisbury, who usually knew what was

---

[8] For an extended account of the partition, see *ibid.*, 163–89, 379–409.

afoot, confessed that he did not understand what was being scrambled for. Granville and Derby regarded it at times as a nightmare, at others, a farce. Gladstone roundly put it down to insanity. All of them deplored the prospect in tropical Africa of yet another empire. Kimberley explained why: "[the climate] is pestilential, the natives numerous and unmanageable. The result... would be wars with the natives, heavy demands on the British taxpayer."[9]

The Economist in 1890 scorned the scramble as "a quarrel of tenth rate magnitude over interests of scarcely any national importance." The trade and finance of most of the region was "infinitessimal"; "the lands of tropical Africa are not usually suitable for a European population and the present inhabitants" would take decades of rough-hewing to civilise.[10] All but the lunatic fringe of British business and politics agreed with this verdict. There was therefore no expensive drive in Britain to build a tropical African empire. *Midas* in the City of London would not invest in one; *Demos* in Parliament would not pay for one, and the means could not be extracted from the poverty of Africa itself.

No actual resources or serious intentions of empire-building inspired the claims and expeditions which the late Victorians sent forward. Their object was profoundly negative. But if it was not practical politics for them to take on more starveling African colonies, neither was it practical politics to let foreign Powers annex the fields of their strategic and commercial interests, however small they might be. They staked out their options on territory merely to exclude rival Powers and they strove to establish them by international agreement in order to avoid colonial responsibility. Up to 1894 their diplomacy largely succeeded in getting international recognition for their claims, except from the French. In this way an extensive area of east and north-east Africa was marked out to exclude the Continental Powers from the Nile, secure Egypt and protect the Suez route to India. In west Africa the lower Niger and the colonial hinterlands were staked off to save them from French and German tariffs. After the diplomacy Whitehall arranged for chartered companies to carry the flag at their private risk. Goldie's Niger Company was advanced to grasp the Muslim emirates to the north of the lower Niger; Rhodes' South Africa Company was set to colonise what was to become the Rhodesias, while Mackinnon's frail East Africa Company was supposed to drive for Buganda. But by the 'nineties two of the three crowned companies could no longer cope. When the East Africa Company went bankrupt, the Victorians characteristically called upon Egyptian and Indian

---

[9] Minute, 6 April 1882, C.O. 806/203, Appendix I, 7.
[10] *The Economist*, 30 Aug. 1890, 1109.

armies and finance to repel the French expeditions from the Nile. By 1895 in west Africa the Niger Company was no longer enough to repulse French military incursions. Some reinforcement from the imperial government in London became inevitable and so at last British expeditions became possible locally. Two years later Chamberlain, the colonial minister broke all the Treasury's shibboleths and organised a west African frontier force of three thousand African troops at an annual cost of over a hundred thousand pounds. It was little enough. But from 1895 the empire began to make the military effort to get the better of the French which they had refused hitherto to get the better of the Africans. When in 1898, French pretensions on the Nile were blown up with the mirages at Fashoda, their challenge to British claims in west Africa went up with them. Ironically the British force which had been raised to stave it off, could now be diverted to put down indigenous resistance to colonial intervention. Incidentally the climax of the scramble threw the pre-colonial system into a crisis which threatened to tip the scales of cooperation heavily against the Africans in favour of the British.

Chamberlain and his officials on the spot seized their opportunity energetically. Ashanti in 1896 and again in 1900 was occupied and its central organisation decapitated. After 1892 treaties of peace and free trade were imposed on the anarchic Yoruba states and by 1903 Lugard with the frontier force at his back had coerced or cajoled the Fulani emirates into cooperation. A sharp defeat of one or two of these organised states served to cow the rest. Yet even after the Benin and Aro punitive expeditions it took years of small forays to bring the headless peoples of south-eastern Nigeria to heel. More than the sum of many small victories however, the baring of the imperial fangs won a reputation of invincibility, and left behind the lion's skin of prestige for a precarious colonial authority after the troops had marched away to their far-off barracks.

Though the forces employed might seem formidable to Africans, they appeared derisory to the British compared with the vast areas of their commitment. Their coercive arm was sufficient to over-awe but not to conquer Africa's rulers comprehensively. Prolonged military occupation of the new protectorates was beyond British colonial power. If widespread African resistance were to be provoked their policing capacity would easily be over-run. Calls for reinforcement from London were regarded as evidence of reprehensible blunders on the part of colonial officials. Their power, so constrained, was enough to manipulate but not to suppress indigenous authorities. If they were now able to force less equal bargains on African rulers, they could not keep the peace without them, nor could they afford the risks of alienating them. As MacGregor, Governor in Lagos put it in 1904.

with their cooperation "punitive expeditions and plots against the government are unknown." "A great chief is a very valuable possession; his authority is an instrument of the greatest public utility, which it is most desirable to retain in full force."[11] To avoid resistance and win acquiescence from chiefs, the terms on offer might be revised but they still had to be very reasonable. They were obliged to stop making war on each other and accept colonial control over their inter-relations, often in return for a small subsidy; they were forced to dismantle their commercial tolls and monopolies and keep the peace within their jurisdiction. In return the British could do no less and no more than leave their control of domestic affairs substantially intact.

What the new protectorates over Nigeria, Gold Coast and Sierra Leone actually represented by 1900 as a result was much less than the areas newly coloured red on the map made it appear. A thin veil of paramountcy had been thrown along the main trade routes into the interior across interstices between one African authority and the next. A few British officials looked after the key towns; the chiefs were left in charge of the countryside. That was all the chiefs meant the colonial governments to do. That was all the Treasury and most politicians in London intended to be done. They had advanced the imperial frontiers, not to govern and colonise the territory, but merely to exclude the French and bring the hinterland into the pre-colonial trading system of the coast. To do more would mean more African resistance, more expenditure and less dividends from trade. There were no stauncher upholders of this traditional policy than the Liverpool merchants themselves. London and Liverpool were at one with the west African rulers in insisting on the revised bargains being kept.

Chamberlain at the Colonial Office from 1895 however dreamed of developing new tropical estates as a business of the imperial government. For many of his officials in west Africa also it was not enough to preside tentatively over a set of corrupt, reactionary native authorities and let the economy stagnate. They aspired to establish close administration in detail over the area on the Indian model. Without the direct intervention of British officials, they argued, the African peasant could not be taxed; without local revenue the British Exchequer would not be relieved, nor could the numbers of white officials required for direct rule be paid. There was no alternative financial solution. The Liverpool lobby was too influential at Westminster for significant increases in import-export duties to be tolerated. In the eyes of this "Indian" school of thought, the chiefs seemed as useless for economic purposes as they appeared to be for tax gathering. They were unable to

[11] Quoted in J.E. Flint: "Nigeria, the Colonial Experience" in L.H. Gann and P. Duignan, (eds): *Colonialism in Africa 1876–1960*, (Cambridge, 1969), I, 246.

conserve the palm and rubber forests which their subjects were over-exploiting to the ruin of the export staples; their control of native lands was supposed to check African economic individualism and thus the cultivation of new staples of cotton, cocoa, coffee and cultivated palms. If the colonial economy was to be developed, British officials must take control over the disposal and use of African land out of the chiefs' hands. The "Indian" school also contended that the long maturing commercialisation of coast society had sapped chiefly authority, so that they were broken reeds also for keeping law and order. If it was to survive, colonial officials should not merely "recognise" chiefs, but choose and direct them in managing their domestic affairs. On assumptions such as these, the first British plan was for scrapping their understandings with west Africa's native rulers and for seizing the colonial opportunity to make another India.

THE FORMATIVE CONFLICT: 1895–1900

The conflict between the new designers and the traditionalists[12] reached its climax at the end of the 'nineties. It was to decide how much colonial government, how much indigenous autonomy there was to be in British west Africa up to 1939. Not a few Christian and semi-Anglicised Africans supported the views of the "Indian" school, while the resistance of indigenous authorities demonstrated the case for the traditionalists and white traders. Out of the conflict between the two sides over the formative legislation, the ineluctable terms for Anglo-African collaboration under colonial rule emerged.

Three portentous issues were settled between 1895 and 1905. Firstly, was the colonial regime able to tax Africans directly? If not, its authority was bound to remain something of a paper tiger. Secondly, could it seize the power to dispose of African land and control land use? If not, Africans would

---

[12] C.S. Salmon stated the crux of traditional doctrine in 1885: The chiefs "need only to be taken in hand ... to answer all those purposes for which British influence would be valuable in West Africa." (C.O. African West 326, Salmon to C.O., 23 March 1885, 4). See also his *Crown Colonies of Great Britain*, (London, 1887), where he advocates self-governing councils of chiefs and British traders to establish order in tropical Africa along trade routes at one-tenth of what colonial officials would cost to do it, (91–2, 101). See also Goldie: "... if dangerous revolts are to be obviated, the general policy of ruling through native rulers on African principles must be followed," (Introduction to Vanderleur, Appendix to D. Wellesley: *Sir George Goldie*, 176). From a similar point of view, Mary Kingsley wrote " ... the sooner the Crown Colony system is ... put under a glass case in the South Kensington Museum, labelled 'Extinct,' the better for everyone," (*West African Studies*, 256). See also E.D. Morel: *Affairs of West Africa*, (London, 1902), *passim*.

keep their previous monopoly of production and supply, and colonial government might not be able to introduce new agricultural staples. Thirdly, were the colonies to be governed indirectly through alliance with the chiefs, or directly in alliance with the educated and commercial African bourgeoisie?

It was African resistance in Sierra Leone and Gold Coast that destroyed the credibility of the "Indian" design. In 1896 Cardew, the administrator in Freetown, sent a few British travelling commissioners and police into the Sierra Leone Protectorate to collect hut tax and free the chiefs' domestic slaves. The Hut Tax war with the Mende and Temne chiefs which ensued from this provocation, incensed the Liverpool traders. They demanded Cardew's dismissal and agitated for a committee of their number to be consulted by the Colonial Office on policy in the future.[13] Chalmers, the Gold Coast Judge, who was called in to investigate the rising, recommended a return to pre-colonial methods. In his view, the tax ought to be withdrawn. British officials should never have taken it upon themselves to interfere with the chiefs' internal affairs and should restrict themselves in future to giving advice. If domestic slavery were abolished, he warned, production and carriage for export would cease.[14] Cardew's plan "had sunk the country into an abyss of debt to carry out a mistaken policy."[15]

The hut tax rebellion of 1897–1898 not only exposed the sketchy nature of colonial authority, it reminded the British that their overlordship hung upon African acquiescence, that acquiescence depended on keeping their end of the bargain and keeping out of the chiefs domestic affairs.[16] The Colonial Office what was more, had learned that West Africans would fight rather than pay tax to the colonial government. So sharp was the lesson of combined African and mercantile resistance that at once Chamberlain vetoed all the schemes for direct tax proposed for the Gold Coast and southern Nigeria though he upheld the hut tax in Sierra Leone where the damage was already done. In 1898 the chiefs of the Gold Coast were rejecting Maxwell's bill for a direct tax.[17] They claimed that as they had never been conquered, their authority

---

[13] "... The revenue collecting passion of the bureaucrats has ruined a trade which took many years of mercantile effort to build," (*ibid.*, 82). See also Manchester Chamber of Commerce to C.O., 7 July 1897, (C.O. African West 533, 139) and 2 May 1898 (C.O. African West 570, 71); also Liverpool Chamber of Commerce to C.O., 9 May 1898, (*ibid.*, 81).

[14] Chalmers insited that the bargains made with the Protectorate Chiefs in the original treaties be kept. These acknowledged "... the character of the Chiefs as the owners and sovereigns of the territory and as independent contracting Powers, unequivocally and universally recognised," (*Report on the Insurrection in the Sierra Leone Protectorate*, P.P., C. 9388, 1899, 9).

[15] Chalmers to C.O., 5 Dec. 1898, C.O. 96/300.

[16] Chamberlain to Cardew, 24 June 1898, C.O. 879/55, 146; and 7 July 1899, P.P. C. 9388, (1899), 166.

[17] Hodgson to Chamberlain, 18 April 1898, C.O. 96/314.

over their own people was independent of the colonial regime. Colonial taxes were therefore illegal because, they contended, they had never conceded such a power to their overlords. Maxwell was breaking the terms of their original agreement. More telling than constitutional antiquarianism, the colonial secretary reported that the tax would have to be collected at the point of the bayonet, even in conquered Ashanti.[18] In the Gold Coast as in Sierra Leone Africans had demonstrated that the money brought in would be much less than the money poured out in extracting direct taxes. The bill was killed along with plans to levy rates on Accra and Sekondi.[19] It was to be several decades before direct taxation was attempted in west Africa again. From now on the Colonial Office rigorously applied the rule of "no colonial taxation without guaranteed African acquiescence." That in effect ruled out the possibility of colonial land revenue. The possibility of an army of British and educated African officials administering their territories directly, was ruled out with it.

At the same time Africa's old rulers were keeping the British to their bargains and repelling colonial attempts to seize control of indigenous economy. Once again the Gold Coast chiefs were in the van. Ever since 1889 their governors had tried to pass laws "to achieve the administration of the public domain for the public benefit... by efficient state machinery."[20] All African land in the earlier versions was to be vested in the British crown. The Colonial Office however warned the governor that such a "social revolution" could not be considered unless native consent could be guaranteed.[21] As the chiefs made sure that it could not, that endeavour was dropped. Maxwell nevertheless resolved that their land should bear its share of taxation. As the chiefs were signing the rights of their people away in concessions to Europeans, the colonial government must take powers to control the disposal of tribal land. The governor also proposed to convert the chaotically commercialised tribal tenures of land in the colony into secure, individual English freehold titles. In this way the enterprising cash crop peasant would be freed from chiefly constraint, and a free market in land created. Several bills were proposed to achieve these objects from 1894 to 1898. All waste land, forest and minerals would have been vested in the crown; the chiefs were to be forbidden to sell concessions without government sanction; tribal land was to be convertible into freehold on demand.[22] Such laws, if passed, would have

[18] Hodgson to Chamberlain, 25 Nov. and 20 and 30 Dec. 1899, C.O. 96/346.
[19] Minutes of Chamberlain and Selborne on Hodgson to C.O. 17 May 1898, C.O. 96/314. C.O. to Treasury, 24 Jan. 1899, C.O. 96/585.
[20] Maxwell to Chamberlain, 11 March 1897, C.O. Africa (West) 531, 59.
[21] Griffith to Knutsford, 25 June 1889, Minutes by Hemmings, 11 Nov. 1889 and Mead, 25 Nov. 1889; and Knutsford to Griffith, 4 Dec. 1889, C.O. 96/202.
[22] Maxwell to Chamberlain, 11 March 1897, C.O. Africa (West) 531, 180.

taken the entire commercial sector of indigenous agriculture out of the chiefs' hands, breaking their remaining authority beyond repair.

In the Gold Coast as in Sierra Leone the chiefs' threats of rebellion combined with the agitation of Liverpool merchants and moralists in Britain to kill the proposals.[23] A deputation of African chiefs and lawyers from the Gold Coast Aborigines Protection Society bearded Chamberlain in Downing Street. All the land in their country, they claimed, was owned by one people or another. There was no waste land for the crown to control. Chamberlain was forced to concede their every point. With the Sierra Leone war on his hands and a South African war in prospect, he dared not risk rebellion in the Gold Coast. He promised that indigenous customary rights and tribal ownership of land would be respected henceforward.[24] Colonial land reform was no more. The powerful minister asked the deputation almost pathetically how they would agree to contribute to the colony's revenue. Rejecting every form of direct tax outright, the chiefs agreed to consider supplying communal labour for public works.[25] That was the end of colonial pretensions to direct the indigenous economy through control and reform of tribal lands. Governments had to content themselves with narrowly drawn concessions, ordinances on the model of that passed for the Gold Coast in 1900.

From the vicissitudes of 1898 the Colonial Office drew a lesson which was never to be forgotten in dealing with proposals by colonial officials for more interference with indigenous authorities. As Chamberlain put it, "*Festina lente* is a just motto in the development of colonies in the possession of barbarous tribes."[26] Rather than risk any more African rebellions the empire resolved to let sleeping dogs lie. No more "Indian" style reforms were to be risked. Ownership of land in the colonies was left in possession of the different ethnic groups and indigenous authorities. To avoid provoking African uprisings, the white planter was to be excluded, as Thomas Lever found when he applied for concessions of palm forest in the nineteen hundreds and nineteen twenties. The only way left of introducing new staples and so of increasing export and local revenue was through the chiefs' influence on the peasantry. By 1900 the policy of native peasant production organised by tribal land authorities had become a political imperative. African resistance

---

[23] Liverpool Chamber of Commerce to C.O., 6 May 1897; Manchester C. of C. to C.O., 7 May 1897; London C. of C. to C.O., 7 May 1897; *ibid.*, 65–77. See also Aborigines Protection Society to C.O., 21 June 1897, *ibid.*, 123–4; Maxwell to Chamberlain, 1 July 1897, *ibid.*, 135–6.

[24] Report of Proceedings of Deputation of Kings and Chiefs of Gold Coast Western Province," 5 Aug. 1898, C.O. Africa (West) 1048, 282–7.

[25] Solicitors for Gold Coast Deputation to Chamberlain, 23 Aug. 1898, C.O. 96/332/23 and Chamberlain Minute, 19 Feb. 1899, C.O. 96/350/14.

[26] Chamberlain Minute, 18 Jan. 1899, C.O. 147/141/1.

had ensured, as the chief agricultural adviser in London put it, that West Africa would never be properly colonised by British capital.[27]

At the same time as these land and tax issues were being decided, colonial officials were trying to equip themselves with administrative powers over African authorities. The outcome was to determine how far the chiefs would be reduced to the status of mere executive agents of colonial government, how far they could retain their inherent rights and powers. All these colonial attempts but one also ended in defeat. In 1896 for example the ill-fated Maxwell proposed a native jurisdiction ordinance intended to quash the Gold Coast chiefs' claims to inherent sovereignty once and for all. They were to be appointed, suspended and dismissed by the governor and bound legally to carry out the administrations' orders.[28] That bill was lost in the same torrent of African vituperation and mercantile objection that destroyed his other proposals.[29] For the next fifty years fear of insurrection deprived the Gold Coast government of the controls over the chiefdoms that Maxwell had failed to establish in 1896.

As a result administration in the colony was frustrated in a confusion of destoolments, faction-fighting and non-cooperation that arose from the continuing freeplay of local politics. It ought to have been easy to seize control of a territory in which commercial influences had eroded the chiefs' authority into molehills; yet it was here that the chiefs in alliance with the prosperous African bourgeoisie and cash crop peasantry succeeded best in turning the molehills into mountains insuperable to white official interference.[30] The Chiefs Ordinance of 1904 empowered the governor merely to confirm the chief who had been elected by his own people, but only if he applied for confirmation! Similarly the Native Jurisdiction Ordinance of 1911 legalised the chiefs' courts without giving colonial officials powers to supervise or direct them.[31] In 1900 the Colonial Office vetoed plans to in-

[27] The Director of Kew Gardens excluded the possibility of British planting enterprise and insisted that prosperity and revenue depended upon the encouragement of native peasant production and a transition from "destructive exploitation of natural products" to "cultural industries," (Dyer to C.O., 21 Feb. 1900, C.O. Africa (West) 635, 180–2).

[28] Rodgers to Lyttelton, 28 Nov. 1904, C.O. 96/420.

[29] *Ibid.*, para. 37.

[30] Rodgers, Govr. of Gold Coast, reported in 1904: "It would ... be impolitic to interfere with election [of chiefs] by the people even if the nominee were not *persona grata* to the Government" (Rodgers to Lyttelton, 18 Oct. 1904, enclosure 13, Memo on Native Jurisdiction, C.O. 96/420).

[31] From 1902 to 1909 the Colonial Secretary, Chief Justice and Secretary for Native Affairs advocated abolishing the Chiefs' Courts and customary law in favour of British law and courts. They argued: "If it is sound policy to educate ... the natives on European lines, then it cannot be sound policy to govern through the Native Chiefs" (Bryan, Memo enclosed in Rodgers to C.O., 19 Oct. 1909, C.O. 96/486/4). The Governors and the C.O. insisted on the principle of native jurisdiction partly from lack of British officials. There were only five District Officers to a

troduce direct administration and crown lands into Ashanti, even though British companies were beginning to mine gold there. Instead "the agency of the native chiefs" was to be used.[32] In the Northern Territory of the protectorate London insisted that it was "impolitic as well as impractical to establish close administration" through British officials.[33]

In Yorubaland meanwhile, once Carter had cowed the states into peace with each other by treaties of protectorate in 1894–1896, colonial intervention with native governments was also halted to avoid African resistance. In 1898 a railway was begun to link Lagos with the Muslim north. Naturally local British officials wanted to take a grip on the internal management of the states through which the projected line would run, particularly Abeokuta. Chamberlain agreed in 1899 to post a British resident there, provided that no risk of Egba resistance was involved. But there was to be no colonial take-over in Abeokuta or any other Yoruba state. *Festina lente* prevailed in the British to such an extent that the necessary jurisdiction over the railway belt was obtained through diplomatic agreements with Abeokuta and the other states involved.[34] They retained their treaties and autonomy inviolate, subject to colonial control of their external relations up to 1914.[35]

Intervention by colonial officials in the indigenous management of South-eastern Nigeria was even more circumspect. British foreign jurisdiction in this area had originated in numberless agreements with petty African leaders to settle trade disputes. From 1891 the handful of vice-consuls under the Foreign Office had been organised into six districts. Even after punitive expeditions had overcome the guerillas of these petty city states and segmented peoples between 1895 and 1902 and imposed orderly free trade on the African monopolists of the region, the tone and purpose of colonial intervention remained diplomatic and commercial rather than administrative. In contrast to their ambition elsewhere, the last thing that local colonial officials wanted here was to establish formal colonial administration. If they did so, they

population of half a million in Ashanti, (Chief Commissioner to Govr., 4 Jan. 1906, enclosed in Rodgers to C.O., 19 April 1906, C.O. 96/441/2). Two Districts of the Colony were without a District Officer; two other Districts were being run by Medical Officers, while a Transport Officer was in charge of the Eastern Province, (Rodgers to C.O., 30 April 1909, C.O. 96/483/3).

[32] Chamberlain to Hodgson, 19 Feb. 1900, C.O. African (West) 623, 17.

[33] *Ibid.*

[34] In 1898 Chamberlain vetoed McCullum's proposal to take Abeokuta under Protectorate on the ground that it was vital to avoid all conflict with the natives, (Chamberlain to McCullum, 30 March 1898, C.O. 147/141/3). Also C.O. to McCullum, 19 Jan. 1899, *ibid.*).

[35] "The Western Province of Southern Nigeria ... is a congeries of native states under indigenous rulers possessing widely varying powers. Each state has ... relations with the British Crown peculiar to itself." The nature and extent of British jurisdiction is very obscure, (J. Anderson, Minute, 10 July 1911 on Egerton to Harcourt, 29 April 1911, C.O. 520/102/2).

would be obliged to abolish domestic slavery on which indigenous authority and the export economy depended. There could be no question of crown land or direct tax in an area without colonial executive agents, and executive responsibility was to be avoided from moral cowardice, for commercial convenience. In 1900 Chamberlain, spurred on by ethical criticism in Britain and confident in the Frontier Force, ordered his officials to abolish slavery, whether native risings were provoked or not. But Liverpool merchants and local officials agitated so strongly that the order was soon countermanded. Such a policy, they alleged, would destroy the social fabric of three-quarters of Southern Nigeria along with its export trade.[36] "If the tribal system is allowed to fall into decay," Acting High Commissioner Probyn pointed out, "it will be necessary to increase to an extent beyond the resources of the Protectorate, the staff necessary for work which is now done under the tribal system."[37] To avoid the disruption of colonial administration a House Rule Ordinance of 1902 legalised the authority of African "Heads of Houses" over their slaves for the next thirteen years. In 1911 a Colonial Office official summed up the results of House Rule in South-Eastern Nigeria and treaties in South-Western Nigeria: "All the energies of the central staff in Southern Nigeria are constantly engaged in "development" ... no attempt seems to be made to guide native policy on proper and uniform lines."[38] There could be no more candid admission that the coming of colonialism had left administration in the hands of indigenous authorities. In this area the officials had deliberately chosen, as in Sierra Leone and the Gold Coast they had been compelled, to achieve free trade and order at the expense of conceding control of domestic affairs to native authorities. They had come indeed to do all that they could to consolidate the chiefs' powers. To win African consent and avoid African discontent had been their over-riding concern.

Of all the British pro-consuls in West Africa, Lugard in Northern Nigeria had the best chance of riveting colonial control on Africa's old rulers. From 1898 to 1903 he had defeated or over-awed the quasi-feudal Fulani regimes with considerable forces. Each of the emirs deployed through a centralised army, bureaucracy, and fief-holders effective power over an extensive area. A Muslim system of direct taxation sustained his grip on his Haussa and animist subjects. Indigenous levers for imperial administration of almost Indian proportions seemed ready to hand. The Colonial Office however did not want to govern a new province, but to promote trade without expenditure. As Chamberlain's Niger Committee recommended in 1898: "Adopt the local

[36] Morel, *op. cit.*, 108.
[37] Probyn to Chamberlain, 15 Sept. 1901, C.O. 520/9.
[38] Anderson, Minute on Egerton to Harcourt, 19 Oct. 1911, C.O. 520/107/7.

native government already existing; be content with controlling their excesses (slave-raiding) and maintaining peace between them."[39] In other words, apply the pre-colonial method of the Niger Company; pacify the trade routes without otherwise interfering in the emirs' territorial affairs. A budget of eighty thousand pounds a year was all that the Colonial Office intended to spend for the purpose. The commerce of the region was worth no more than that.[40]

The administrator of the territory had bigger ideas of what should be done. Though Lugard ended with a reputation as the classic inventor of African "Indirect Rule," the Colonial Office regarded him in the beginning as the most ferocious direct ruler in British West Africa. In no other dependency did British officials plunge so deeply into African government as his did at first in Northern Nigeria. He made himself the kingmaker of emirs, where everywhere else colonial officials were leaving the choice of chiefs to Africans. His letters of appointment claimed that the emirs' only authority derived from the British, when everywhere else the inherent authority of chiefs was recognised. Where officials in other territories had failed to collect direct tax, Lugard levied tribute on the emirs and reformed their traditional fiscal systems; and where others kept hands off African domestic affairs, his residents intervened between the emir and his headmen and redistributed fiefs. More than that, his administration was able to assume control of waste land and minerals. Such was the persistence of pre-colonial traditions of non-intervention in the Colonial Office that all this was castigated as direct rule.[41] Lugard as a result became the most unpopular and distrusted colonial official in Whitehall. The cost of what he was doing rose to nearly one-half a million pounds a year by 1905. His estimates were cut back. Fewer residents compelled him to reduce his interference.

Yet Lugard acknowledged in principle the critical importance of equations of collaboration and resistance. In 1904 he reported on "the danger incurred by having a handful of British with no class who in a crisis can be relied on

[39] Cooke; *British Enterprise in Nigeria*, 179; C.W. Orr: *The Making of Nigeria*, (London, 1911), 79.

[40] Treasury Minute, 30 June 1899, P.P. C. 9372, 3–4. "The European element is too small and individually changing to really govern the natives, and it is through the chiefs that this must actually be done," (Moor to C.O., 18 Aug. 1898, C.O. African (West) 550, 301). This was the Niger Committee's view. No attempt to introduce direct tax should be made, (Report of Niger Committee, 4 Aug. 1898, *ibid.*, 285).

[41] Antrobus of the C.O. minuted in 1905: " ... The system of administration which Sir F. Lugard is seeking to establish is too elaborate. There is no desire on the part of H.M. Govt. ... to govern otherwise than through its own [native rulers] ... but the tendency of Sir F. Lugard's administration is to destroy the influence of the native rulers and to govern the country by white officials," (Minute, 22 July 1905 on Lugard to Lyttelton, 26 April 1905, C.O. 446/45/2).

to stand by us, and whose interests are wholly identified with ours."[42]
Distrusting the loyalty of the Fulani oligarchs in this role, he proposed to
import more reliable collaborators and bring in an army of Muslim Indian
labourers, clerks and fighting men.[43] His masters in London angrily rejected
his scheme. Indians would only stir up more trouble with the Africans.[44] The
Colonial Office censured Lugard's interventionist policies severely. They
were provoking African disaffection as the Satiru and Muntshi Risings
showed.[45] He was rebuked for assessing his officials by the amount of tax they
collected; in the same breath he was criticised as a spendthrift at the British
Exchequer's expense; he was too militaristic and sent too many punitive
expeditions.[46] As the Colonial Office saw it, his tendency was "to destroy the
influence of the native rulers and to govern the country by white officials."[47]
From 1905 onwards the imperial government thwacked him back into line.
Much of what he had been doing seemed unnecessary, extravagant and far
too risky. Lugard was compelled at last to stop his officials from interfering in
the working of emirate government, unless it was through the ruler at the top.
Not until then could his method be called truly indirect. Even then he was
driven to it, and even so his administration remained interventionist
compared with the practice of the other British West African dependencies.

THE MEANING OF INDIRECT RULE

Many more examples of the repulse of the colonial regime's attempts to
justify its name and take ruling power from indigenous authorities could be

[42] Lugard to Lyttelton, 19 Jan. 1904, C.O. 446/38/1.

[43] *Ibid.* See also Lugard's Report on Northern Nigeria 1900–01, C.O. African (West) 580, 123.

[44] Minutes by Antrobus and Ommaney, 15 March 1904 on Lugard to Lyttelton, 19 Jan. 1904,
C.O. 446/38/1.

[45] See Winston Churchill's castigation of Lugard in 1906: "The continuance... year after
year of these sanguinary ... operations will so soon as they come under public attention, excite
general dissatisfaction. I see no reason why... these savage tribes should not be allowed to eat
each other without restraint.... we are simply drifting along upon the current of military
enterprise and administrative expenditure... we should withdraw from a very large portion of
these territories which we now occupy nominally, but really disturb without governing... we
should concentrate our resources upon the railway and economic development of the more
settled and accessible riparian or maritime regions," (Minute on Lugard to Elgin, 17 Jan. 1906,
C.O. 446/52/1). Elgin commented: "We engaged in the game of grab in the African continent and
we cannot escape the consequences," (Minute, 28 Feb. 1906 on *ibid.*).

[46] Lugard rattled his sabre in justifying his Sokoto expedition in 1903: "The policy of
conciliation has been followed... as far as it legitimately can be with due regard to the dignity of
the Sovereign whom I represent, and the prestige which is another name for self-preservation in a
country occupied by millions and ruled by a few scores," (Lugard to Chamberlain, 15 Jan. 1903,
C.O. African (West) 718, 4).

[47] Antrobus Minute, 22 July 1905, on Lugard to Lyttelton, 26 April 1905, C.O. 446/45/2.

cited. The point is that, except perhaps in Northern Nigeria they failed. They were either vetoed by financial constraint and the over-riding concern in London to avoid rebellion and win African cooperation, or they were baffled by the resistance of Africa's old rulers, British merchants and moralists. The Sierra Leone rebellion and the continual threat of risings in Gold Coast impressed the British with a sense of the fearful risk involved in any positive step to actually govern these territories. Even had they wished to do so, they could not. It is true that the necessity of excluding the French had strengthened the force of the British colonial impact sufficiently to recon-struct these areas into pacified, free trade zones. But by 1905 the reinforce-ment was dribbling away again. A reviving sense of humanity in Britain combined with a return of Treasury parsimony inhibited the use of further punitive expeditions.[48] The lack of finance was responsible for the lack of force. Consequently British officials had to behave like curators tip-toeing round an ethnological museum lest they knocked over the exhibits or the exhibits knocked them over. There was no indigenous fiscal system for them to exploit as there was in India. To impose central taxation on chiefs and peasants proved normally beyond their powers. Like the American colonists earlier, west Africans refused to be taxed to finance imperial rule and so did the Liverpool merchants. The chief representatives of British expansion resisted colonial government as fiercely as did African chiefs. The rulers as a result had not the money, men or power to rule. They over-ruled indigenous authorities largely through prestige – a commodity which served only so far as they let sleeping dogs lie and let well alone.

The terms for Anglo-African collaboration that emerged from the for-mative conflicts of 1894–1906 and persisted into the era of "Indirect Rule" differed surprisingly little from those of the pre-colonial system on the coast. By and large Africans retained their economic and political control of production and supply, though their tolls and monopolies had been knocked down; European agencies still provided the capital and marketed the exports. By and large the chiefs still governed their people in practice by inherent right rather than as executive agents of the colonial administration. Over the greater part of the new West African empire, colonial officials neither chose the native authorities nor did they intervene in their domestic affairs; and the chiefs retained the tribute and taxes of their people. It is true that in some areas the chiefs acted with respect to the views of the district officer, but it was also true that the district officer made sure that his orders would be acceptable before issuing them. In the early colonial system as in the pre-colonial

[48] As for footnote 45.

understandings, colonial intervention in indigenous matters was normally restricted to the purposes of peace for trade.

It is easy therefore to exaggerate the break with the pre-colonial collaborative system that annexation involved. The transition may look dramatic in constitutional form and pro-consular heroics, and the shooting had been real enough. Yet if the force of the colonial regimes seemed formidable to Africans, it seemed tiny to British officials in comparison with the possibilities of disaffection and revolt. As they depended on the cooperation of Africa's old rulers, so they curbed their pretensions within their subjects' tolerance for their demands. Essentially the advent of colonialism thus represented not so much the construction of a new collaborative system but the extension of an old one from the coast inland. The British still had to work through indigenous allies and political processes, though they had altered the overall frame in which they worked; but because their power to uphold that framework derived from African acquiescence, their ability to reform the bargains of cooperation remained marginal.

There is a sense therefore in which the British never really governed their west African colonies. Their rule over them was much more a function of indigenous political economy than it was of the expansion of Britain. The highly superficial, formal imperial context may have been new, but the terms for African acquiescence in it were old and had changed remarkably little. Far from west Africans being take prisoner by British imperialism, British imperialism was the prisoner of its chiefly, west African collaborators. Beside the glittering spires and armed towers of Indian empire, the West African appears like a temporary awning for a parish fête. Where the Indian revenue was counted in millions, the African was saved in thousands. On the strength of its taxes India had borrowed two hundred and fifty millions by 1914, the Gold Coast two millions by 1939. India's rulers had an army of a quarter of a million men at their back; Africa's overlords were lucky if they could call a single battalion to their aid. Where the Indian pro-consul conquered and commanded therefore, the African district officer could only negotiate. Scant pickings and intractable resistance make but a puny empire. African governors could rarely govern; they merely backed and supervised indigenous rulers; they could not suppress them, they merely manipulated indigenous politics if they saw a chance. They could not transform, they only scratched the surface of Africa's historic continuities.

In this limbo between the expansion of Europe and the contraction of Africa to which the casual cartography of the diplomats of the 'eighties had consigned them, British officials henceforward had no choice but to justify their comparative impotence in the theology of "Indirect Rule." Its dogma inspired their theory and practice in West Africa up to 1939. Lugard defined it as "Rule by native chiefs, unfettered in their control of their people, yet subordinated to the control of the Protecting Power in certain well defined directions."[49] Tentative empire on this principle was erected into a system. There was nothing for it but make a virtue of necessity and preserve native institutions intact. "It is necessary," Lugard declared," that the inevitable change should be as gradual as possible, so that existing institutions may have time to adapt themselves."[50] The district officer was present merely to hold the ring of peace while waiting for them to evolve organically according to their own teleology. As late as 1934, Cameron, another philosopher of the school wrote, "The great aims to be followed throughout are those of building on the existing organisations and ideas of the people themselves, assisted by sympathetic advice, to develop their own local institutions."[51] A lofty and humane gloss might be put upon it, but the aim was to keep things quiet and justify it. The Colonial Service had no power to do otherwise. This was the bargain with their collaborators, and it was Africa's old rulers that shielded them against subversion by the educated African. The purpose of the colonial regime remained negative and conservative. So, the negative motives for acquiring territories which were admittedly unsuitable for either the British kind of expansion or the British sort of empire on the cheap, projected themselves in half a century of negative colonialism. This was the real meaning of the long reign of Indirect Rule.

[49] From *The Dual Mandate*.
[50] *Ibid.*
[51] Sir D. Cameron; *Principles of Native Administration*, (Dar-es-Salaam, 1934), 33.

PART V

EPILOGUE

9. EUROPEAN EXPANSION
AND THE CIVILIZATION OF MODERNITY

by

S.N. EISENSTADT

I

The subject of European expansion is a complex one for the very simple but basic fact that while on the one hand the expansion which began in the sixteenth or seventeenth century has indeed transformed the world outside Europe, yet on the other hand this transformation has led to something very different from what was envisaged at any stage of this expansion; especially from what was envisaged during the most intensive stages of this expansion, in the nineteenth and early twentieth centuries. In these periods, there developed a widespread assumption later on most fully articulated in the literature on modernization, that, the world would become more and more similar to the West.[1]

It is a simple observation that experience has proved otherwise. Certainly the world has become transformed, and very profound changes have taken place throughout the world, but the world has not become similar to the West or to Europe. Rather this transformation has taken a great variety of forms, which may seem to be entirely different from what has happened in Europe, or from what Europe thought it was bringing to the world through this expansion.

Perhaps we may here be dealing with the fulfillment of a prophecy, if one can call it that, of an eminent Dutch historian Jan Romein,[2] who claimed, I believe, that just as the nineteenth century was European, the twentieth

---

[1] On this see in greater detail, S.N. Eisentadt, *Tradition, Change and Modernity*, New York: John Wiley, 1973, esp. Part I.

[2] Jan Marius Romein, *The Asian Century: A History of Modern Nationalism in Asia*, in collaboration with Jan Erik Romein. Translated by R.T. Clark, Berkeley: University of California Press, 1962, *id.*, *A World on the Move; a History of Colonialism and Nationalism in Asia and North Africa from the Turn of the Century to the Bandung Conference*, translated by J.S. Holmes and A. Van Mark, Amsterdam, Djambatan, New York, Institute of Pacific Relations, 1956.

century will probably be Asian, and by then, in addition, the world will reverse from the deviation manifested by that European phase. He claimed that the very pluralistic type of social, economic and political conglomeration; the development of relatively autonomous, pluralistic units not guided by any central political power, is something unusual in history, a deviation from the common human pattern. Since then scholars have reiterated without necessarily referring to Romein's work that what has happened until now in the countries beyond Europe is a return to some of the common patterns that existed in the traditional societies, especially those of Asia. It has been claimed that these Great Traditions, other than the European, are now re-absorbing whatever impact Europe has had on them, according to their own precepts and are reshaping it in their own image and not in Europe's.

These claims can be seen as a reaction against the first assumption of many earlier studies of modernization, that, haltingly, intermittently, but surely, the whole world would become more and more similar to the West. Outstanding among these theories have been the "classical" theories of modernization, and later on the theories of convergence of industrial societies, a theory which refers back to Marx, in a sense, but which has been taken up by non-Marxists like Clark Kerr. [3]

The basic model which emerged out of all the central research on modernization assumed that the conditions for development of a viable, growth-sustaining modern society were tantamount to continuous extension of socio-demographic and/or structural indices, and to total destruction of all traditional elements. According to this view, the more characteristics of structural specialization could be found in a society and in its component organizations, the higher the society ranked on various indices of social mobilization, and the more thorough the disintegration of traditional elements in the process, the more would a society be able to develop continuously – to deal with perennially new problems and social forces and to develop a continuously expanding institutional structure, to increase its capacity to absorb change and, implicitly, to develop other qualitative characteristics of modern societies such as rationality, efficiency, and a predilection for liberty. When scholars working within this paradigm addressed themselves to the investigation of the problems of transition from a traditional to a modern setting, they developed a series of assumptions which guided the first group of researches dealing with problems of modernization.

The first assumption was of the almost total co-variance of rates of change

---

[3] On this see in greater detail S.N. Eisenstadt, *Tradition, Change and Modernity*, (see note 1.)

in various institutional areas and of the very close and concomitant interrelations of almost all the major aspects of "development," or of modernization, in all major institutional spheres of society. This assumption predicated that the processes of modernization of the different economic and political institutional spheres tended to coalesce in relatively similar patterns. This co-variance was very often formulated in terms of the systemic "needs" and/or prerequisites of the modern economic, political, or cultural system, when the basic outputs of one of these systems were often conceived as providing the prerequisites for the emergence and functioning of the other.

Second was the assumption that once the institutional kernels of such systems were established they necessarily would lead to the development of similar irreversible structural and organizational outcomes in other spheres and to the general process of sustained growth and development, and by that presumably move in a general common evolutionary direction. This assumption could be found with different degrees of explicitness in many economic and political analyses – whether in Rostow's "stages of economic growth" or in the first analysis of the development of political institutions in the so-called New Nations. It tended to merge with another assumption: namely that the continuity of modernization, of "sustained growth," of continuous development in any institutional sphere, was usually assured after the initial "takeoff." It was these assumptions that guided many of the initial researchers on modernization and, in particular, those attempting to explain the variability of transition of modernity.

In the first studies of modernization, the "systemic" qualities and possibily homeostatic tendencies of transitional societies were subordinated to their presumed "dynamic" tendencies to develop in the direction of the end-stage of modernity. Transitional societies were seen as developmentally impermanent, even though it was sometimes recognized that some societies may "halt" at a certain, even early, stage. Different non-modern societies were compared in the degree to which the "weight" of tradition and primordial attachments resisted the impingement of the potential forces of modernization that came from inside or outside. While there was growing recognition of the possible diversity of transitional societies, it was still assumed that such diversity would disappear, as it were, at the end-stage of modernity.

These general assumptions were also shared by the various theories of the convergence of industrial societies. Both the theories of modernization and those of the organizational dynamics of institutions – economic, industrial, political – which provide the dynamic force or structure of any complex society, claim that cultural differences are of secondary importance in the processes of modernization and industrialization. Both of them have as-

sumed that as the world becomes more and more developed industrialized societies will become relatively more similar, because the internal
dynamics of modernization or industrialization create certain organizational and institutional problems which will obliterate any major differences
between these societies. Such differences are stronger at the starting points
and will be evident in the period of transition, but once societies become more
modernized, developed and industrialized, the more similar they will become.
True, there will be still areas of folkloristic usages and customs which will
vary greatly from one society to another. But the image of modern and
industrial societies, as it was conceived in many of these theories, was that of a
world which becomes more and more homogeneous because of the strong
drive of basic technology and industrialization and, to some degree, because
of political tendencies to grow in participation.

II

Somehow reality did not fully bear out these theories, even though there was a
very important kernel of truth in them. Historical and anthropological
studies have shown that the dynamics of different countries and societies
today, as they are "reacting" to the impact of Europe, cannot be understood
in these terms. A whole spate of criticism of the theories of modernization and
of the convergence of industrial societies developed but will not be discussed
here in detail. It is sufficient to point out some of the highlights. Perhaps the
most crucial aspect was the recognition of the systemic viability of the so-
called transitional systems. This is first, and most clearly, done by Fred
Riggs,[4] especially in his work on the Sala model which was primarily based on
his studies of the Philippines and Thailand. Riggs attempted to show how a
previously traditional system tended to develop into a new type of social or
political system under the impact of forces of modernization coming from the
West. Further, that such a new system, often described as "traditional,"
develops systemic characteristics and properties of its own, creating its own
mechanism of stability and self-perpetuation.

These reconsiderations of the tradition-modernity dichotomy were connected with a reappraisal of the importance of historical continuities in
shaping the directions of societal development. Even in the first stages of

---

[4] F.W. Riggs, "Agraria and Industria: Toward a Typology of Comparative Administration"
in W.J. Siffin (ed.), *Towards a Comparative Study of Public Administration*, Bloomington,
Indiana: Indiana University Press, 1959. *id.*, *Administration in Developing Countries*, Boston:
Houghton Mifflin, 1964.

research on modernization it was realized that some of the differences between the structural and symbolic contours of differing modern societies might be related to their respective historical traditions. Initially, such continuity was perceived as persistence of some broad cultural orientations with little attention being paid to the more structural aspects of modern societies – an approach very often related to, or derived from, the "culture and personality" school. The further development of concepts, such as that of political culture, provided a very important link between such cultural orientations and more specifically structural aspects of behavior. Later, recognition grew that such differences may also persist in crucial structural areas – such as the rules of the political game, the various aspects of social hierarchy, etc. – and that these variations might be influenced by the historical traditions of these societies where a very large degree of continuity with these traditions may be noted. Some scholars of the Maghreb have pointed out that in order to understand Maghrebian politics it is necessary to study Ibn Khaldun, and not Marx, de Tocqueville, or Max Weber.[5] J.C. Heesterman has very profoundly illuminated Indian politics in terms of the polar divisions between the Brahmin, the saint or renouncer, and the ruler (or the dominant caste).[6]

Perhaps one of the most important developments in this context was the concept of "patrimonialism" to describe the political regimes of several of the new states.[7] The use of the term "patrimonial" to depict these various regimes was a reaction to the inadequacies of the central assumptions of the major studies of modernization, as well as to later concepts like those of "breakdown," "political decay," or "transitional" societies. The inadequacy of these assumptions was emphasized by showing that many of these societies and states did not develop in the direction of certain modern nation-states. Furthermore, it was demonstrated that these regimes did not necessarily constitute a temporary "transitional" phase along an inevitable path to this type of modernity. Third, there was an indication that some internal "logic" nevertheless was present in their development. And last, the possibility that at

---

[5] E. Gellner, "The Great Patron – A Reinterpretation of Tribal Revolutions" in *Archives Européennes de Sociologie*, 1: 61–70, 1969.

E. Gellner, *Saints of the Atlas*, London: Weidenfeld and Nicolson, 1969.

J. Waterbury, *The Commander of the Faithful – The Moroccan Political Elite – A Study of Segmented Politics*, London: Weidenfeld and Nicolson, 1970.

Y. Lacoste. *Ibn Khaldoun – Naissance de l'Histoire. Passé du Tiers Monde*, Paris: Maspéro, 1966.

[6] On this see J.C. Heesterman, "Tradition and Modernity in India." *Bijdragen Taal-, Land- en Volkenkunde* vol. 119 (1965), pp. 237–273.

[7] See S.N. Eisenstadt. *Traditional Patrimonialism and Modern Neo-Patrimonialism*, Sage Studies in Comparative Modernization. Beverly Hills, London: Sage Publications, 1973.

least part of this logic or pattern could be understood and derived from some aspects of the traditions of these societies was pointed out. Extremely illuminating studies have substantiated the claim that the European or Western episode in the history of mankind may be a very transitory one. This claim seems to be even more substantiated by the fact that there has been a very important shift of power within the world international system. This is most drastically shown in the great upsurge of the importance of the oil companies. Even more interesting perhaps is the central place which an Asian country, Japan, has taken at least in the international economic system. There has been the great resurgence of China as well.

III

This, however, is not the whole story. It would be a rather simplistic interpretation of the works of many of these scholars – and of contemporary reality – to say that what we are witnessing now is simply a return to the traditional patterns with perhaps the addition of some new technology. The picture is much more complicated, and we would not do justice to the complexity of the contemporary world picture if we only stressed this point of return to other non-European, traditional patterns. The historical development connected with the impact of the West is much more complex. It may, of course, be that one century hence all this will recede and Western impact will be of only historical interest. According to present indications, however, it is rather doubtful that this will happen very soon.

In order to understand this process more fully, the main point that should be emphasized is that the expansion of Europe should be seen not only in terms of a series of concrete and discrete activities, economic, political and so on, but rather as a case of the spread of a new civilization, of a new great tradition – not unlike for instance, the spread of Christianity or of Islam or the establishment of the Great Historical Empires. As in the case of these civilizations, the civilization of modernity was also changed through its diffusion. It was not the same as it was when it spread in the countries of its origin, but neither did it leave all the older civilizations, cultures or great traditions unaffected, or only affected externally.

What was the nature of this modern European civilization? What are its major characteristics? I wish to emphasize the unique elements, not those things which it has in common with other imperialist and colonial dominations, or other cultural civilizations. It seems to me that the most important of these characteristics has been the most far-reaching undermining of traditional civilizations that has ever occurred in history together with the creation of new international systems within which take place continuous shifts in power, influence and centres of cultural model-building.

It has already been stressed in this volume by Profs. Braudel, Zürcher, Schöffer and Heesterman that the most interesting thing is that through the expansion of Europe, and later of the United States, Russia and Japan, as continually new centres of power expanded, the old institutional balances that existed in different civilizations were destroyed, above all the relations between the local units and the center. Now it is true that, even today, when we look at many societies in Africa, Indonesia or in China in the 1930s and 1940s, there are still very important regions in which the old traditional ways of economic life, and to a smaller degree of political life, still seem to be going on. But the important thing is that in most of these societies more and more local units were not only externally affected, but were taken into wider economic systems of a different order from those that previously existed. They have become more and more related to central markets and to international fluctuations. Not only was there some sort of relationship between what happened in China and what happened in Europe, for this had always been the case, as external events affecting one another, but there took place a certain unification and hierarchization of the economy of the different regions of the world, and the effect of the central units upon the local ones became more continuous – even if those affected did not understand what was happening. This situation is something rather unusual and it was very characteristic of the expansion of Europe. Many possibilities opened up, but whatever balance existed between the local segments and the center was destroyed. New ways had to be found to integrate them.[8]

This process developed not only in the economic and technical fields. What was perhaps even more interesting – and this has not been stressed enough in the literature – is that this was also true of the political and cultural field itself. As the very term modernization implies, in most of these societies the traditional legitimation of the political order has been destroyed. Traditional attachments persisted, but with very few exceptions the traditional rulers could no longer claim their old type of legitimation. There are still some exceptions to this, but, as of now, it is obvious that these are exceptions. And experience shows that, even for those rulers, it is not very easy to maintain the traditional type of legitimation.

Another aspect that should be stressed is that the· whole relationship

[8] The point has been recently put forward in great detail by I.M. Wallerstein, *The Modern World System; Capitalist Agriculture and the Origins of the European World-Economy in the Sixteenth Century*, New York: Academic Press, 1974.

between the center and the periphery of society has been changed.[9] The periphery has started to impinge very strongly on the centre in the name of such ideals, or symbols, as equality, solidarity, participation and so on. These themes are not new in any civilization. They can be found in almost all civilizations, but mostly in movements of rebellion and heterodoxy. They were not usually the symbols of the center. One of the things that characterized traditional civilizations is that they possessed very good mechanisms through which movements of rebellion and transformations were absorbed by the centre. China is one of the most interesting cases. New dynasties were very often created from rebellions, but, whenever they were so created, the symbols of rebellion, if they were very heterodox, were immediately changed and incorporated into the old traditional symbols.[10] All this has changed very profoundly with modernization. Although historians may differ as to exactly when it happened, whether sometime in early modern Europe, around the Reformation, the Counter-Reformation, or during the Revolutionary periods of the Great Rebellion in England and the American and French Revolutions, yet, in all these cases, occurred the profound change through which the themes which were usually associated with rebellion were incorporated into the central symbols of society and started to generate their own continuous dynamics. This is what is generally meant by the spread of revolutionary ideologies and images concomitant with modernization and this was one of the great impacts of the West, of Europe, on all, or most, civilizations throughout the world. Not only was traditional legitimization undermined but also new connections were opened up between movements of protest and changes at the centre – generating the spread of revolutionary symbolism throughout the world. It should be stressed that this was revolutionary symbolism because quite often the institutional changes that came about were perhaps not very revolutionary in themselves. It is this impingement of the periphery on the centre and the continuous relations between them in terms of what we call "revolutionary imagery," combined with technological and economic changes, that have been one of the most profound impacts of the West on most traditional civilizations.

But contrary to the assumptions of many of the earlier studies of modernization, these two types of change – the symbolic, cultural and political, and the economic and technological, did not always go together. Although the directions were similar, the tempo was not always the same. There was

---

[9] On this see in greater detail: S.N. Eisenstadt, *Tradition, Change and Modernity*, (see note 1), esp. Part III.
[10] On this see in greater detail: S.N. Eisenstadt, *The Political Systems of Empires*, New York: The Free Press, 1963, Ch. XI.

often the spread of economic changes, with the political and cultural aspects lagging behind, or the other way around. There was no one-to-one relationship, as was assumed in earlier studies.

IV

Closely related to this "revolutionary" aspect of modernity has been the second major aspect of the new historical reality created by the expansion of Europe, namely, the creation of a series of international almost world systems and the concomitant tendencies to continuous changes within them.

Thus, first it should be stressed that these were almost "world-wide" systems and that there developed several such "systems." From the point of view of a purely schematic analysis we can of course say that there is only one international system, but if we look at it in terms of historical, socio-political and cultural dynamics, from the sixteenth century on, we witness the continuous construction not just of one international system, but a series of international systems, having some very peculiar characteristics, rather new in the history of mankind.

It is well known, of course, that from the sixteenth century on, more and more parts of the world were taken into the international economic system, first into the commercial capitalist, later into the industrial capitalist and, still later, into a much more complex international industrial system which already contained different types of economic regimes, such as capitalism, Soviet Communism and other types. They have, at the same time, been continuously interacting, very often giving rise to extremely surprising consequences, as the developments of the last few years have clearly shown. Given the international nature of the system, there may occur within them very interesting and unpredictable shifts of economic and political power.

It was not however, only an economic international system that developed. Side by side there developed also similar political and ideological systems. These systems, in all these spheres, are almost world-wide, and gradually more and more parts of the world have been and are being incorporated in all these international systems.

Although these different systems originated in the same place, basically Europe, and although they were closely interrelated, yet they were not coterminous or identical; each of them has a dynamic of its own, and often they reacted one against the other. Although they were connected with one another, the centres of power and influence within each of them were not identical. Thus, the international cultural system, based on the revolutionary ideologies expounded above, tended to react very strongly against the problems created by the international economic system.[11]

Because of this, the types of international system that developed here were rather new and unique in the history of mankind. International systems existed, of course, before, as for instance the Chinese international system, on which quite a lot of work has been done. A very interesting book edited by J. Fairbanks[12] pointed out how there has been a very important pattern of international relations in Chinese history, concerned with expansion and so on. But this was an imperial pattern, more or less directed from one centre, which at least tried to control all the different aspects, economic, political and ideological. Although it was never fully successful in this, of course, the tendency was there. This was not the case in the spread of Islam but, although there was never one imperial system, there was at least the idea of one community that would develop and the ideal itself created certain types of dynamics.

However, it is only with the expansion of Europe that we have the creation not of one system, but of several, almost world-wide systems which are not directed from one centre but are pluralistic and multi-central, each of which may generate its own dynamics and its own reactions to the others. Within these systems there are continuous shifts of power, influence and of cultural, social and political model building, which interact continuously, and it is they that create part of the dynamics of the new world scene. The crucial point here is that, in terms of the international system, this type of impact generated a continuous predisposition towards change. That is why the term "reaction", i.e. reaction to the European expansion, is unsatisfactory. There was not only a one-time reaction, or series of reactions, to Europe. There developed a series of processes through which new forces were continuously being generated throughout the world as a continuous reaction to what existed before.

Thus, to comprehend the particular dynamics of any specific society, we must take into account these unique aspects of the European expansion or rather of the spread of this civilization which should perhaps be called the civilization of modernity, rather than Western civilization, because, in principle, it may persist, even if the West becomes insignificant. It is only in this context that we may also understand the persistence of old traditions. To understand the Maghreb, we do have to read Ibn Khaldun. We do have to

[11] These points have been elaborated in greater detail in S.N. Eisenstadt, "Some Preliminary Observations on the Pattern of Transformation of Traditional and Modern and Imperial International Systems." Paper for Commission of the 9th World Congress of Political Science, Montreal, Height, 1973.

[12] J. Fairbank (ed.), *The Chinese World Order; Traditional China's Foreign Relations*, Cambridge: Harvard University Press, 1968.

remember the old Indian traditions of the ruler, the Brahmin and the re-nouncer. We do have to remember something about the Mandate of Heaven or the cosmic symbolism of old Japanese polity. This is true because they provide very important clues as to the ways in which different civilizations and societies have been coping with the new problems which emerged in con-junction with this civilization of modernity and which are entirely new. Ibn Khaldun did not know anything about industrialization. He did not know as much as we know now – and certainly would not have phrased it in these terms – about the politicization of the masses. The modern revolutionary imagery was outside the scope of his vision. What he did know was a cer-tain pattern of tribal or patrimonial politics which may still persist. But this pattern has been confronted with new problems.

But, it is not only these economic, political and cultural problems that are new. The new international systems also have a great influence on which of the traditional patterns may become predominant in a certain society. No great civilization has had just one tradition or just one cultural model. As was mentioned earlier, in every such civilization there were heresies, rebellions or "anti" movements, and their ideologies have become more important. The shaping of the concrete reconstruction of the tradition of any single society within this new framework has been very much dependent on the nature of the different models available in this reservoir of traditions, images and modes of coping with problems on the one hand and the relative place of different societies and civilizations within the new international sphere on the other.

V

I would like to illustrate these somewhat general and abstract propositions that I have put forward by one concrete problem. In this, I am really exploiting a seminar held several years ago in Jerusalem on the topic "Socialism and Tradition."[13] First of all, this seminar did not accept the usual view that there is necessarily a basic dichotomy between socialism and tradition. Rather, we posed the question in a different way. We looked at socialism itself as a new tradition, part of this new civilization that is emerging. Socialism has been one of the most important symbols which have been incorporated into the traditions of many of these new societies. This is not to say that it was completely pervasive or even to claim that it will remain

[13] On this see in greater detail: S.N. Eisenstadt and Y. Azmon (eds.), *Socialism and Tradition*, New York: Humanities Press; The following exposition is based on modernization presented and analysed in this book.

so. In some cases it will, in some it will not, because there are differences in this incorporation: the socialism of Ne Win in Burma, of Mao, of Stalin or of the African socialists – they all use very similar symbols, but the meaning is obviously different. Can we discover any pattern in this great variety of uses of these symbols?

Before this, we have to ask an even more paradoxical question. Why, of all the symbols, was socialism the most pervasive? After all, socialism is a product of the European experience. Some scholars, including the late George Lichtheim and an Australian by the name of Eugene Kaminka who has followed him, have said that socialism is the reaction to the tension between the ideals of the French Revolution and the outcome of the Industrial or capitalist revolution. Basically, socialism is a protest in terms of equality, fraternity and so on, that is in terms of the basic premises of modernity, against the realities of European industrialization. It is wholly based in European tradition and experience.[14]

Given these specifically European historical roots of socialism, the question arises: Why was it so successful in spreading beyond Europe to countries and civilizations where both cultural traditions and structural, economic, or political conditions differed greatly from those in Europe and within which the specific structural conditions which were so important in the spread of socialism – that is, the spread of industrialization – developed, if at all, but very haltingly?

How can we then explain this success of socialism in spreading beyond its points of origin and into conditions seemingly entirely different from those of its origin? Why was socialism more successful than the "European" religions such as the different branches of Christianity, or than movements like liberalism? Why has it been even more forceful than indigenous movements of protest – sometimes even absorbing them into its own fold?

The clue to the special position of socialism and communism is to be found in some aspects of the encounter of the non-Western, non-European societies with modernity as it spread from Europe; in some of the unique aspects of the processes of modernization as compared with other situations and movements of change in the history of mankind. The unique characteristic of this movement is the fact that it was based on the assumption of the possibility of an active creation by man of a new socio-political order, an order based on premises of universalism and equality. The spread of these assumptions through the world was combined with far-reaching structural-organizational changes, especially in the economic and political fields; and it took place

[14] *Ibidem*, p. 13.

through a series of social, political, and cultural movements, which, unlike movements of change and rebellion in many other historical situations, tended to combine both orientations of protest and of centre-formation. Through this spread there developed a tendency to a universal, world-wide civilization in which different societies – and especially the first, the European one – served as reference points, from which they judged their own place and each other according to these premises of universalism and equality, thus serving for each other as negative objects of protest as well as models of emulation in terms of these premises.

The most crucial fact here is this combination in one movement of rebellious orientations, protest, and intellectual antinomianism alongside strong tendencies towards centre-formation and institution-building – all of them of specifically modern flavor and connotations.

To bring out the specific characteristics of socialism from this point of view, it might be worthwhile to make a comparison with the Great Religions or Traditions of the past, on the one hand, and with other movements – such as the revolutionary movements related to the English, French and American Revolutions which developed in the first stages of European modernity, on the other.

Then we see, first, that this dual character of socialist movements is also to be found in the Great Religions and the revolutionary movements which ushered in modernity in Europe – and not in other movements of rebellion or of millenarianism and heterodoxy in the history of mankind. And second, organized political protest was joined with more elaborate intellectual heterodoxy there than in these other movements.

Unlike, however, the Great Religions, the major emphasis of socialism was "this-wordly" – politically, socially and economically. It was "this world" that served as the focus and source of socialism's major transcendental orientations – usually undermining the validity of any other-wordly legitimation to these orientations. And unlike other revolutionary movements of modernity – such as the English, French or American Revolutions or the Enlightenment – socialism was the first overall modern movement of protest which was oriented not only against the premises of traditional systems of authority but also against the modern institutional systems – political, economic and ideological – which developed in the first phase of modern European society.

It was this tendency to continuous combinations of these various orientations and elements and the fact that it was these elements that were the most pervasive ones in the spread of socialism that indicate that socialism and communism, as it developed in Europe from the beginning of the nineteenth century, very quickly crystallized into a tradition of sorts, composed of many different elements and components which can indeed be, to some degree, "decomposed" in different situations, even if retaining some basic common cores.

Socialism developed in the European settings, greatly changing the structure of European societies, spreading beyond Europe – and it was especially its spread beyond Europe that contributed to change in the international systems. This spread was possible through the development of symbolic parallelism – in terms of the perception of relative standing and relative deprivation according to the universalistic principles of modernity – between the development of the working class in Europe and of the new nations in the modern international system. In this sense those who claim that class struggle, instead of remaining within the nation, has become international and that the "new" countries were as the proletariat of this new international struggle, have indeed put their finger on a very important aspect.

Truly enough, the exact structure of the relations between different countries in the world is, of course, entirely different from those of classes within the same society: instead of being internal it is international; instead of being related to the internal division of labor, it is mostly related to ideological, international and political stances. Hence also, the whole dynamism of the spread of socialism in these countries differs from its initial development in Europe. But with all these differences there has indeed taken place a symbolic transposition and parallelism between the conditions of development of socialism in its original European setting and the situation in which many non-European societies found themselves as a result of the spread of modernity. It is due to this symbolic transposition that the attraction to the socialist tradition in non-European countries can be explained. It is due to the fact that the socialist tradition is the one modern international tradition in which the protest against the concrete constellation of modernity may be worked out in terms of identity of participation in the premises of the modern world itself.

The special attraction of socialism in general lay in the fact that it proved to be the best channel through which it was possible to develop some active participation in the new modern (i.e. Western), universal tradition together with some selective negation of many of its aspects in general and of the West in particular. Socialism made it possible for the elites and strata of many non-European societies to combine the incorporation of some of the universalistic elements of modernity in their new collective identity without necessarily denying either specific components of one's identity or the continuously negative attitude toward the West.

This symbolic transposition of the initial ideology of socialism from European to non-European settings has been greatly reinforced by the combination, in the socialist tradition, of the orientations of protest with that of institution-building and centre-formation mentioned above. Thus, the respective groups and elites in these societies were enabled to refer both to the tradition of protest and to the tradition of centre-formation in these societies and to cope with the problems of reconstruction of their own centres and traditions in terms of the new setting in which they were put. The important thing about socialism is that it made it possible to rebel against the institutional realities of this new civilization in terms of its own symbols. Therefore it was an expression of some commitment to this new civilization while at the same time judging the realities of the situation according to these new ideological premises. As mentioned, there may be some interesting parallels with Islam. Islam was also universalistic and egalitarian, but did not always deliver the goods. Although the situation was different, the parallel is very interesting to explore.

It was thus that socialism became one of the basic generators of change in the modern international setting.

VI

These, then, are the general reasons for the attraction of socialism. But this attraction was very differential. Not all societies have incorporated the socialistic symbols into their new symbols of collective identity, and they differed as to which aspects of the socialist tradition they incorporated. Once again, I wish to emphasize that I am not concerned with small groups of socialist or communist intellectuals, which can be found in all societies, with the exceptions of Kuwait, Saudi Arabia and maybe Nepal – although even there they may come. We have here before us two problems – first which societies have, and which have not, incorporated some symbols of socialism into their central traditions; and second what are the conditions which explain the differential absorption within the first type of societies, of different aspects of the socialist tradition?

A list can be constituted of these societies which have incorporated the symbols of socialism into their traditions, or have attempted to do so at certain periods. And there are a few others which obviously have not. Russia, China and Burma under U Nu and Ne Win have done this. This last instance may not be considered serious, but symbols are serious, even if they are not lived up to. African and Islamic socialism may be more or less important, but in all these countries there have been attempts to incorporate socialism. There have also been societies which have not incorporated these symbols, however strong their socialist policies and however strong socialist parties may have been. Japan has never done this, although of course there were socialist parties in Japan. India to a much lesser extent has not, although it did try to implement some socialist policies. There may be differences of opinion as to how socialist the policies were, but they were claimed to be so. However, it seems that socialism has not yet been incorporated into the Hindu pantheon, although the time may come. There has been national planning and socialist politics but socialist symbols were not incorporated into the central symbols of the society.

How can this differential attraction of socialist symbols be explained? It should be emphasized again that there is not something inherent or unchanging in the nature of these societies which will make them always interested in incorporating socialism. In certain periods of time, in certain historical situations this was done.

It seems that the receptivity to socialist symbols as components of central symbols of collective identity is dependent, first, on the degree to which the traditions of the respective societies (or of their respective elites) contain within themselves strong universalistic elements which transcend the given tribal, ethnic or national community, as well as strong utopian and millenarian elements and orientations. Thus, it was in Western Europe, Russia and China and to some degree in the Middle East countries, in which such universalistic and utopian elements were predominant (but not in Japan or India, where they were missing) that there developed a strong pre-disposition to the incorporation of socialist symbols. Again, it is important to remember that socialism, as it appeared throughout the world, was a specific symbol of a new universal civilization because of its very strong utopian and millenarian dimensions, whose transposition into social and political reality was attempted. As against this, in Japan or India which did not tend to incorporate socialism, the Utopian and millenarian tradition of protest was very weak. This is especially true in Japan, but to a smaller degree in India, because everything is always available there. As Professor Heesterman pointed out to me, however, in India, such millenarian traditions as existed only had a very limited access to the central core of tradition and were pushed aside from any continuous political work. So long as they persist in the traditions of these particular societies, the weakness of these elements made them less predisposed to the incorporation of socialism.

Second, the receptivity to the central symbols of socialism which is dependent on the degree to which these universalistic orientations and elements existed in the Great Tradition of the affected societies, also depends on the security and cohesion of these societies as their traditions become undermined by the process of being drawn into the new international system, and on the degree to which in this process there develops a discrepancy between their aspirations to participate in the universalistic Great Tradition and their ability to forge out, continue, or maintain their own Great Traditions with strong universalistic elements.

Thus, in Europe, such symbols were forged out, as we have seen, as part of European tradition and of the processes of its reshaping in the nineteenth and twentieth centuries. In other countries it was the ways of incorporation into the new European-dominated international settings that influenced the strength of such predispositions to incorporate the socialist symbols into their symbols. Thus, here again, we see that it was Russia and China – whose own strong traditions as centres of a Great, potentially universalistic, Tradition were very sharply undermined – that were highly predisposed to the incorporation of such symbols.

On the other hand, the cases of Japan, Latin America, and to some degree Africa, indicate that as long as their cultural identity was maintained in some positive way in its relations to the West and its international system – whether through attainment of strong standing without any strong changes in their own self-conception, as was the case in Japan, or through the acceptance of their own part in it, as was the case for a very long time, but seems to be no longer, in Latin America – the predisposition toward the incorporation of socialist symbols into their central symbols was very small and limited to some extremely marginal elites which were not successful in influencing the centre and/or broader groups.

The picture in African and Middle Eastern societies indicates some different constellations of the factors determining predilection to incorporate different aspects of socialism. In most African societies, the process of colonialism has drawn relatively simple political and cultural units with very weak – if any – Great Traditions into the new international orbit and has implicated, at least among the more educated and urbanized elites, a very strong predisposition to participation in the new broader setting of such New Great Traditions. It was in this context that the ideology of African socialism tended to develop among some of these groups.

In the central Islamic countries the predilection of some elites to incorporate into the central symbols of their societies those of socialism was also very strongly connected with the weakening of many elements of their own Great Traditions – and especially the uncertainty about the relations between the new emerging political centers and the universalistic claims of

Islam. At the same time, the persistence of this ambivalence as well as of
the fact that Islam is a universalistic tradition, resulted here also in the
selection of some general socialist symbols as well as of broad socialist
political programs – though not in the development of the institutional and
organizational aspects of societies.

Here it is indeed very significant that the predisposition to the incorporation of socialist symbols has been weakest in those African groups or
societies within which there persisted or developed a strong Islamic identity
which assured them of the possibility to participate in an already existing
Great Tradition. At the same time the fact that these groups stood on the
relative periphery of the centers of Islam saved them from the turbulation and
problems of the more central Islamic countries. In many such countries
symbols of socialism were simply incorporated into the general Islamic
symbols of the collectivity; while at the same time such groups, with their
relative security of participation in a Great Tradition, did not share the
turbulence of the center.

VIII

Similarly a number of conditions had influence on whether the whole
"package deal" of socialist *Weltanschaung* or only the political, social or
cultural symbolism and/or programs were incorporated into the central
political symbols of their respective societies. They also influenced the degree
of motivational commitment which such symbols evoked, and the extent to
which symbolism and/or concrete centre-formation and institution-building
or rebellion were emphasized in the incorporation of socialist traditions.

Among the most important of these conditions – in addition to the
universalistic and utopian elements in the respective traditions of these
societies or of their elites – have been the strength or weakness of their centers,
i.e., the degree to which these centers have commanded a high degree of
commitment; the degree and the nature of the major orientations of these
centers and especially the differential emphasis within them on prestige and
power; and the degree of internal solidarity of their respective elites and the
degree of internal pluralism within them.

The propensity to accept all of socialism as a package deal into their central
symbols was greater in those societies in which the universalistic orientation
and the utopian elements in their respective traditions were stronger, and
insofar as the actual process of undermining impinged on strong cultural and
political centers which commanded a high degree of commitment and whose

undermining gave rise to strong "totalistic" movements. While such tendencies could develop among almost any elite or group, yet on the whole, the influence of such elites could be greater where they developed in societies with strong but relatively closed centres, i.e. societies which placed a strong emphasis on power and prestige orientations – of which Russia and China provide the clearest illustrations. In Burma or Ceylon with their tradition of "weaker" centres and greater emphasis on passive and adaptive attitudes to the centre – as well as in Latin America with its Spanish patrimonial heritage – the predilection to accept socialism as a package deal was weaker. Except among very marginal groups which attempted to forge out new far-reaching symbols of collective identity, socialism was mostly a selected broad cultural orientation. Similarly, given the relatively low degree of intra-elite solidarity, there developed here only relatively weak tendencies to institution-building or concrete centre-formation, while at the same time a strong tendency developed to emphasize the symbols of collectivity and centre-formation.

In contrast, in Europe the more pluralistic tradition of the centre – combined as it was with relatively strong commitments to it – worked on the whole against the tendency to acceptance of the package deal of socialism and contributed to the differential selection of different aspects of socialism. The selection that took place here was, given the strong universalistic tradition, first, toward incorporation, especially of social and social-political programs, into the existing political symbols. Secondly, given also the relatively strong cohesion and solidarity of these groups, there developed here also a relatively strong emphasis on the institutional and organizational as well as the motivational aspects of socialism.

The relative emphasis on protest as against centre-formation and institution-building was mostly influenced by the position of respective groups in their internal social or international power situation and by their perception of their place in their own society or in the international setting. Thus, very often – as in Russia or Africa – elites changed their respective emphasis from protest to centre-formation when they became ruling elites and new "oppositionary" groups within the society tended to a strong protest orientation couched in the terms of socialism to use against the ruling elites and their interpretation of socialism.

IX

The preceding analysis stresses another point made above which may now be better illustrated: namely that there is nothing permanent in the mode of reception of different aspects of socialism. This is not a one-time reaction to Europe. It is not just because of European impingement that in China there was a predilection to socialism. For a long time there was no such predilection, and for a certain period there was a struggle against it. In other societies, there was no such predilection at all. Rather this new situation has created dynamics of its own, within which there may develop continuously changing situations, so that at one phase of the development there are elites, groups of leaders or revolutionaries who are successful in building up the imagery of socialism and taking it into the points of common identity. Once they are consolidated, the symbols of socialism cease to be symbols of protest and become symbols of power and solidarity and so recede from importance. They will be taken up in other places where this dynamic is being recreated.

So this is not a one-time reaction, which remains static and freezes in its own new mold. Rather, in itself it generates new forces, whether of protest or solidarity. Accordingly, the pattern of absorption of different aspects of socialism will vary in different societies according to a combination of their own traditions and their place in the continually changing international system, different groups selecting different aspects of this new civilization. The selection is greatly influenced by the traditions of the particular society, but the traditions themselves are not something immutable. Rather, they are reconstructed by incorporating into themselves elements of this new civilization. It is impossible to understand what is happening unless one emphasizes these new elements and their relations with the more traditional aspects. But moreover, the process of selection is greatly influenced by the dynamics of this new international system, which is itself changing, but which is a very powerful force. So, to return to my opening remarks, it is certain that the transformation of the world as it has occurred under the impetus of European expansion, has followed paths entirely different from those that were foreseen by this expansion, in either political, intellectual or scholarly guise. But it has not brought a simple resurgence of the old traditions. Rather, it has created an entirely new reality in which different civilizations are incorporating new symbols and new realities and reconstructing themselves by a combination of the impingement of new forces on them, their own traditional forces and their place in this new system.

Hence while it may very well happen that the relative importance, in this new system, of Europe and of the West, will recede or decline – this does not mean that the new civilization will not continue through its own dynamics however great may be the shifts in the importance of different models within it.

NOTES ON THE CONTRIBUTORS

F. BRAUDEL (1902) was professor at the *Collège de France* and President of the *Ecole des Hautes Etudes, VIe section*.
His publications include:
La Méditerranée et le monde méditerranéen à l'époque de Philippe II, (2 vols.) Paris 1949. (English translation: *The Mediterranean and the Mediterranean World in the Age of Philip II*, London 1972/'73, 2 vols.)
Civilisation matérielle et capitalisme (XVe–XVIIIe siècle), Paris 1967. (English translation: *Capitalism and Material Life 1400–1800*, London, 1973.)
Ecrits sur l'histoire ["Writings on History"], Paris 1969.

H. BRUNSCHWIG (1904) is *Directeur d'études* at the *Ecole des Hautes Etudes*.
His publications include:
Mythes et réalités de l'impérialisme colonial français, 1871–1914, Paris 1960. (English translation: *French Colonialism, 1871–1914. Myths and Realities*, London 1966.)
L'avènement de l'Afrique noire ["The Awakening of Black Africa"], Paris 1963.
Le partage de l'Afrique noire ["The partition of Black Africa"], Paris 1971.

S.N. EISENSTADT (1923) is professor at the Eliezer Kaplan School of Economics and Social Sciences, Hebrew University of Jerusalem.
His publications include:
The Political Systems of Empires, New York/London 1963.
Israeli Society, London 1967.
Tradition, Change and Modernity, New York 1973.

J.C. HEESTERMAN (1925) is professor of Indology at Leyden University.
His publications include:
The Ancient Indian Royal Consecration, The Hague 1957 as well as various articles on Indian history, dealing particularly with modernization processes.

J.L. MIÈGE (1923) is professor of history at the *Université de Provence* and Director of the *Institut d'Histoire des Pays d'Outre-Mer* at Aix-en-Provence.
His publications include:
Le Maroc et l'Europe ["Morocco and Europe"], Paris 1961–1964 (4 vols.).

L'impérialisme colonial italien de 1870 à nos jours ["Italian Colonial Imperialism since 1870"], Paris 1968.

Expansion européenne et décolonisation de 1870 à nos jours ["European Expansion and Decolonisation since 1870"], Paris 1973.

R.E. Robinson (1920) is fellow of Balliol College and Beit Professor of the History of the British Commonwealth, Oxford.

His publications include:

Africa and the Victorians. The Official Mind of Imperialism (with John Gallagher), London 1961.

(ed.) *Developing the Third World: the Experience of the Nineteen-sixties*, Cambridge 1971.

I. Schöffer (1922) is professor of Dutch history at Leiden University.

His publications include:

Het nationaal-socialistische beeld van de geschiedenis der Nederlanden ["The National-socialist View of the History of the Netherlands"], Arnhem/Amsterdam 1956.

(ed.) *Zeven Revoluties* ["Seven Revolutions"], Amsterdam 1964.

A Short History of the Netherlands, Amsterdam 1973 (2nd ed.).

H.L. Wesseling (1937) is professor of contemporary history and director of the Centre for the History of European Expansion, Leiden University.

His publications include:

Soldaat en Krijger. Franse opvattingen over leger en oorlog, 1905–1914 ["Soldier and Warrior. French opinions on army and war, 1905–1914"], Assen 1969 and various articles dealing with imperialism.

E. Zürcher (1928) is professor of East Asian history at Leiden University.

His publications include:

The Buddhist Conquest of China. The Spread and Adaptation of Buddhism in Early Medieval China, Leyden 1959 (2 vols.).

(ed., with W.F. Wertheim) *China tussen eergisteren en overmorgen* ["China between Yesterday and Tomorrow"], The Hague 1963.

(ed., with D.W. Fokkema) *China nu, Balans van de Culturele Revolutie* ["China Now, The Outcome of the Cultural Revolution"], Amsterdam 1973.

INDEX